T0355059

MANIFESTATIONS *of*
GRACE

STEVE STEWART, TH.D.

WESTBOW
PRESS°
A DIVISION OF THOMAS NELSON
& ZONDERVAN

WestBow Press books may be ordered through booksellers or by contacting:

WestBow Press
A Division of Thomas Nelson & Zondervan
1663 Liberty Drive
Bloomington, IN 47403
www.westbowpress.com
844-714-3454

ISBN: 978-1-6642-6661-2 (sc)
ISBN: 978-1-6642-6662-9 (hc)
ISBN: 978-1-6642-6660-5 (e)

Library of Congress Control Number: 2022908615

Print information available on the last page.

WestBow Press rev. date: 05/14/2022

CONTENTS

INTRODUCTION

The subject of grace has been written about by many authors who have approached the subject from a wide variety of angles. Nothing I could say in this work would ever add anything of any consequence to the multitudinous volumes that have already been written, and it is not that purpose for which I write.

So, to the question of why I felt another work on grace was needed. Actually, it's not at all that I thought another volume was needed, but that possibly the subject could be approached in a slightly different way. In this work I will attempt to look at how grace manifests itself in the lives of individuals. Grace is a necessity in the life of everyone, and every person is the recipient of grace.

Believer and non-believer alike all experience the grace of God. There is a general administration of the grace of God which is the common experience of humankind. There is grace to be seen in the natural course of things as it is by God's grace that the natural order is kept intact. Grace is seen in the fact that individuals – whether they believe in the Lord Jesus Christ or not – experience good things, and actually display good works.

God is good, and all good things flow from Him. Goodness is evident even in the life of those who would curse God's name. Humankind, in general, is the recipient of the good things of God, thus we have the term common grace.

There have been tremendous contributions to humanity through the good works of believer and non-believer alike. Non-believers prove to be good parents, good spouses, good employees and employers. Many have been great philanthropists, donating huge sums of money and other resources to wonderful causes. So many have contributed to the human family as medical researchers, scientists, technology experts, educational institutions and so many other fields.

The goodness of man is possible only because of the goodness of God. And the experience of God's grace is only possible because He is the giver of all good gifts in the lives of believers and non-believers alike. The Bible speaks of the rain falling on the just and the unjust. This is common grace. It is no respecter of persons. The individual who curses God with every other breath enjoys the same bountiful rainfall as his God-fearing neighbors. Oftentimes the non-believer's family enjoy financial success, family unity, and physical heath, while the God-fearing Christians across town experience financial hardship, family dysfunction and chronic health issues. Good things and bad things happen to the God-fearing and the godless all the same.

Still another way the term common grace can be understood is in relation to God's working in the governments of man. Paul reveals to his readers in Rome that the governments of the world are all ordained by God. He has established them for the restraint of evil in society. The authority of established governments is granted by God for the rewarding of good behavior and the punishing of bad behavior.

This work, however, is focused not so much on common grace, but rather specific manifestations of grace. It is also not looking at God's grace in the lives of unbelievers except in indirect ways. It will focus more on the working of grace in the lives of believers. Attention will be given to non-believers as grace impacts them through the work of grace in the life of a believer.

Special Note

As you read the pages of this work you will notice that there are no footnotes. The reason for this is that this book is written from knowledge gained through twelve years of Biblical/theological education and forty years of pastoral ministry. I have benefited from so many in the classroom as well as in the study. I was privileged to sit under the teachings of great men and women of God, and to read the writings of Bible scholars and commentators. I have listened to countless sermons and attended dozens of Bible conferences. It is with a spirit of gratitude that I give credit to those from whom I have been taught, and with a word of sincere appreciation to those whose words and teachings have so impacted my life and ministry.

DEDICATED TO

This work is dedicated to the following:

- First and foremost, this book is dedicated to the Lord Jesus Christ. It is by His grace in my life that I have been saved, sealed, and am now in the process of sanctification. To Him be the glory both now and forever, Amen!
- Second, I dedicate this book to my wife, Teresa. She has been by my side for forty-eight years and counting. She has been a faithful wife and mother. Now I, along with our children arise and called her blessed!
- Third, it is with joy that I dedicate this work to our three children and their families: Bryan and his wife Tammy, and children Gaige, Trinity and Jayden; Joshua and his wife Amanda, and children Luke and Levi; and Charity, and her daughter Luna Rey.

Special Thanks:

- Special thanks to my dear friends, Mike and Marilyn Grenfell. They very graciously gave of their time to proof-read this manuscript, calling attention to grammatical and syntactical errors, as well as sharing suggestions on how to make the book more 'readable'.
- Thanks also to the many professors, mentors, and fellow pastors who have helped 'sharpen the iron' as we have discussed doctrine, theology, practical application of the text, and so much more.

CHAPTER 1

Scriptural Emphasis on Grace

But grow in the grace and knowledge of our Lord and Savior Jesus Christ. To Him be the glory both now and forever.

Second Peter 3:18

Amazing Grace
Amazing Grace, how sweet the sound
That saved a wretch like me!
I once was lost, but now I'm found
Was blind, but now I see.
Twas grace that taught my heart to fear
And grace my fear relieved;
How precious did that grace appear,
The hour I first believed.
Through many dangers, toils, and snares
I have already come;
Tis grace that brought me safe thus far,
And grace will lead me home.
When we've been there ten thousand years
Bright shining as the sun;
We've no less days to sing God's praise
Than when we first begun.
Amazing Grace – John Newton

The Bible places a tremendous amount of emphasis on grace. You can't read very far into the pages of Scripture before coming across this powerful biblical concept. The word "grace" is found 138 times in the Bible, but the emphasis on grace is evident far more than the number of times the word is found. And, as we see in the words of Peter, we are admonished to grow in the grace of our Lord and Savior, Jesus Christ.

In this book, attention will be given to the multi-faceted concept of grace, with chapters dealing with the different ways in which grace is manifested in the world at large, as well as in the lives of individuals. But to begin, it would be wise to invest some time in striving to come to a deeper understanding of the emphasis grace is given in the Bible. Reading through the Bible, one becomes aware very quickly of the overwhelming emphasis on grace, and the desperate need for grace.

Grace in the Old Testament

One might be a bit confused when reading through the Bible due to the fact that the Old Testament and the New Testament are often viewed as having distinctly different emphases. It might appear that the Old Testament leans more toward the judgment and wrath of God, whereas the New Testament leans more toward the love and grace of God. How are we to reconcile this seeming discrepancy?

It needs to be understood, first and foremost, that there is not a discrepancy between the two testaments. The Bible presents a progressive revelation of God, from the first word in Genesis to the last word in Revelation. And, the Bible presents the ongoing saga of the history of man – the creation of man, the fall of man, the depravity of man, and the redemption of man. This unfolding story begins in the Old Testament, where we see the plans and purposes of God begin to unfold.

We don't have to read very far into the Old Testament before we see the expression of God's grace. A few examples will be sufficient to clearly illustrate that God's grace is just as evident in the Old Testament as it is in the New.

ADAM AND EVE

To begin our survey of grace in the Old Testament, there are a few foundational principles that need to be reviewed. First, the Bible teaches clearly that God created humankind, not as a collective whole, but with the creation of one couple – Adam and Eve. God's instruction to this couple was clear and concise. It is found in the following words:

> And the Lord God commanded the man, saying, "Of every tree of the garden you may freely eat; but of the tree of the knowledge of good and evil you shall not eat, for in the day that you eat of it you will surely die."
>
> (Genesis 1:16-17)

Second, it is interesting as well as essential to note that at this time Adam and Eve had no children. It was just the two of them in the Garden of Eden, enjoying the bounty of God's creation. And it was indeed bountiful! The imagination is not sufficient to truly envision what it must have been like in the garden. The trees in the garden bore all manner of luscious fruit. Each of them was there for their enjoyment and pleasure. Adam and Eve could enjoy the fruit of all trees in the garden with the exception of one: the tree of the knowledge of good and evil. Adam and Eve were forbidden to eat from that particular tree.

Third, it was Adam and Eve, still alone in the garden, who decided to go against the instructions from God. The story is familiar. They chose to disobey God's command and decided to eat of that forbidden fruit. And this is where the fact that they had not yet given birth to any children becomes so significant. Remember, God had clearly told them that if they ate fruit from the forbidden tree, they would die that day. However, after they ate of the fruit, they lived hundreds of years. How are we to

3

understand what appears to be a glaring mistake in Scripture? Why did they not die that day?

God could have carried out His pronouncement of death within that twenty-four-hour period of time. It would have meant that He would have to start over, with the creation of another pair of human beings. It would require the repeat of the consequences of eating fruit from the forbidden tree. It would have required the newly created couple doing what Adam and Eve did not do. It would call for obedience to God's command to never eat the forbidden fruit. And, God would have been perfectly just in carrying out the death penalty immediately.

However, He did not carry out the prescribed sentence immediately, at least not in terms of a twenty-four-hour day, and not in terms of physical death. This should not be of concern to the modern reader, because the Bible makes it amply clear that God does not reckon time the same way we do. There is an important verse that teaches this concept clearly. The apostle Peter makes the following statement:

> But beloved, do not forget this one thing, that with the Lord one day is as a thousand years, and a thousand years as one day.
>
> (2 Peter 3:8)

Much time has been spent, and many ideas have been shared, as to what exactly Peter had in mind when he penned those words. For our purposes, we will simply take this statement at face value, and understand it to mean that time places no restrictions on God. He dwells outside of time. Time is His creation, part of the created order, but does not constrict God in any way whatsoever.

If we apply that verse to God's decree that Adam and Eve would die "in that day," then in God's eyes their death could have occurred at any time within a thousand years, and still have been within a day. So, physically, they did indeed die "that day."

But the point we need to see is that God could have carried

out His decree of death the moment Adam and Eve disobeyed had He chosen to do so. Instead, He showed grace toward the wayward couple. He took the skin of an animal to cover their nakedness, banished them from the Garden, and carried out His decreed punishment, but in His own timing, and for His own purposes.

In keeping with His decree, the earth was put under the curse brought about by the disobedience of this first couple, and humankind has been suffering the consequences ever since. The fact that God allowed Adam and Eve to continue living, to bear children, and to reach an age of hundreds of years is truly an act of grace.

So what does this have to do with Adam and Eve being alone in the garden when they chose to disobey God's command? Had they already given birth to children prior to their act of disobedience, then the children would have been presented with the same choice as Adam and Eve. But, because they disobeyed prior to have any children, then their children inherited the sin nature that has now been passed down to all humankind. Each of their children were born with that sin nature and were thus accountable to God for their personal sinfulness. As is each person who has been born since that initial act of rebellion in the garden of Eden.

Therefore, the amazing grace of God is seen, not only in Adam and Eve, but in all of their descendants as well. The grace of God is magnified exponentially as we consider this initial act of grace between God and His human creation.

NOAH

Another beautiful example of God's grace in the Old Testament is witnessed in Noah. Consideration of Noah must begin with a review of what has transpired between the time of Adam and Eve's disobedience and the historical era of Noah. There are approximately eleven hundred years between the creation of Adam and the birth of Noah. Much happened in those hundreds of years. One thing of grave importance to note is that the Bible makes it abundantly clear that there was a consistent move toward depravity. Man, in his state of fallenness, moves further and further away from God and His demands for holiness. Genesis records for us the following depiction of the sinfulness of humanity at the time of Noah:

> "Then the Lord saw that the wickedness of man was great in the earth, and that every intent of the thoughts of his heart was only evil continually. And the Lord was sorry that He had made man on the earth, and He was grieved in His heart. So the Lord said, 'I will destroy man whom I have created from the face of the earth, both man and beast, creeping thing and birds of the air, for I am sorry that I have made them.'"
>
> (Genesis 6:5–7)

What a sordid record of the wickedness of man. The eating of the forbidden fruit was just the beginning of the downward spiral of man into total depravity. Please make note of the phrase, "every intent of the thoughts of his heart was only evil continually." This is a tremendously difficult thing to comprehend. Humans had become so wicked that God saw nothing of any redeeming value. No one had a thought for God or the things of godliness.

It appears that humankind once again, in a total state of disobedience and disregard for the things of God, is at a point of no return. God was grieved that He had created humans and decided to wipe all of humanity off the face of the earth. And once again, as observed in the story of Adam and Eve, He would have been perfectly justified had He chosen to destroy humanity entirely. When consideration is given to the depth of humankind's depravity as they have given themselves totally over to the dictates of fleshly desires, it is no wonder that God is so indignant toward them.

But we can be eternally grateful for the words recorded in the very next verse:

> But Noah found favor in the eyes of the Lord.
>
> (Genesis 6:8)

Out of all the masses of humankind populating the earth at this time in history, only one man and his family found grace, favor, in the eyes of God. So, once again, there will be a new beginning. Because of the evil of mankind, God sends a great flood, wiping out all humankind, with the exception of Noah and his family. His instructions to Noah are clear about what he is to do to prepare for this worldwide deluge. Noah and his three sons carry out the plans for building an ark large enough to house the four of them along with their wives – eight people in all – and two of every animal on the earth (seven of all clean animals) so that the earth could be repopulated after the floodwaters subside. What a tremendous portrait of grace.

Once again, God had every reason and right to completely rid the earth of all humankind. They had rebelled against God, broken God's law, and become a law unto themselves. It is a reflection of God's boundless love, and a display of His astonishing grace, that humankind survived the devastation of the global flood.

DAVID

From the time of Noah to the time of David we must move ahead approximately 1800 years. So much has happened during these intervening years: the calling of Abraham, the birth of Isaac, of Jacob (Israel), and of the twelve sons of Israel from which the twelve tribes of the nation would come. After that we have the record of the birth of Moses, who is used by God as the deliverer of the people of Israel after they had spent more than four hundred years in Egyptian bondage. After Moses' death Joshua succeeded him as leader of the people of Israel. Joshua then led the people into the promised land.

Following Joshua there are the tumultuous years that are recorded in the Book of Judges, in which the people of Israel go through approximately four centuries of a cycle of rebellion, repentance and restoration. And finally, we come to the time of the kings. The first king of Israel is Saul, son of Kish, of the tribe of Benjamin. His tenure as king proved to be disastrous, and God removed him from the throne, replacing him with David. God revealed His plan to remove Saul in these words:

> But now your kingdom shall not continue. The LORD has sought for Himself a man after His own heart, and the LORD has commanded him *to be* commander over His people, because you have not kept what the LORD commanded you.
>
> (1 Samuel 13:14)

The man here referred to as the one who will replace Saul is none other than David. And the truly amazing thing about this is the testimony God gave of David: He says David was a man after God's heart. This testimony borne of David is spoken by none other than God Himself. What an astounding thing to consider. God stated that David is a man with a heart for God. This is truly a remarkable thing to consider given some things we know about David.

When one studies the life of David it becomes evident very quickly that he was a man prone to moments of weakness in which he sinned grievously against the Lord. This makes the statement of David being a man after the heart of God all the more amazing.

David had given in to sinful lusts when he engaged in sexual relations with Bathsheba. Then, when he discovered she was now pregnant through their sexual liaison he tried to cover it up by having her husband, Uriah, placed on the front line of battle, and then having the army retreat from around him. This resulted in Uriah's death. He then had Bathsheba brought to his palace where he married her, which resulted in his having to engage in deceit in order to cover up his sinful activities. He hid his sinful actions a full year and did not come to confess until confronted by the prophet Nathan.

This does not sound like the actions of a godly man, and yet, God testified of David that he was a man after the heart of God. How are we to understand this assertion? Does it mean that God was pleased with David's actions? Of course not. That is the very reason God sent Nathan to confront David over his sinful actions. Then how are we to reconcile these difficulties?

The answer can be seen, at least to the satisfaction of this writer, with the reaction of David when confronted by Nathan:

I have sinned against the Lord.

(2 Samuel 12:13)

Granted, David did not make this confession until he had been confronted by Nathan and had heard the indictment Nathan pronounced against him. But when he was finally confronted, he quit trying to cover it up. Neither did he try to deny his actions. Rather, he openly confessed. He openly acknowledged his sin.

Perhaps it is this spirit of contrition and brokenness when confronted about his sinful actions that helps us understand God's testimony of David. Yes, David made some enormous mistakes. Yes, he willfully disobeyed God. Yes, he then tried to cover it all up. But also yes, he made full confession when finally confronted. Should he have gone to God in confession before being confronted by Nathan? Absolutely. But the fact is also true he could have continued to try to cover it up by denying it even after being confronted.

And yes, he received the grace of God. Now granted, the text tells us that he still had to suffer consequences for his actions. Sin always has a price. Someone has said that sin will always take you further than you want to go; it will keep you longer than you want to stay; and it will cost you more than you want to pay. This all became reality to David.

This all becomes so painfully clear in the charge brought against David. Nathan reveals God's disapproval by pronouncing the following sentence:

> Now therefore, the sword shall never depart from your house, because you have despised Me, and have taken the wife of Uriah the Hittite to be your wife. Thus says the LORD: "Behold, I will raise up adversity against you from your own house; and I will take your wives before your eyes and give *them* to your neighbor, and he shall lie with your wives in the sight of this sun. For you did *it* secretly, but I will do this thing before all Israel, before the sun."
>
> (2 Samuel 12:10–12)

David's sin led to him suffering the consequences of his actions. However, in the midst of it all he still experienced the amazing grace of God.

This should teach us a very important Biblical principle. God's grace of forgiveness is available to all who will sincerely repent and seek forgiveness from God. This truth is spoken beautifully and powerfully in the first epistle of John.

> If we confess our sins, He if faithful and just to forgive us our sins, and to cleanse us from all unrighteousness.
>
> (1 John 1:9)

The grace of forgiveness is a reality for those who will meet God on His terms. When we fall to the temptation to commit an act of sin against God, He will immediately bring about conviction of that sin. When we respond with confession and repentance, then we experience the wonder of God's limitless supply of forgiveness. David is a perfect example of the imperfections of our fallen nature, and of the availability of God's willingness to forgive. More consideration will be given to David in the chapter on salvaging grace.

JEREMIAH

Another example of God's amazing grace in the Old Testament is the prophet Jeremiah. His life bears testimony to his commitment to carry out God's calling, but it also bears testimony to one who struggled with that calling. Jeremiah spent years wrestling with God's call for him to be a prophet. It was an intense struggle as he tried to make sense of the initial explanation God offered him as he received the call to preach the Word of God to people who would not listen.

This struggle is seen clearly in his response to the call of God:

> Then the word of the Lord came to me, saying, "Before I formed you in the womb I knew you; before you were born I sanctified you; I ordained you a prophet to the nations." Then I said: "Ah, Lord God! Behold, I cannot speak for I am a youth."
>
> (Jeremiah 1:5–6)

Jeremiah responded to this initial calling of God by offering the excuse that he can't carry out God's call because he is just a youth. So many others have followed in the footsteps of Jeremiah, giving God their excuses for not accepting His call. Excuses are so easy to manufacture in our minds. Some might say they can't follow God's call because they are too young, while others say they are too old. Some say their children are too young, so they will have to follow God's call later, while others might say that their children are too old, and they will have to get them through college before they are able to follow that call. Still others might say that they are unable, unequipped, unqualified, or untrained, to accept such a challenging call from God. Yes, excuses are easy to come by.

So how does God respond to Jeremiah's initial excuse? He responded with words of challenge and words of encouragement:

> But the Lord said to me: "Do not say, 'I am a youth,' for you shall go to all to whom I send you, and whatever I command you, you shall speak. Do not be afraid of their faces, for I am with you to deliver you," says the Lord.
>
> (Jeremiah 1:7–8)

God assures Jeremiah that even though he was young, he had no need to worry because God was going to be with him. This should have been an encouraging thing for Jeremiah to hear. It is a promise that God had repeated so many times to others who came before Jeremiah.

God had promised Abraham that He would be with him and make of him a great nation. Later, He made gave the same promise of His presence to Moses, as He called him to be the deliverer of the people of Israel from their Egyptian bondage. When Moses was succeeded by Joshua, God repeated the same promise to him, telling Joshua to be strong and courageous because God would be with him just as He had been with Moses.

So now God once again repeats the promise of His presence to Jeremiah, as Jeremiah presents his feeble argument to God that he is but a youth who cannot possibly perform this assignment.

And when we think about what exactly his mission and

ministry would be, we might better understand why he did not want to answer God's call. God tells Jeremiah exactly what to expect as he engaged the people of his beloved nation with the message of God:

> "Then the Lord put forth His hand and touched my mouth, and the Lord said to me: 'Behold, I have put My words in your mouth. See, I have this day set you over the nations and over the kingdoms, to root out and to pull down, to destroy and to throw down, to build and to plant.'"
>
> (Jeremiah 1:9-10)

Obviously, Jeremiah's ministry was not going to be an easy one. And yet, he was to take heart in knowing that God would be with him to deliver him. God was sending Jeremiah to the people to warn them of impending consequences for their actions if they did not repent. God was sending a message of grace for the people if they would turn back to God.

However, what I would like to focus on is not God's grace to the people, but His grace to Jeremiah. The first chapters of the book of Jeremiah reveal that the prophet struggled with the calling of God, and the ministry assignment God had gave him. It came to a point of crisis in the twentieth chapter of Jeremiah's prophecy:

> O Lord, You induced me, and I was persuaded;
> You are stronger than I, and have prevailed.
>
> (Jeremiah 20:7)

The King James Version of the Bible translates this verse, "O Lord, thou hast deceived me, and I was deceived." The prophet feels that God had, in some way, been less than honest with him. Of course, this is the prophet's perception of the activity of God in his life. All he really had to do was remember the commission

God had extended in the first chapter, where God told him plainly that his ministry would consist of rooting out, of pulling down, of destroying, and of throwing down. It should not have taken Jeremiah by surprise to be treated viciously by his family, as well as the nation at large. Remember, God had spoken plainly to Jeremiah, revealing to him from the outset of his ministry that things would not be easy as he fulfilled God's calling.

> Behold, I have put My words in your mouth. See, I have this day set you over the nations and over the kingdoms, to root out and pull down, to destroy and throw down, to build and to plant.
>
> (Jeremiah 1:9-10)

And this is where we see clearly the grace of God extended to Jeremiah. Even after the prophet lashes out at God, God still graciously used Jeremiah to speak God's message of warning to the nation. Yes, Jeremiah suffered tremendously as he performs his ministry, and yet God did as He promised back in chapter one: He delivered the prophet from the people. And that message is valid for those whom God calls still today. His grace will prove to be all-sufficient to carry out His plan. The message and ministry God calls one to perform might lead down a path of suffering of a kind that we feel we could not survive, and yet God provides us with the grace to keep going.

Jeremiah is a perfect example of the grace of God at work in the life of an individual who accepts the challenge of God's call on his life. Many who have accepted the challenge of God's call have experienced heartache and grief as they have faithfully discharged their duties in service to God. Some places of ministry prove to be filled with pain and hardship as the ministry is performed. Opposition arises from within and without as those who dislike the message turn their attacks on the messenger. Many pastors leave the ministry altogether because they cannot handle the pressures of pastoral ministry.

Jeremiah wanted to quit. He wanted to walk away from the challenging ministry God called him to perform. He struggled intensely with that call, and with the cost of giving himself to it. But in the end, the grace of God sustained him, and enabled him to finish the race the Lord had set before him.

Grace in the New Testament

The New Testament is replete with examples as well as exhortations concerning God's grace. The writers of the books of the New Testament had much to say about this matter of grace, through personal experiences with God as well as with inspired instructions from God.

JESUS CHRIST

We must begin with Jesus Christ Himself if we are to understand the New Testament concept of grace. And the place to begin, of course, would be at the beginning of His earthly life. John, in his Gospel, gives us much needed insight into this matter by stating the following:

> "And the Word [Jesus Christ] became flesh and dwelt among us, and we beheld His glory, the glory as of the only begotten of the Father, full of grace and truth... And of His fullness we have all received, and grace for grace."
>
> (John 1:14, 16)

It is obvious from these important words that Jesus is the full expression of the grace of God. To understand grace all one must do is look at Jesus. His grace is evident in His life, His work, His teachings, His words, His exhortations, His sacrificial death, His resurrection, and His ascension. Each aspect of Jesus's life is an expression of His grace.

First, His birth is a definite expression of the grace of the Father. God the Father, in an act of unmerited love, from eternity past, decreed that Jesus would be the source of salvation for fallen humanity. The apostle John, in the book of Revelation, penned these words in declaration of this amazing truth:

> All who dwell on the earth will worship him, whose names have not been written in the Book of Life of the Lamb slain from the foundation of the world.
>
> (Revelation 13:8)

Out of the abundance of the Father's love, mercy, and grace, Jesus was ordained from before the creative activity of God to be the One who would give His life in sacrifice so that sinful humankind might be redeemed from their state of fallenness.

And then, Jesus came into the world through the miracle of the virgin conception. This, too, was an act of grace. Jesus could not have been conceived through the usual means of conception, because to have been conceived through physical union between a man and woman would mean that He would have been born with a sin nature, just like all of humankind. But for Him to be able to provide salvation from sin, He had to be perfectly sinless. Thus, the need for the virgin conception, which was an act of God's amazing grace in making sure the birth of Jesus protected His perfect, sinless nature while at the same time providing full humanity so that He might give His life as the propitiating sacrifice which could appease the justifiable wrath of God.

And that same grace is still available to us today. The Bible states that there is never any change in Jesus, but rather that He is always the same. He is constant and consistent: the never-changing God of the universe, who extends grace to all who will accept it.

His life then was a continual expression of that grace. Through His words He taught the importance of receiving God's grace, and the means through which this might become reality. Then, beyond the acceptance of that grace in salvation, He showed us how to be sanctified by that same grace through which we are saved.

His teachings were a testament to God's grace as He taught man how to have a relationship with the Father. His miracles were testimonies to His grace, as He provided healings of different kinds, manifesting His grace to those in need. Jesus's life was the full expression of grace, and the means of accepting, embracing, and appropriating that grace.

His death, burial, and resurrection are the crowning heights of His grace, as He fulfilled the will of His Father in giving Himself as the means of salvation. Through His death He took the sting out of ours. Through His burial He was able to suffer the fullness of the penalty of our sin. And through His resurrection He won the victory over death, hell, and the grave. Grace that is sufficient for all.

THE HOLY SPIRIT

So, if we identify Jesus Christ as the expression of God's grace, then it would also be appropriate to identify the Holy Spirit as the extender of that grace. Jesus, indeed, is the means through whom sinful human beings receive the grace of God in salvation. Then it is through the ministry of the Holy Spirit that saving grace and sanctifying grace comes to fruition in the life of the individual. This work of the Holy Spirit manifests itself in many different ways. The following will offer a quick summary of this work.

One thing the Holy Spirit does that could be identified as a work of grace in the life of the unbeliever is the work of conviction. Jesus referred to this amazing work in the following statement:

> It is to your advantage that I go away; for if I do
> not go away, the Helper will not come to you; but
> if I depart, I will send Him to you. And when He

has come, He will convict the world of sin, and of righteousness, and of judgment: of sin, because they do not believe in Me; of righteousness, because I go to My Father and you see Me no more; of judgment, because the ruler of this world is judged.

(John 16:7b–11)

Jesus speaks clearly in this passage of the essential role the Holy Spirit will play once Jesus had ascended back to the Father. His ministry is one of conviction, bringing about an awareness of sin and the need for repentance. He will convict the world of righteousness based on Christ's completed work and His return to His pre-incarnate position at the right hand of the Father. And He will convict the world of judgment, revealing the truth about the judgment of Satan, the ruler of this world.

The Holy Spirit is also involved in a teaching ministry in the life of the believer. This is an extremely important aspect of the Holy Spirit's involvement in bringing the believer in Jesus Christ to a more intimate understanding of Jesus' work. According to the book of Acts, the Holy Spirit continues the work Jesus started during His earthly ministry. Jesus continues His discourse on the work of the Holy Spirit in the next few verses of the text quoted above:

I still have many things to say to you, but you cannot bear them now. However, when He, the Spirit of truth, has come, He will guide you into all truth; for He will not speak on His own authority, but whatever He hears He will speak; and He will tell you things to come. He will glorify Me, for He will take of what is Mine and declare it to you. All things that the Father has are Mine. Therefore I said that He will take of Mine and declare it to you.

(John 16:12–15)

One of the key responsibilities of the Holy Spirit is to guide the believer into truth. The world is filled with error. Theological error, philosophical error, political error, societal error, moral error, ethical error, behavioral error, and cultural error, to name just a few. How are we to know what is truth and what is error? The Holy Spirit will guide the believer into the truth. He will personally see to it that the truth of God's word is protected from the attacks of sin-hardened men.

There are so many other aspects of the ministry of the Holy Spirit, but we will give consideration to just one more. He is involved in the distribution of spiritual gifts which enable the individual believer to serve God. Paul speaks of this role of the Holy Spirit in his correspondence with the Corinthians.

> There are diversities of gifts, but the same Spirit. There are differences of ministries, but the same Lord. And there are diversities of activities, but it is the same God who works all in all. But the manifestation of the Spirit is given to each one for the profit of all.
>
> But one and the same Spirit works all these things, distributing to each one individually as He wills.
>
> (1 Corinthians 12:4–7, 11)

Each individual believer receives at least one spiritual gift through the ministry of the Holy Spirit. It is not the choice of the individual to choose which gift(s) he has, but the Holy Spirit distributes according to His will. The believer is then to develop his gift and use it for the profit of all. The ministry of the local church runs efficiently and effectively if each individual member of that body is doing their part, using their gift, for the glory of God and the profit of the entire body.

It is obvious from these examples that grace is a Biblical concept that runs throughout the entirety of scripture. In the following pages we will attempt to look at a number of different nuances of grace as we strive to determine how it plays an important role in the life of each individual believer in the Lord Jesus Christ. The chapter topics are not written in any particular order, so as you peruse the table of contents you might see a topic that is of special interest to you. I would encourage you to read that chapter first as you dive into the manifestations of grace.

POINTS TO PONDER

1. If you were asked to share your understanding of the Biblical view of grace, how would you do it? Are there any key words, phrases, or examples you would use to give your explanation?

2. Some believe that there is a distinction between the emphases of the Old Testament and the New Testament. Do you agree with this assessment? Why or why not?

3. Several examples were given from both the Old Testament and New Testament. Can you identify yourself with one or more of these individuals?

4. If so, which one(s), and why do you identify with them?

5. List any Biblical examples of grace that come to mind. Why would you identify these as examples?

CHAPTER 2

Sovereign Grace

For even if there are so-called gods, whether in heaven or on earth (as there are many gods and many lords), yet for us there is one God, the Father, of whom are all things, and we for Him; and one Lord Jesus Christ, through whom are all things, and through whom we live.

(1 Corinthians 8:5–6)

O Worship the King

Oh, worship the King, all-glorious above,
Oh, gratefully sing His pow'r and His love;
Our Shield and Defender, the Ancient of Days,
Pavilioned in splendor, and girded with praise.

Oh, tell of His might, oh, sing of His grace,
Whose robe is the light, whose canopy space;
His chariots of wrath the deep thunderclouds form,
And dark is His path on the winds of the storm.
Robert Grant

P aul states clearly in the verse quoted on this chapter's title page that there is one God, the Father, **of whom are all things**, and one Lord, Jesus Christ. Since all things come from this one God, then it only stands to reason that if there is any such thing as grace it must of necessity come from Him. God is the initiator of grace, the distributor of grace, and the sovereign ruler over the work of grace.

God's sovereignty is most commonly thought of in relation to His action in the salvation of human beings. There are many verses in Scripture that would validate the claim that God does indeed act by His own sovereign power in salvation (a topic that will be covered in detail in chapter three), but in this chapter focus will be given to a much broader view of sovereignty, and specifically sovereign grace.

Sovereignty can be thought of in terms of God's omnipotence. He is an all-powerful Being, possessing power to accomplish all He chooses to accomplish. This concept of sovereignty is evidenced in many ways and is clearly seen in many passages in the Bible.

For example, the very beginning of the biblical record reveals the sovereign power of God in creation. The first two chapters in the Book of Genesis record for us God's creative activity. According to these records, God, by His power to accomplish His purpose, simply spoke the created order into existence. The opening words of the Bible state clearly the creative activity of God:

> In the beginning God created the heavens and the earth.
>
> (Genesis 1:1)

This verse reveals several aspects of God's being that set the tone for the remainder of the entire Biblical canon. If one can embrace these truths, then, by faith, there will be little problem embracing the teachings of the remainder of the Bible.

The Eternality of God

First, this verse would reveal to the reader the eternal nature of God. The phrase, "In the beginning," reveals an aspect of God that must be understood correctly, or the reader of scripture could easily miss, or at least misinterpret, one of the most important of His attributes.

The Bible teaches that God had no beginning and will have no end. It is imperative that we understand that the "beginning" referred to in this verse is not a reference to the beginning of God. Rather it is a reference to the beginning of God's creative activity. Note carefully that the verse does not say, "In the beginning *of* God", but rather "In the beginning God." Again, we must understand that God had no beginning. A few verses of Scripture will illustrate this truth.

> Then Abraham planted a tamarisk tree in Beersheba, and there called on the name of the Lord, *the Everlasting God*.
>
> > (Genesis 21:33)

> Before the mountains were brought forth, or ever You formed the earth and the world, even *from everlasting to everlasting You are God*.
>
> > (Psalm 90:2)

> *The eternal God* is your refuge, and underneath are the *everlasting arms*...
>
> > (Deuteronomy 33:27)

> For thus says the High and Lofty One *who inhabits eternity*, whose name is Holy...
>
> > (Isaiah 57:15) (emphasis added
> > on each of these verses)

24

These verses provide an enormous amount of evidence that supports the biblical claim that God is truly an eternal Being. Some might object that there is no empirical evidence that would validate this claim. However, for those who embrace the first verse in the Bible by faith, it is relatively easy to embrace the rest of the biblical record as well. And this is the testimony of Scripture. Carefully read these words from the Epistle to the Hebrews:

> Now faith is the substance of things hoped for, the evidence of things not seen. For by it the elders obtained a good testimony. By faith we understand that the worlds were framed by the word of God, so that things which are seen were not made of things which are visible.
>
> (Hebrews 11:1–3)

When faith is removed from the formula then we are left to ourselves to explain the intricacies of the created order. But, when faith gives us eyes to see the unseen, when faith gives the ability to understand that the worlds were framed by God Himself, when we begin to believe the biblical report, then we need no other explanation. The eternal God is the answer.

Granted, it is difficult to embrace an idea that is presented as truth if there is no empirical evidence to substantiate that claim. There are many who deny the account of creation in the biblical record due to the fact that there is no "hard" evidence to scientifically prove it. After all, no one was there to witness the creation of the universe. All we have is an ancient text that records a description of God's creative activity.

But the same argument could justifiably be raised against those who embrace the "big bang" theory of the origination of the universe. No one was there to record the explosion. No one was present to give a written account of exactly how it took place. No one was there to record what the material was, and where the material originated that was used to "build" the universe.

And even further, what, or who, caused the bang? There has to be an original cause behind it all. It didn't just happen by chance, or coincidence, did it. If so, chance would have to be embraced as an entity of some sort, with the power to bring about the massive explosion out of which the entire universe came. So where did chance originate? Nothing can happen by chance, unless chance has the ability to cause something to happen.

But for those who would argue for the massive, big bang explosion all those billions of years ago, not only does there need to be an explanation of the cause of the explosion, but also there has to be an explanation of the material used in the explosion. If not, then the material of the universe was in existence prior to the explosion, and somehow, out of the explosion all that preexisting material had to somehow lock into orbital patterns that have, at least on one tiny planet called Earth, been able to produce life.

It seems obvious that the record of the sovereign work of the eternally existing God offers a much better explanation. However, whichever explanation one might choose to embrace, it demands belief by faith in something that cannot be empirically or experientially explained. The Bible presents a substantial argument for creation by an eternal Being, referred to in scripture as "God".

This leads us to a second observation about the sovereignty of God.

THE CREATIVE ACTIVITY OF GOD

Since God is an eternal being, with no beginning and no end, then we can embrace by faith that it was by His choice that the heavens and the earth were created. There is the evident work of a Creator, a Designer, behind the intricacies of God's marvelous creation. As stated in the previous section, some would have us believe that the creation came about by mere chance: that through some cataclysmic explosion billions of years ago everything came into existence. Somehow, through this "big bang", planets and stars and moons and galaxies all were birthed into being. These heavenly bodies somehow are then locked into an orbit circling the center of every given galaxy. This resulted in the earth being locked into an orbital rotation around the sun at just the right distance to produce the process of evolution and maintain life. Then, over a period of an unknown span of time, and through the process of evolution, from the beginning of a one-celled amoeba developed every form of life on planet earth.

This theory of evolution has been accepted by many as scientific fact, rather than what it actually is: theory. It is an attempt to give explanation to the existence of the heavens and the earth without having a divine Creator in the formula. When God is removed from consideration, then the imagination of man can run headlong into the black hole of the uncertain and the unknown.

I will admit that I am no expert on the theory of evolution. I do know enough about it to know that it has far too many unknowns to give answer to every question and concern of many who, like me, have a desire to know the truth. As a matter of fact, it would take a great deal more faith to believe in the theory of evolution than it would to believe in the testimony of the Bible. And please note, either one would take belief in something that cannot be proven empirically. There is the need to either accept the Bible's teaching on the subject, or man's teaching.

The Bible states clearly that God created the heavens and the earth. The word translated "created" literally means to bring something into existence. It does not mean that God took preexisting matter and formed it into the vastness of the universe. Rather, it means that God created the vastness of the universe out of absolutely nothing. It means that prior to the creative work of God, nothing, outside of God Himself, existed.

That is such a mind-blowing thing to consider. Have you ever thought of nothing? Can you even think of nothing? For a moment, try this mental exercise. Go back in your mind to a time before time. Back beyond the existence of man. Back before the existence of the stars and the moons and the planets. Back before anything existed. Back to that point where there was nothing but God.

Can you do it? Can you think of nothing? It is actually an exercise in futility. It is impossible to do because even your thought of nothing would be something. It is literally impossible to think about nothing. But, if we are to understand this first verse in the Bible, we must understand that there was a point in the past where absolutely nothing existed, except God.

And out of the vastness of absolute nothingness, God brought everything into existence. God created the heavens and the earth. The first chapter of Genesis then unfolds for us six consecutive days of creation, and how God spoke everything into existence within the confines of those six days. He is the eternal God who, by His own choice and to serve His own purposes created the heavens and the earth, crowning His creative work with the creation of man and woman. Therefore, this first verse in the Bible clearly teaches the eternality of God and the creative activity of God.

THE AUTHORITY OF GOD

Then, it also clearly teaches the amazing attribute of the authority of God. Since it is true that God is the eternal God of the universe, and that by His power and for His purpose He created the heavens and the earth, it only stands to reason that He has authority over that which He made. He is, indeed, sovereign.

Oftentimes, God's sovereignty is thought of in terms of the role He plays in man's salvation (which will be discussed at length in chapter three). However, the Bible gives a much broader view of God's sovereignty. God is truly and totally in control of His created order. There are so many different ways this truth can be discussed and has been discussed at length through the writings of multitudes of authors. For the purposes of this work, a broad overview of this topic will be offered.

Through many examples of God's activity in relation to the created order, and specifically in relation to the earth and its inhabitants, the authority of God becomes quite clear. The creation account in the first chapter of Genesis establishes the fact of the authority of God in an unquestionable manner. One might deny the truth of this account, but if the account is taken at face value it leaves no room for doubt about the authority of God over creation.

Beyond that, the Bible is replete with examples that would further validate this claim. Again, just a few of these examples should be sufficient to make this point, all from the book of Genesis. The four major events recorded in the book of Genesis – the creation, the fall, the flood, and the tower of Babel – are clear indicators of the authority of God in relation to the created order. Then, the four main characters in the book of Genesis – Abraham, Isaac, Jacob (Israel) and Joseph - show us clearly the authoritative work of God in relation to His human family.

THE CREATION

Discussion has already been made of the creation account, so a quick review will suffice. With absolute authority, God brought everything into existence out of sheer nothingness. God created the heavens and the earth, and then, meticulously and methodically, He completed His creative activity after a series of six consecutive days of creation. To better understand the Bible's teachings on this subject, a few verses might prove to be helpful.

> In the beginning was the Word, and the Word was with God, and the Word was God. He was in the beginning with God. All things were made

through Him, and without Him nothing was made that was made.

(John 1:1–3)

By faith we understand that the worlds were framed by the word of God, so that the things which are seen were not made of things which are visible.

(Hebrews 11:3)

For by Him [Jesus Christ] all things were created that are in heaven and that are on earth, visible and invisible, whether thrones or dominions or principalities or powers. All things were created through Him and for Him. And He is before all things, and in Him all things consist.

(Colossians 1:16–17)

These verses clearly establish the authority of God in His creative work. And please note carefully the phrase, "And He [Jesus Christ] is before all things, and in Him all things consist." The word "consist" literally means that it is in Christ that all things are held together. The planets and stars are locked into orbital patterns because Jesus Christ has thus ordered the universe. And these orbital patterns will hold in place until God sees fit to intervene.

THE FALL OF MAN

The second major event in the book of Genesis is the fall of man. God had created Adam and Eve and placed them in the Garden of Eden. Everything they could ever possibly need was provided for them in that garden. It must have been a glorious place, far above our ability to even imagine. It would also have been a wonderful place to reside, with everything humankind would need to live a fulfilling, meaningful, and contented life. Even the animals were subject to this human couple.

The greatest thing about Adam and Eve residing in Eden was the fact that God was there, in their very presence. He conversed with Adam and Eve in the most personal and intimate way. What a glorious place this must have been: heaven on earth! God dwelling, walking, talking, enjoying fellowship with His human creation. Our minds are ill-equipped to grasp this concept. Oh, yes, we have the privilege of conversing with God through the vehicle of prayer. We are ushered into the presence of God as we, in humility, confession, and adoration, bow before the God of the universe. But it is still vastly different. God was present with them in a very unique way. The Genesis record tells us that He walked and talked with Adam in the garden in the cool of the day.

But into this beautiful scene enters the arch enemy of God: Satan. The record is found in the third chapter of Genesis. God had provided abundantly for Adam and Eve in the Garden of Eden and had instructed them they could eat from every tree in the garden except one: the tree of the knowledge of good and evil. Satan enters the picture and places the seed of doubt in their minds about the word of God.

> And the woman said to the serpent, "We may eat the fruit of the trees of the garden; but of the fruit of the tree which *is* in the midst of the garden, God has said, 'You shall not eat it, nor shall you touch it, lest you die.'"
>
> Then the serpent said to the woman, "You will not surely die. For God knows that in the day you eat of it your eyes will be opened, and you will be like God, knowing good and evil."
>
> (Genesis 3:2–3)

God's command was clear: don't eat fruit from the tree of the knowledge of good and evil or you will die. Satan's deceit was just as clear: You will not die! Deceit was the tool, and doubt was the goal. Satan simply planted the seed of doubt in the minds of Eve and Adam. And the plan worked. They gave themselves over to the deceit of Satan, ate of the forbidden fruit, and suffered the dire consequences God had pronounced. Thus, man fell into the pit of disobedience, and the results have been devastating. Each and every human being born into this world have inherited the sin nature passed down by Adam and Eve. The earth, and all in it, is now under the curse of God.

Man's plunge into the depths of spiritual darkness spiraled out of control, leading up to the decision of God to completely destroy humanity. Read these somber and sobering words in the Genesis account that relate to the reader the reason for God destroying the world of humankind with a global flood.

> Then the Lord saw that the wickedness of man was great in the earth, and that every intent of the thoughts of his heart was only evil continually. And the Lord was sorry that He had made man on the earth, and He was grieved in His heart. So the Lord said, I" will destroy man whom I have created from the face of the earth, both man and beast, creeping thing and birds of the air, for I am sorry that I have made them."
>
> (Genesis 6:5–7)

This might cause some to question, and even doubt, God's sovereignty. How are we to understand the statement that God was grieved in His heart that He had created man? Is it possible that the wickedness of man caught God off guard? Did it take Him by surprise? Thinking back to the garden of Eden, and Adam and Eve's decision to eat of the forbidden fruit, are we to think that their action was not foreseen by God? Does God's sovereignty mean that He was somehow involved in Adam and

Eve's disobedience? Did He cause it to happen? Did Adam and Eve have no choice in the matter?

There has always been a great divide among theologians and Bible scholars concerning this matter. We might think of several contemporary events to illustrate this point. Consider, for example, the terrorist attack on the United States on September 11, 2001. Did God orchestrate the events of that day? Was it God's preordained plan to have almost 3000 people killed as they went about their normal activities? Or what about the tsunami on December 26, 2004, that killed more than 250,000 people? Or Hurricane Katrina in late August of 2005, that took more than 1800 lives and resulted in costs estimated to be more than one hundred twenty-five billion dollars. Or so many other destructive events that resulted in massive death and devastation.

Does God, in His sovereignty, orchestrate events such as these? If God is indeed sovereign, wielding all-power to accomplish all His purposes, does it mean that He is the cause of everything that happens?

It is true that the Bible teaches certain acts of devastation were a direct result of God's sovereign omnipotence. It is clearly taught that God caused several episodes of drought, famine, and blight in the Old Testament. These were ordained by God to call His people to repentance. There are other times that these same types of events are to be viewed simply as results of the curse God has placed on the earth because of the fall, and not a result of God's direct orchestration of those events.

But each of these is a testimony to God's sovereign power. Devastating floods, earthquakes, hurricanes, tornados, volcanoes, and other such catastrophic events happen because of the curse. But they all happen within the parameters of God's sovereign will.

And so, we are to understand the wickedness of man. Yes, it grieved God's heart that man had become so completely evil, which led to the destruction of humankind. But it was not because God orchestrated the wickedness. It was because God allowed

33

Adam and Eve to commit that first act of disobedience, and we have all followed in their footsteps, because God has allowed us, within the parameters of His sovereign rule, to make choices pertaining to our own desires. And those desires are motivated by the sinful nature we inherited from the very first couple. God hasn't preordained the sinful actions of man but has allowed man to make these choices for himself.

THE FLOOD

This brings us to a consideration of the third major event in the book of Genesis: the flood. God had made the decision to destroy the earth with a global flood. If the Bible is taken literally, and the account of the flood is understood to be a literal event, then who could possibly question the sovereignty of God? His power is evident in this event perhaps more than any other event recorded in Scripture. God had created Adam and Eve and given them the command to multiply and fill the earth. That command had been fulfilled as now, in the days of Noah, the population of the earth had grown exponentially. Approximately 1100 years elapsed between Adam and Noah. The lifespan being so much longer then than it is now means that couples could have many more children than is common today. There is no way of knowing what the exact population would have been, but it could have possibly been in the billions. Perhaps that helps us better understand the gravity of this event.

It was God's intent to completely destroy humankind. However, we come to a pivotal verse in the sixth chapter of Genesis:

> But Noah found favor in the eyes of the Lord.
>
> (Genesis 6:8)

Again, this might cause some concern about God's role in devastating natural catastrophes, along with concern about why

34

God would choose to save Noah and his family while destroying the rest of humankind. Also, could this action of God be viewed as being unfair as He destroys everyone except one family? What gives God the right to act in such a way?

When I was a boy, I enjoyed assembling model cars. This was a tedious task, as those model kits contained many small pieces which had to be separated from their molds, and then put together using model glue. Then, more time would be spent in painting the assembled model, and finally and painstakingly placing those pesky decals on the finished product.

Oftentimes I would then display the cars on a shelf for all to see. After all, these were my masterpieces. I wanted to show them off, to hear the accolades of those who would gaze at the beauty of my models and tell me what a talented model builder I was.

After building many of these models, I began taking them off the shelf and playing with them. At first, I did this carefully, not wanting to damage my works of art. Eventually, though, I started becoming more adventurous with my creations. And it all culminated with using these models in demolition derbies. I banged them together, pretending to crash them as the drivers tried to be the last car running.

One day I had a brainstorm. I began to think how exciting it would be to see the cars crash together and burst into flames. So, I would douse two of the cars with lighter fluid, and as the cars went around the demolition track, chasing each other, trying to crash into the other cars, I would smash them together while lighting a match, causing the cars to burst into flames.

Please understand that this is an extremely feeble attempt to illustrate God's sovereignty, but bear with me for just a few more moments. I had built the models. Granted, I built them out of material that already existed. I did not bring anything into existence, as God did. But I was the creator of these models. Then, just as I had decided to create them, I decided to destroy them. They were mine. They belonged to me. I had the right to do with them as I pleased.

Let's now apply that feeble illustration to God's sovereignty over His creation of humankind. He had provided for man. He had given man instructions on how to enjoy life in the garden paradise He had given them. And now, man had abused the creation, disobeyed the Creator, and had turned their hearts to evil continually. So, God decided He would destroy what He had created.

It is only logical to understand that He had every right to act in this way. He could have chosen to destroy Noah and his family along with the rest. He could have chosen to create another human couple, place them in a garden paradise, command them to be fruitful and multiply, and start all over. Rather, He chose to do it the way He did: He saved Noah and his family and made a new start with them. This was the sovereign choice of the omnipotent God who created it all.

THE TOWER OF BABEL

Once again the earth became populated with vast numbers of humans. Over the next three centuries multitudes of babies were born. This brings us to our consideration of the fourth major event in the book of Genesis: The Tower of Babel.

This is certainly one of the most interesting stories in Scripture. And once again, it provides the reader of the Bible with more insights into the sovereignty of God as He makes another determination that will affect the entire human race. The story of the Tower is found in Genesis 11.

> Now the whole earth had one language and one speech. And it came to pass, as they journeyed from the east, that they found a plain in the land of Shinar, and they dwelt there. Then they said to one another, "Come, let us make bricks and bake them thoroughly." They had brick for stone,

and they had asphalt for mortar. And they said, :Come, let us build ourselves a city, and a tower whose top is in the heavens; let us make a name for ourselves, lest we be scattered abroad over the face of the earth."

(Genesis 11:1–4)

As the population grew, and as earth's inhabitants began to spread out, there arose the desire among the human family to maintain unity. There was the desire to stay together, to build a name for themselves, and to protect what was theirs. The emphasis is so very easy to see: self-centeredness and pride. It is all about them.

It is interesting to note the contradistinction between the actions of the people and that of God. They are building a tower that will reach up into the heavens. It was to be a massive structure, one that would be the centerpiece of their new society. Obviously, it was their attempt to show how powerful and intelligent they were. Using the most modern of materials they began the work of building up and up and up. Up to the heavens!

But God, Whose residence is heaven, comes down. Once again, we see a clear demonstration of His sovereignty. This event is a display of God's omniscience as well as His omnipotence. His ability to know all things, coupled with His ability to accomplish all things, sets the tone for this encounter with those who are striving to thwart His command to fill the earth. God simply, by an act of His will, confounds the languages of the people, and scatters them abroad in language groups. They are now fulfilling the command to fill the earth, whether they had the desire to do so or not.

These four major events – the creation, the fall, the flood, and the tower of Babel – are all graphic displays of God's sovereignty and of His grace. But there are also four major characters in the Genesis record – Abraham, Isaac, Jacob, and Joseph. They are also displays of sovereignty and grace.

ABRAHAM

Abraham is one of the great characters in the Biblical narrative. He holds a prominent place in the Old Testament as being the one whom God chose to be the father of the Hebrew nation. The record of the calling of Abram (his name before God changed it to Abraham) is found in Genesis 12:

> Now the Lord had said to Abram: "Get out of your country, from your family and your father's house to a land that I will show you. I will make you a great nation; I will bless who bless you, and I will curse him who curses you; and in all the families of the earth shall be blessed."
>
> (Genesis 12:1–3)

A few matters of extreme importance should be noted as consideration is given to Abraham. First, God took the initiative in confronting Abraham. It was clearly God's choice of Abraham, and not Abraham's choice of God, that is in view here. God chose Abraham for the task He was going to bring about. He could have chosen anyone out of all the human family alive on earth at this specific moment of human history, but for reasons known only to God, Abraham was chosen.

Why did He choose Abraham? Was there something about this particular man that caught God's attention? Was Abraham a man of devout faith, with a heart set on seeking God and following obediently God's will? Actually, there is no indication in the unfolding story that would lead us to believe that Abraham was seeking God at all. By all indications it appears that Abraham's father was a pagan, worshipping the gods of the land. This truly makes the story even more amazing when we consider the sovereign grace of God.

God chose Abraham. Period. Then, He instructed Abraham on what he was to do: leave his country, his family, and his father's house. Everything that was comfortable and familiar God was calling him to leave behind. It would be a clean break for Abraham: a fresh start with a clean slate. God obviously wanted Abraham to be in a place – physically as well as spiritually – where he could discard the old and replace it with the new things God wanted to give him. In order for Abraham to embrace this God who was completely new to him, he would have to get away from those gods he had been taught to worship.

So what does Abraham do? He obeys. He begins a journey to – well, to where he did not know. He was only told by God to leave his country and go to a place God would show him. Again, a clear display of God's sovereignty and grace. But Abraham would have to obey these instructions in order to experience what God had promised: to make of Abraham a nation through which all nations of the earth would be blessed.

The ultimate outcome of this divine calling of God on Abraham's life was that he would become the father of the nation of Israel, and the father of spiritual Israel: the church. Only a sovereign God could make such audacious promises, and then keep them. It was by His sovereignty and His amazing grace that the unfolding drama of the history of Israel as well as the unfolding glory of the church of Jesus Christ could be fulfilled through the calling of God on the life of one man.

But there was a bit of a problem to overcome – at least a problem in the eyes of Abraham and his wife, Sarai. Abraham was 75 years old when he first received the call of God recorded in the passage quoted above. God was going to make of Abraham a great nation, but Abraham and Sarai had no children which meant there was no one through whom this promise could be fulfilled. Here, again, we note the sovereign grace of God.

God appears to Abraham once again and assures him that his reward will be great.

After these things the word of the Lord came to
Abram in a vision, saying, "Do not be afraid,

Abram. I am your shield, your exceedingly great reward." But Abram said, "Lord God, what will You give me, seeing I go childless, and the heir of my house is Eliezer of Damascus?" Then Abram said, "Look, You have given me no offspring; indeed one born in my house is my heir!"

(Genesis 15:1–3)

Even though God gives these words of encouragement, Abraham seems to be somewhat perplexed as to how this promise could possibly be kept. He has no heir, other than a slave by the name of Eliezer.

Sometimes we may feel as Abraham must have felt. We read of God's grand promises in Scripture, and we, perhaps, see others who seem to be experiencing and enjoying those promises. But all we personally experience is heartache and grief, suffering and pain. We read of the amazing generosity of God in providing for His children, but we struggle to make ends meet as we have more outgo than income. We see others who are blessed with health and happiness, but all we have is sickness and sadness.

It may cause us to question the goodness of God. Maybe it could cause some to doubt God's ability to carry out His promises. Or that God's promises are for someone else, but not for me. But let's learn a lesson from Abraham. He was 75 years old when God made those fantastic promises found in the 12th chapter of Genesis. It was not until twenty-five years later that God blessed Abraham with his son, Isaac. God's timing in fulfilling His promises may leave us confused and could possibly cause us to question what He might be up to, but He always keeps His word.

This truth is clearly seen in the life of Abraham. When he was 100 years old, and Sarah was 90, God fulfilled His promise that they would have a child. After all those years of experiencing the inability to conceive and bear a child God opened Sarah's womb and allowed her to conceive and give birth to Isaac, the child of promise. And, just as God had promised, all nations of the earth have been blessed through him. All because of the sovereign grace of God.

Far too often we hear of people who have lost their faith, turned their backs on God, and walked away from what at one time was a life of commitment and service to God's glory. Many become disillusioned because they don't see God working in their lives as they see Him work in other's. Perhaps they have succumbed to some of life's troubles and tribulations, and they are wondering why God has not intervened in their life as He has in so many that they have known.

We can learn from the example and experiences of Abraham and Sarah that God keeps His word, but does so on His own timetable, and in accord with His own purposes. But even if He does not come through for us as He has for others, it doesn't mean that He has broken His word. It could be that He is simply letting us know that the time isn't right. Abraham and Sarah had to learn this lesson as they waited twenty-five long years to see the fulfillment of God's promises.

ISAAC

Isaac is the second of those four major characters in Genesis. It is through Isaac that the family line of Abraham is carried forward. And once again the sovereign grace of God is displayed in the most amazing of ways.

Isaac was truly a miracle child, being born to Abraham and Sarah at the ages of 100 and 90, respectively. Earlier, after the initial calling of God to Abraham, years passed without their seeing the promise of God fulfilled. This resulted in their trying to take matters into their own hands by having Abraham have a child through a sexual liaison with Hagar, Sarai's handmaid. This son was given the name Ishmael, who would be fifteen years old when Isaac was born.

God made great promises to Abraham regarding Ishmael even

though he was not the son of promise. However, the descendants of Ishmael and the descendants of Isaac have experienced tensions that continue to exist to the present day. Hardly a day goes by that we don't hear news of some battle of words, if not actions, between the descendants of these two families of Abraham. This illustrates what happens when we try to work out God's plans on our own, using our reasoning skills to try to figure out what we should do. Had Abraham and Sarai simply been patient they would have seen how wonderful God's plan was, and how He would have brought it all to pass.

God did indeed keep His promise to Abraham, and Isaac was born. We continue to see the sovereign grace of God at work in Isaac as God providentially guides and provides in his life. A couple of events in Isaac's life will be sufficient to illustrate this point. The first is found in Genesis 22. God speaks to Abraham once again with a most unusual and unexpected word of instruction. No one would have ever expected to hear God command Abraham to carry out the awful deed He gives here. Remember, Isaac is the son of promise through whom the descendants of Abraham are to come. And yet God gives this horrific command. Read these words carefully, and try to imagine the horror Abraham must have felt as he heard God's command:

> Now it came to pass after these things that God tested Abraham, and said to him, "Abraham!" And he said, "Here I am." Then He said, "Take now your son, your only son Isaac, whom you love, and go to the land of Moriah, and offer him there as a burnt offering on one of the mountains of which I shall tell you."
>
> (Genesis 22:1–2)

We can't even begin to imagine the consternation and confusion Abraham must have felt to hear this word of command.

Isaac is the one through whom the family line was to come. He was the one though whom the nation was to grow into a multitude beyond number. If Isaac is offered as a burnt offering, how then is the family line to be carried on?

This story, even though it is true in every detail, and is a picture of Abraham's total trust in God and his faithfulness to God, is also a prophetic picture of the work of God the Father and God the Son. It depicts the amazing grace of God the Father in giving His Son, Jesus Christ, as the sacrificial Lamb who would pay the penalty for humankind's sin.

But it is also the true story of one man being willing to obey the command of God even though it was a truly heart-wrenching thing to consider. Isaac, who questions his father as to why they did not bring a lamb to sacrifice, hears Abraham reply in simple faith, "God will provide a lamb." And that is exactly what happened: God provided a lamb for Abraham's sacrifice, and God the Father provided the Lamb, Jesus Christ, for the ultimate sacrifice.

Then, there is a second episode in Isaac's life that once again illustrates the sovereign grace of God. It also presents us with another prophetic portrait of the work of God the Father and God the Son. But this story introduces us to a third person, the oldest servant in Abraham's household.

> So Abraham said to the oldest servant of his house, who ruled over all that he had. "Please, put your hand under my thigh, and I will make you swear by the Lord, the God of heaven and the God of the earth, that you will not take a wife for my son from the daughters of the Canaanites, among whom I dwell; but you shall go to my country and to my family and take a wife for my son Isaac."
>
> (Genesis 24:2–4)

This story beautifully illustrates the role of the three Persons of the Trinity in the process of salvation. God the Father, illustrated by Abraham, commissions the household servant, who represents the Holy Spirit, to go to Abraham's own family to seek a bride for Isaac, who represents Jesus Christ. Again, as stated before, this application does not negate the truth and veracity of the historical event as recorded in this passage, but in addition to the truth of the story it also illustrates the wonderful truth of the Father, the Son, and the Holy Spirit all working together to secure the salvation of the lost.

The sovereignty of God is clearly displayed in His providential guidance as Abraham's household servant arrives in the country of Abraham's family. After asking God for leadership as he sought a bride for Isaac, the plan unfolds before him as if he had meticulously prepared every detail of the journey. He comes into direct contact with Rebekah, the daughter of Bethuel who, according to the account in Genesis, was the grandson of Abraham's brother, Nahor. This is yet another display of God's sovereign grace.

As the Genesis account continues to unfold, we see how important Isaac's role is in the working out of God's sovereign plan. Isaac was forty years old when he and Rebekah were married. After being united as husband and wife, it was soon discovered that she was unable to conceive. Isaac went to the Lord in prayer asking that He would grant her the ability to bear children.

> Now Isaac pleaded with the Lord for his wife, because she was barren; and the Lord granted his plea, and Rebekah his wife conceived.
>
> (Genesis 25:21)

It is obvious that Isaac saw Rebekah's inability to conceive as a matter that could be remedied by God. He prayed for the Lord to intervene in his wife's life, and the clear implication is that he recognized God's sovereignty over the physical care and well-being of individual human beings.

Could it be that in our modern world, with all the advances in medical science and research, that we have come to place very little confidence in God's ability to intervene in our lives when we are faced with health issues? I am not suggesting that we quit seeking medical attention when the need arises, as God has granted those in the medical field the abilities they have, and the knowledge they possess, to perform amazing medical feats. But could it be that we place more faith in their ability to heal than we do on seeking God's assistance? It is certainly true that there was not a plethora of medical experts to turn to in Isaac's day, so he did not have the privilege of taking Rebekah to the nearest doctor's office. But what we can learn from his actions is that he undoubtedly trusted God with the barrenness of his wife. He turned to the Lord, took his request to the Lord, and then trusted in the Lord to handle the problem. And what was the outcome of his prayer? The verse quoted above gives the answer: The Lord granted Isaac's prayer request and Rebekah conceived.

JACOB (ISRAEL)

Not only did she conceive, but she was blessed in this pregnancy to be carrying twins. However, the Genesis account goes on to record that Rebekah was having some type of difficulty in her pregnancy. Not having the tools and technology available today, there was no way of knowing exactly what was causing the struggle she felt going on inside her. So once again, as we saw in Isaac's prayer to God on behalf of his wife, we now see Rebekah going to God with her question.

> But the children struggled within her; and she said, "If all is well, why am I like this?" So she went to inquire of the Lord. And the Lord said to her: "Two nations are in your womb, two peoples shall be separated from your body; one people shall be

stronger than the other, and the older shall serve the younger."

(Genesis 25:21–23)

The children were born and given the names Esau and Jacob. There are several observations that should be made as consideration is given to these two brothers. First, we once again see the recurring theme that has already been noted: God's sovereignty. Through His response to Rebekah, He revealed that the older would serve the younger. Esau, who was born first, was the oldest by mere moments, but he was the eldest of the two boys none-the-less. And God, having revealed to Rebekah that the older would serve the younger, shows once again His sovereignty.

A second observation is the astounding fact that God could use someone such as Jacob. His name - which literally means supplanter, or deceiver - reveals the kind of person Jacob would be. As he and Esau grew into adulthood, Jacob used deceit and trickery to manipulate others to get his own way. As a result of this, a wedge began to develop between Jacob and Esau. Tensions grew as Jacob consistently used deceitful measures and tactics to accomplish his desires, which were sometimes very questionable. This all reached a point of no return when Rebekah came up with a plan to assure Jacob would receive the blessing from his father before Isaac died. Jacob's plan, of course, was to give Esau the blessing of the first born before Jacob died.

> And it came to pass, when Isaac was old and his eyes were so dim that he could not see, that he called Esau his older son and said to him, "My son." And he said to him, "Here I am." Then he said, "Behold now, I am old. I do not know the day of my death. Now therefore, please take your weapons, your quiver and your bow, and go out to the field and hunt game for me. And make me

savory food, such as I love, and bring it to me that
I may eat, that my soul may bless you before I die."

(Genesis 27:1–4)

Esau, being the first-born, would be the recipient of the
blessing of the oldest son. However, Rebekah devised a plan
through which Jacob would deceive his father, making him think
that he was Esau.

> Now Rebekah was listening when Isaac spoke to
> Esau his son. And Esau went to the field to hunt
> game and to bring it. So Rebekah spoke to Jacob
> her son, saying, "Indeed I heard your father speak
> to Esau your brother... Now therefore, my son,
> obey my voice according to what I command you.
> Go now to the flock and bring me from there two
> choice kids of the goats, and I will made savory
> food from them for your father, such as he loves.
> Then you shall take it to your father, that he may
> eat it, and that he may bless you before his death."
>
> Genesis 27:5–10)

It seems that Jacob got his deceitful nature honestly. Isaac
and Rebekah had done their children the great disservice and
injustice of playing favorites. The account in Genesis makes it
clear that Esau was Isaac's favorite, while Jacob was Rebekah's.
And it is quite clear that Rebekah was a deceiver, just as Jacob.
The entire episode of Jacob stealing the blessing of Isaac was a
plan concocted by Rebekah. She is the one who came up with
the idea of using deceit to trick Isaac into giving the blessing to
Jacob instead of Esau, as Hebrew custom and practice required.

Parents, let's be warned: We cannot overestimate the
influence we have on our children. They learn so much from us
by listening to what we say, observing what we do, and imitating
everything they hear and see. When we watch our children, it

will amaze us of how much of their behavior is nothing more than an imitation of what they observe in us. Their mannerisms will mimic ours. Their vocabulary will be a carbon copy of what they hear from us. They learn by watching and listening. This truth is seen clearly in this story of Rebekah and Jacob. She was a deceiver, and so was he. He learned his behavior by watching his mother.

It is truly amazing that God would use someone like Jacob. However, there is a great truth we can learn from this story: God uses broken people. No one is beyond experiencing God's grace. There are so many examples of this in Scripture: Moses, Abraham, David, Samson, Paul, Peter, and others illustrate this truth vividly. And, to that list you can add your name. No matter how broken you were/are, God can still use you in remarkable ways.

After this act of deceit in which Jacob stole Esau's blessing, Esau was infuriated and promised to kill Jacob. Rebekah, in fear for Jacob's life, tells him to go back to her family until Esau's anger subsides. Jacob follows the instructions of his mother and leaves, escaping Esau's wrath. What he probably expected was to leave for a brief time and then return home. This, however, was not the case. He ended up staying away twenty years, during which he fathered twelve sons who would eventually become the tribal heads of the twelve tribes of Israel. This chapter in God's unfolding plan is a powerful testimony to His sovereign grace and reveals the truth that He performs His will through His works in real time in real history.

It is clear that God chose Jacob to be the next in line as God's plan unfolds. Abraham, Isaac, and Jacob are truly examples of God's sovereign grace as He continues His work of bringing about redemption for fallen humanity. As stated earlier, Jacob fathered twelve sons. One of those sons would be next in line to carry on the providential plan of God, and again we see God's sovereign choice.

By logical reasoning, and because of the traditions and customs of the day, it would be reasonable to think that Reuben, the first-born son of Jacob, would be the son of choice. But again, we see that God does not work according to tradition and custom. Not only does He pass over the first-born, but the second, and the third. God chooses Judah to be next in line in the lineage of Jesus Christ, through Whom the plan of redemption would be fulfilled. However, it is not Judah, but Joseph, through whom the sovereign activity of God is seen as the story of Genesis continues to unfold.

JOSEPH

Once again, we see parental favoritism. It is clear from the account in Genesis that Jacob favored Joseph above his other sons. This caused a great deal of jealousy to develop between the brothers, which can easily be understood. The other brothers saw how much favor Jacob placed on Joseph, and it caused them to burn with animosity.

> Now Israel loved Joseph more than all his children, because he was the son of his old age. Also he made him a tunic of many colors. But when his brothers saw that their father loved him more than all his brothers, they hated him and could not speak peaceably to him.
>
> (Genesis 37:3–4)

Jacob's favoritism was clear for all to see, and it caused a huge chasm to develop between the brothers. The text makes it clear beyond doubt: they hated Joseph. This led to the brothers devising a scheme to get rid of Joseph. They would have killed him had not Reuben intervened on his behalf. But they did sell him to a band of Ishmaelite traders who took him to Egypt and sold him there to a man by the name of Potiphar, an officer of Pharaoh.

This led to a series of events that took Joseph through years of twists and turns and ups and downs. He was elevated in the household of Potiphar because Potiphar realized that Joseph was blessed by God, and he was being blessed as a result. However, Potiphar's wife set her affections on Joseph, trying day-by-day to seduce him. He refused to give in to her enticements, stating that it would be a sin against God. Potiphar's wife then accused Joseph of trying to seduce her, and for that he was thrown into prison.

There, in prison, he was still blessed by God and was eventually released from prison and elevated in the court of Pharaoh. It was through this remarkable, even miraculous chain of events that Joseph was ultimately used by God to save his family during seven years of famine.

There are so many invaluable lessons to be learned from the experiences of these four Biblical characters. The grace of God is evident in the lives of each of the four. His grace does not always work out in their lives as they probably would have liked, but in the end they could see the handprint of God in all of their life experiences.

We can learn that God sometimes works in inexplicable ways that we may never fully understand in this physical life. As consideration is given to each of these four men it is obvious that things did not always work out the way they would have planned if given the opportunity to do so. I have shared with many young couples who were contemplating marriage that they need to always expect the unexpected because life will assuredly present them with several challenging situations as they go through their life journey together.

Through these four men – Abraham, Isaac, Jacob and Joseph – the sovereign grace of God is unmistakable and impossible to miss. Had a man, or a committee of men, tried to come up with such a plan as this it most certainly would not have been the same choice of individuals, and the same series of events that eventually led to the unfolding of God's redemptive plan. God acts according to His will, elevating those whom he chooses to elevate, and bringing down those whom He chooses to bring down. His plans unfold according to His purposes, and His will is accomplished according to His power.

The sovereign grace of God is seen throughout the entirety of Scripture. We will turn our attention now to different manifestations of God's grace in the ensuing pages of Scripture.

POINTS TO PONDER

1. How would you define the term "sovereign"?
2. How would you explain the sovereignty of God?
3. What are the four major events found in the Book of Genesis?
4. Who are the four major characters found in the Book of Genesis?
5. How do you understand the statement that "it grieved the heart of God that He had made man?"
6. Do you think it is possible for God to change His mind?
7. How do you explain the fact that God used people such as Jacob, who was known for his deceitful ways, in fulfilling His plans?

CHAPTER 3

Saving Grace

For by grace you have been saved through faith, and that not of yourselves; *it is* the gift of God, not of works, lest anyone should boast. For we are His workmanship, created in Christ Jesus for good works, which God prepared beforehand that we should walk in them.

(Ephesians 2:8–10)

Jesus Paid It All
I hear the Savior say,
"Thy strength indeed is small,
Child of weakness, watch and pray,
Find in Me thine all in all."
Jesus paid it all, all to Him I owe;
Sin had left a crimson stain,
He washed it white as snow.

Lord, now indeed I find,
Thy power, and thine alone,
Can change the leper's spots,
And melt the heart of stone.
Jesus paid it all, all to Him I owe;
Sin had left a crimson stain,
He washed it white as snow.
Elvina M. Hall

P robably one of the most controversial theological topics of discussion and debate revolves around the matter of God's activity in man's salvation. There are so many theoretical and theological arguments revolving around this subject, to which many volumes have been written striving to explain the intricacies of God's work in bringing about the amazing grace of salvation.

As has been noted in the previous chapter, God is able to accomplish His will through His work in real time and real history. He worked through faulty men – Abraham, Isaac, Jacob, and Joseph – to set the course in motion which would ultimately lead to the lineage through which Jesus Christ would come. Through these examples, coupled with the astounding work of God in those four major events in Genesis – the creation, the fall, the flood, and the tower of Babel – God's sovereign power is revealed in remarkable ways.

Giving consideration to these matters should help us realize that nothing is beyond God's ability to accomplish, and He does accomplish everything necessary for making it possible for sinful man to be reconciled to a holy God. In this chapter, attention will be given to several different topics of concern when we think about God's sovereign grace as displayed in the work of salvation.

GOD'S FOREKNOWLEDGE OF THE NEED OF SALVATION

The Bible makes it amply clear that God has all knowledge of all things – past, present, and future. This is an amazing attribute of God that is truly astounding when we give it serious consideration. To think that God can know everything that has ever happened or ever will happen is remarkable.

First, consider the fact that He knows everything in the past: perfectly. There are no flaws in His memory. He doesn't concern Himself with historical revisionism, rewriting it to fit into His purposes and plans. He has perfect recall of every minute detail of every event that has ever transpired. Not only the big events that impacted history, but even the most insignificant occurrences imaginable. He remembers what Abraham was wearing that first day He spoke to him in Ur of the Chaldees. He remembers what David ate for breakfast on the first anniversary of being king of Israel. He remembers what Jeremiah was thinking – yes, thinking, not doing – as he sat in the cistern after being incarcerated. And He remembers every act, every thought, every deed of your entire life. His knowledge of the past is perfect.

We can know some things about the past. We study history in school, and we learn certain details and facts about events that happened long before our lifetime. But we would have to admit that all we know about the past is very limited. And even what I know of the past is not perfect. My knowledge of the past is not only limited in scope, but unreliable in accuracy. Some of the details have become muddled in my mind. Historical dates are sometimes forgotten.

Not so with God: His knowledge of the past is perfect and complete. He has perfect remembrance of every detail, not forgetting anything, ever.

Then, He also has perfect knowledge of the present. And this is full knowledge of everything going on in the world at any given moment. He knows what is happening in the United States, in Russia, in Baghdad, in the closed-door sessions of Washington, DC, in the living room of your home. But it goes far beyond that. He also knows what is going on in the vast far corners of the universe. Nothing escapes His knowledge. Nothing can be done that He is not fully cognizant of.

Again, I have an extremely limited knowledge of the present - emphasis on the word limited. I have some idea about what is going on in my home, in my family, on my job, etc. But still it is extremely limited in scope. I have no clue what is going on in Washington, DC. Decisions are being made there daily that affect the lives of all Americans, and we are for the most part oblivious as to what those decisions are. Even in relation to my immediate family my knowledge of what is going on in their lives is so small. My two sons and their families live several hundred miles from me. I know very little about what is happening in their day-to-day experiences. Our knowledge is limited, but God's is perfect. He knows everything in the past and the present.

Then, He also knows perfectly everything that will happen in the future. This is probably the most problematic of the three phases of God's omniscience. One of the main reasons liberal scholars have problems with the Old Testament prophets is because God revealed to them things that would not happen for hundreds and sometimes even thousands of years. For Him to do that, He must of necessity have the ability to know all things, including things that are hundreds, even thousands of years in the future.

Before we go further into the subject of God's sovereign grace in salvation, a topic of extreme importance needs to be addressed briefly. How are we to relate the subject of God's foreknowledge with His preordaining certain things to happen? If, for instance, God by His foreknowledge knows that something will happen, does that mean that it must happen? Is it possible for man to circumvent the knowledge of God?

If the answer to that question is yes, then we must understand how it affects God's omniscience. If He foresees an event as taking place in the future, but that event does not take place because of a choice of man, then that means God's ability to know all things failed. If then, that ability failed, even on only one occasion, it means that God does not have the attribute of omniscience. That would cause serious problems for those who believe the Bible to be the inerrant Word of God. Perhaps a few verses will help clarify the matter.

> Remember the former things of old, for I am God, and there is no other; I am God, and there is none like Me, declaring the end from the beginning, and from ancient times things that are not yet done,

saying, "My counsel shall stand, and I will do all
My pleasure."

(Isaiah 46:9–10)

For there is not a word on my tongue, but behold,
O Lord, You know it altogether.

(Psalm 139:4)

Oh, the depth of the riches both of the wisdom
and knowledge of God! How unsearchable are His
judgments and His ways past finding out! 'For who
has known the mind of the Lord? Or who has first
given to Him and it shall be repaid to him?' For of
Him and through Him and to Him are all things,
to whom be glory forever. Amen.

(Romans 11:33–36)

And there is no creature hidden from His sight, but
all things are naked and open to the eyes of Him
to whom we must give account.

(Hebrews 4:13)

These few verses are only a sample of the many others in
scripture that validate the omniscience of God, and how His
knowledge of all things necessitates the occurrence of those
things. If God knows it, it must be so.

But how are we to understand God's foreknowledge of
future events and His preordaining certain events to happen?
Are foreknowledge and preordination the same thing? If so,
why confuse things by using two different words to describe the
same activity of God? And if not, how are we to understand the
difference between the two?

Foreknowledge means to know beforehand. It is knowing
something will happen before it actually takes place. In relation
to God, it means that He knows everything there is to know.

Nothing can ever happen that will take Him by surprise. He is never caught off-guard by anything.

We have a very limited ability to know certain things before they happen. For example, we can know that the sun will rise tomorrow at a certain time. This is based for the most part on the knowledge that it has consistently happened every day in the past. However, our knowledge of that future event is not guaranteed. There could come the day that the sun does not rise. Our knowledge of the future is based on our faulty knowledge of the past. God's knowledge of the future is not based on the past, but is complete and reliable because of His ability to know all things.

But His perfect foreknowledge of every event that will happen in the future and His ability to preordain certain events to take place in the future are not the same thing. Having now considered God's omniscience, let's try to come to a better understanding of how God's sovereign grace is related to the miraculous work of salvation. We will give further consideration to the relationship between His foreknowledge and His preordination as we continue.

GOD'S PREORDAINED
METHOD OF SALVATION

Having the ability to know all things, past, present and future, would mean that before God created humanity, He would have already known how the first human couple, Adam and Eve, would respond to the command concerning the forbidden fruit. Their act of disobedience in the Garden of Eden did not take God by surprise. And truly, this makes the story of God's redemptive plan even more fascinating. Let's review a verse quoted in an earlier chapter:

> All who dwell on the earth will worship Him,
> whose names have not been written in the Book

of Life of the Lamb slain from the foundation of
the world.

(Revelation 13:8)

Since reference is made to Jesus being the Lamb slain from
the world's foundation, we would understand that the act of
God's preordination would have taken place before the creation.
This act would mean that God foreordained a method through
which salvation would be available for fallen, sinful man.

Let's return now to the relation between God's
foreknowledge – His ability to know everything before it
happens – and His foreordination – His ability to preordain
an event, guaranteeing it will happen. If God's ability to know
something is going to happen necessitates it happening, then His
foreknowledge of Jesus being the sacrificial Lamb necessitated it
taking place. But here, it was not only a matter of foreknowledge,
but a matter of preordination. God ordered this event to happen
from before the foundation of the world. In a very real sense we
could understand this to mean that God preordained Jesus to die
for the sins of humankind based on His foreknowledge of Adam
and Eve's committing that first act of rebellion in the garden of
Eden.

Thus, the method of salvation was through the Lamb, Jesus
Christ. Take just a moment to dwell on that truth. Before He
created us, He had already foreordained His Son to be the Lamb
who would take away the sin of the world. This is truly amazing.
We have no record of God's activity prior to His creation of
this universe. Perhaps He had already created other universes.
Perhaps He had previously involved Himself in other creative
activities. There is no way of us knowing what He had busied
Himself with in precreation nothingness.

But we do know what He did when He decided to create
this universe. He created everything with the full knowledge
that man would rebel, which would result in the imputation of
God's curse on man. He also had the full knowledge that to bring

about salvation for sinful man He would have to give His Son as sacrifice to pay the penalty for sin. Knowing all of this, He created us anyway. As Paul said in the verse quoted above, "Oh, the depth of the riches both of the wisdom and knowledge of God! How unsearchable are His judgments and His ways past finding out!" Our finite minds cannot possibly begin to comprehend His wisdom and knowledge. It is through the vehicle of faith that we embrace the wonderful truths presented in scripture.

GOD'S PURPOSEFUL MEANS OF SALVATION

God's sovereign grace is clearly seen in His preordained method of salvation. We can also note that His grace is seen in His purposeful means of salvation. The means of His salvation is just as amazing if not more so as His method.

The Bible presents us with the truth that God in His fullness – God the Father, God the Son, and God the Holy Spirit – is at work in salvation. As has already been noted above, God the Father is the originator of the plan. Of course, we are not to think that any of the three Persons of the Trinity acted alone in the matter. They all worked in conjunction with the others. However, it does seem possible to understand components of salvation as being the work of one of the three. God the Father assigned God the Son the role and the task of being the sacrificial Lamb. He predestined this plan from eternity past and has brought it about in real history.

God the Son's role is to act in obedience to the Father's assigned task of giving His life as a sacrifice to pay the penalty for sin. In this act of sacrifice Jesus actually appeased the wrath of the Father. Every human being was under the curse of God's judgment on sin, and it is only through this redemptive work of Jesus Christ that God's gracious gift of salvation could be administered to us.

Then, God the Holy Spirit's role is to make known to sinful

man this amazing work of God. He accomplishes this through the conviction of sin, the making known of the Savior, and the communication that Jesus Christ is the only means of salvation. The work of the Trinity is, of course, much more complicated than that, but this is the gist of God's purposeful means of salvation.

GOD'S ELECTIVE WORK IN SALVATION

At the beginning of this chapter, it was mentioned that the subject of God's work in salvation is perhaps one of the most controversial of all theological topics. If that is indeed true, then the subject of God's elective work in salvation must be the crown of that controversy. What exactly is the elective work of God? How does it work in the life of an individual who is presented with the Gospel? Is everyone who is numbered among the elect of God necessarily going to be saved, or is it possible for one of the elect to reject the Gospel? And then what about the non-elect? Are they eternally doomed because of their non-elect status, or can they decide on their own to accept the gift of salvation?

These are all difficult questions. Not only are they difficult, but there is no consensus on the answers. Answers stretch from one end of the theological spectrum to the other. On one end of that spectrum are those who believe God has preordained every individual either to heaven or to hell, with no one having any real choice in the matter. On the other end are those who believe man has absolute free will and will experience no compelling action of God at all in their final choice. Scattered on that line between these two extremes are all sorts of different attempts to give explanation to this extremely important and controversial Biblical doctrine.

In discussing this matter attention must be given to the subject of the free will of man and the total sovereignty of God. Is there any way to reconcile these two seemingly contradictory and irreconcilable ideas? That has not been accomplished yet to the satisfaction of everyone, and this is not an attempt to be the one who finally ties it all together. What will be done in this book is to give an overview of passages which seem to support both sides of the debate, with the hope that we might draw from those passages a reasonable explanation for the seeming conflict between free will and sovereignty.

First, there are several passages which would appear to teach the free will of man. Free will can be thought of as the ability of man to make the choice to believe or disbelieve, to accept or reject, the message of salvation. The following is a list of verses that appear to clearly support the free will of man:

> For God so loved the world that He gave His only begotten Son, that whoever believes in Him should not perish but have everlasting life.
>
> (John 3:16)

> But as many as received Him, to them He gave the right to become children of God, to those who believe in His name: who were born, not of blood, nor of the will of the flesh, nor of the will of man, but of God.
>
> (John 1:12–13)

> I call heaven and earth as witnesses today against you, that I have set before you life and death, blessing and cursing; therefore choose life, that both you and your descendants may live…
>
> (Deuteronomy 30:19)

> For this is good and acceptable in the sight of God our Savior, who desires all men to be saved and to come to the knowledge of the truth.
>
> (1 Timothy 2:4)

For there is no distinction between Jew and Greek, for the same Lord over all is rich to all who call upon Him. For whoever calls on the name of the Lord shall be saved.

(Romans 10:12–13)

Many other passages could be added to this list, but these should be sufficient to show that there is scriptural support for the belief in the free will of man. The references to 'whoever' and 'all men' would appear to be all inclusive. The argument could be thought of as follows: if God desires all men to be saved, and someone (whoever) believes in God's gracious offer of salvation, then they will be saved. This, then, is coupled with the statement in John 1:12 that Jesus gave the right to become sons of God to those who believe the message of salvation and receive the gift of salvation. These verses would appear to support the idea that man has the sovereign ability to either receive or reject the offer of God's gift. This would mean that God actually, in a very real sense, relinquishes His sovereignty to the free will of man, placing man in a position of authority over God.

Free will is the ability of an individual to choose between different possible choices. When I go to a restaurant, I have the capacity to choose freely if I want steak or chicken, or perhaps to even go vegetarian and forego the meats altogether. When I decide to purchase a new vehicle, I have the capacity to choose the make, model, and color of the one I purchase. When I get up in the morning to start my day, I can choose what clothing I will wear, what I will eat for breakfast, and what route I will take to my destination. Choices: we make countless numbers of them every day. And yes, they are real choices made because of our personal desires and preferences at any given moment. God created man with this ability.

However, that ability was damaged in the garden of Eden when Adam and Eve decided to disobey God. To understand this a little better, it would probably be helpful to review the account of the beginning of humankind. Adam and Eve – and Jesus Christ - were the only human beings who had true free will. The first couple was created as perfect humans, placed in a perfect paradise, where they enjoy perfect fellowship with the perfect God of the universe. They had the capacity to make free choices based on their desires at any given moment. Given the opportunity to choose to obey or disobey the prohibition of God concerning the forbidden fruit, they freely chose to disobey. This resulted in God's curse, which had been previously pronounced to Adam and Eve, being placed on them. And, since Adam is the head of the entire human race, all descendants from the first couple are born with a sin nature.

Augustine, considered by many to be one of the greatest theologians of the early church, shared some helpful insight in this matter. He stated that in the pre-fall state man was able to sin and able not to sin; in the post-fall state he was not able not to sin; in the regenerated state he is able not to sin; and in the glorified state he will be unable to sin.

This statement does not speak directly to the subject of God's elective purposes in salvation, but it does help us clarify the matter of free will before and after the fall. Adam and Eve were able to sin or not to sin. We, however, are not able not to sin. Therefore, based on God's pronouncement of the curse of death on anyone who sinned, we can make some observations about the matter of free will in the post-fall state.

Individuals make choices every day, as stated previously. Some are of little consequence while others are life changing. Some may even be a matter of life or death. However, every choice we make is tainted by our sin-nature. We make good choices, and we make bad choices. Someone may decide to marry a certain individual, and not long into their married life they become aware that they have made a horrible mistake. Someone else may decide to purchase a house in a certain neighborhood without doing any research into the school system their children will be attending. They soon find out that it is an extremely poor school system that has the lowest rating in the state. A very poor choice made because of not using the ability to do research before deciding. Of course, these are very poor examples, but they do provide us with a little insight into the fact that we do have the ability to choose.

But now let's consider the matter of salvation. Are we free to choose or to reject this amazing gift of God? Again, the Bible speaks clearly to this subject.

> As it is written: "There is none righteous, no, not one; there is none who understands; there is none who seeks after God. They have all turned aside; they have together become unprofitable; there is none who does good, no, not one."
>
> (Romans 3:9–10)

Before looking at more verses, let's be sure to read these verses carefully once again, noting the phrase, "there is none who seeks after God". None. No one. Everyone has turned aside from God and seeking the things of God.

This is such an important assertion made by Paul, so we must not pass over it lightly. Once again, for the sake of clarity, focus on those words, "none" and "no one". Not a single, solitary person since the fall of Adam and Eve in the garden has sought after God. We all go our own way, seeking after the things that bring pleasure and gratification to our personal desires and preferences. But God is not being sought. If He did not take the initiative to seek us none would ever be saved. Dwell on that thought a few moments before reading the next few passages.

> And this is the condemnation, that the Light has come into the world, and men loved darkness rather than light, because their deeds were evil. For everyone practicing evil hates the light and

does not come to the light, lest his deeds should
be exposed.
(John 3:19–20)

But the natural man does not receive the things of
the Spirit of God, for they are foolishness to him;
nor can he know them, because they are spiritually
discerned.
(1 Corinthians 2:14)

No one can come to Me unless the Father who
sent Me draws him, and I will raise him up at the
last day.
(John 6:44)

For many are called, but few are chosen.
(Matthew 22:14)

Blessed by the God and Father of our Lord Jesus
Christ, who has blessed us with every spiritual
blessing in the heavenly places in Christ, just as He
chose us in Him before the foundation of the world,
that we should be holy and without blame before
Him in love, having predestined us to adoption as
sons by Jesus Christ to Himself, according to the
good pleasure of His will…
(Ephesians 1:3–6)

These are powerful passages of scripture which speak directly
to the matter of God's elective work in salvation. We were at
one time dead in our trespasses and sins (see Ephesians 2:1).
Spiritually dead. What can a dead person do? Absolutely nothing!
A physically dead person cannot stand, speak, walk, laugh, etc.
So it is with a spiritually dead person. He has no ability to do
anything at all. He can take no part in the work of salvation.

When we take into account all the passages quoted above, there are several things we can deduce. First, no one seeks God. No one! We have no desire to know Him or to have a relationship of any kind with Him. We have all gone our own way, seeking after those things that bring personal fulfillment and satisfaction.

Second, the only ones who have a desire to know Him are those who receive His call. Jesus makes this clear in His statement, "No one can come to Me unless the Father draws him." Some may object by arguing that the Father draws everyone and then leaves the final decision to the individual. But look again at Jesus' words in Matthew 22:14: "Many are called, but few are chosen." The "many" in this verse could be thought of in terms of the entire human population – past, present, and future. This is what might be referred to as the general call of God. Every person receives this call.

But out of the general call, there are those who receive an effectual call. These are the chosen ones. It is these who are brought out of death into life. Spiritual death gives way to spiritual life as one is brought to life by the work of the Spirit of God. Before this takes place in the life of an individual, he remains dead in his trespasses and sins.

Third, those who receive the general call but not the effectual call make a real choice. They choose to reject God's offer of salvation because they are left to make their decision while in a spiritually dead state. Paul states assertively that the natural man cannot receive the things of the Spirit because they are spiritually discerned. The natural man, being spiritually dead, cannot comprehend the things of God.

Fourth, this matter of God's election is not based on man's goodness. Had He elected according to the goodness of man, no one would be saved. We have, after all, turned to our own selfish and self-serving ways. We are dead in our sins, having no desire to know God.

An interesting fact is that every time the word "elect" is used in the Bible when speaking of God's activities with man, God is always the subject and man is always the object. Man is always the recipient of God's elective purposes. Man never elects God; God always elects man. This is yet another example of God's sovereign work in bringing about the salvation of sinful man.

Fifth, the non-elect make a very real choice: they choose to reject the offer of God's grace in salvation. Thinking once again about the Bible's teaching that no one seeks God helps us understand this truth. Since the fall of man in the garden of Eden, man has been affected by the sin nature passed down from Adam and Eve. We make choices – real, personal choices – that affect every area of life. As noted previously, even lost individuals can make good choices because of the goodness of God operative in their lives. But, when given the choice to either accept or reject the offer of salvation, they choose to reject because they have no desire to seek God. It is a real choice they make. If it were not for God's gracious intervention in the lives of the elect, no one would be saved.

And finally, the term "free will" never appears in Scripture, but the term "predestination" does. Bottom line is that if God left us to choose for ourselves, each and every human being would choose to reject His offer of saving grace. He sovereignly, from eternity past, adopted those who would be saved. For those who would argue that this is unfair of God, let's remind ourselves that He created us, He owns us, and He has every right to do with us as He wills.

GOD'S EFFECTIVE WORK IN SALVATION

This brings us to one final consideration on the topic of saving grace: the effectual work of God. There are many different passages that speak to this subject, but what may very well be the pivotal passage for this subject is found in the following verses:

> For whom He foreknew, He also predestined to be
> conformed to the image of His Son, that He might

be the firstborn among many brethren. Moreover, whom He predestined, these He also called; whom He called, these He also justified; and whom He justified, these He also glorified.

(Romans 8:29–30)

There is a chain of events found here that gives us insight into the effectual work of God in bringing about salvation in the lives of His elect. Predestination – calling – justification – glorification. Special note needs to be made of the fact that three of these verbs – predestined, called, and glorified – are all past tense. This would lead us to believe that these all took place in eternity past. Paul states definitively in the first chapter of Ephesians that God chose us from the foundation of the world. If that is the correct understanding of this passage, then it means that the predestination, calling, justification and glorification all took place when God made His decision to elect some for salvation.

In conclusion, it must be understood that this is a theological topic that will continue to be debated until Jesus comes for His bride at the rapture of the church. For now, we simply must agree with Isaiah, when he said:

For as the heavens are higher than the earth, so are My ways higher than your ways, and My thoughts than your thoughts.

(Isaiah 55:9)

We cannot possibly understand the majestic work of God in salvation. It is far beyond our ability to reconcile two Biblical teachings that seem to be irreconcilable. It should cause us to adore God even more knowing that He is working out His plans according to His will and good pleasure. And, for those who are the called and chosen of God, let us bask in the knowledge that He, by His grace and for His glory, has added our names to the Lamb's book of life.

In bringing this chapter to a conclusion, and in testimony to my personal understanding of God's work in bringing about salvation in the life of an individual, I will share my own salvation experience. It was my great privilege to be reared in a Christian home by godly parents. My siblings and I were not taken to church and dropped off by our mother and father, but we were taken to church with them.

This practice went on until I reached my teenage years. I talked my parents into allowing me to attend church with some of my friends while my parents continued to attend their church. What they did not realize was that my friends and I "cut" church as much, if not more, than we attended. It was about this same time that I began to rebel against many of the things that I had been taught while attending church.

In my mid-teen years I began to smoke, drink, and use marijuana. I also started playing drums in a rock and roll band. My life began to spiral downward as I became more and more involved in these worldly activities. My selfish desires and goals took precedence over everything I had been taught.

At the age of twenty-one I met Teresa Harrington, the woman I would marry in 1973. For a brief while after our wedding I "cleaned up" my life, but it only lasted a very short time. I soon was right back at my old activities. After four years of marriage and the birth of our first child, Teresa and I had decided to divorce. I was so committed to making it big in the music industry that I felt as if I had no time for her or our son. They were only a distraction that kept me from realizing my ambitions.

At the request of my parents, the pastor of the church where they continued to attend had been to our house on several occasions. I'm still amazed after all these years that he kept coming back because every time he came I treated him so rudely, trying to give him reason to never return. But he kept coming back. Time after time he came. But it was doing no good. I was convinced that I wanted nothing to do with church, or with Jesus Christ.

It was on Thursday, September 8, 1977. I was on my way to work that Thursday morning, and it was on that ten-mile drive that I heard God speak to me, personally and powerfully. I'm positive that had you been with me that morning you would not have heard His voice as I did. But for me, it was the most unbelievably powerful thing I had ever experienced. It was through that encounter with the Living Lord that I became convinced of my desperate need of salvation.

I went home that evening and shared with Teresa what I had experienced that morning. After sharing every detail with her I then told her that I would like to go to church on Sunday morning. She laughed, thinking that I must be joking. After all, I was chasing my dream of making it big as a drummer in a rock and roll band.

I persisted, telling her again on Friday morning, then all day Saturday, that I wanted to go to church. She refused to go with me, so I went without her. Please understand that I had not been to church for years, except on the rare occasion of a Christmas or Easter Sunday, just to appease my parents.

I arrived at the church, went in and sat on the very back row. The pastor was the very same one who had been to our house many times. After the morning worship, I spoke with him about coming to our house to talk with us about the Lord. He told me that he would come on Tuesday evening at seven. He arrived, and patiently explained to us the plan of salvation (which I had heard so many times in my younger years), and at 10:45 that evening God graciously and powerfully saved both me and my wife, healed our broken marriage, and shortly after called me into pastoral ministry.

I have shared that lengthy testimony with you to share my understanding of the amazing work of God in salvation. I had heard the message many times in my life. I had been given many opportunities to make a decision to trust Jesus Christ as my personal Savior. However, I had never felt the need. As a matter of fact I had pretty much made it a huge joke every time I heard anyone share this wonderful news with me.

That Thursday morning as I made my way to work, any thought of Jesus Christ was as foreign to me as anything could possibly be. But it was on that morning that He spoke personally to me. He called me, and that calling proved to be effectual in bringing me to salvation.

Had I made real choices to reject the message of salvation on every previous opportunity? Was it a real choice on those occasions when the pastor came to our home to share with us the good news of salvation? Yes – these were real choices. Then, when God spoke so powerfully to me on that Thursday morning, did I make a choice to accept His invitation? Absolutely! Was it a real choice, based on the opportunity to accept or reject? Yes. But it was a choice I made to accept Him because of a choice He had made to save me from the foundation of the world.

But what about those who hear the message, receive the general call that is issued to all men, and reject. Did they have a choice? Yes. But because there is none righteous, not even one, the choice they make is in keeping with their state of unrighteousness. They choose to reject the offer of salvation because of their predisposition toward unbelief.

God, in His amazing grace, has seen fit to adopt the elect into His forever family of faith. If you have experienced the new birth, now having your name written in the Lamb's Book of Life, then rejoice with great joy that He chose you from the foundation of the world to be His child.

Hallelujah! What a Savior!

POINTS TO PONDER

1. How would you explain God's preordained method of salvation?
2. How would you explain God's means of salvation?
3. How would you explain God's elective work in salvation?
4. What do you think Jesus meant when He said, "Many are called, but few are chosen?"
5. Is there a distinction between what is referred to as a "general call" and an "effectual call?"
6. What is the relationship between God's foreknowledge and His election?

CHAPTER 4

Salvaging Grace

When I kept silent, my bones grew old through my groaning all the day long. For day and night Your hand was heavy upon me; my vitality was turned into the drought of summer. I acknowledged by sin to You, and my iniquity I have not hidden. I said, "I will confess my transgressions to the Lord," and You forgave the iniquity of my sin.

Psalm 32:3-5

Just As I Am
Just as I am, without one plea,
But that thy blood was shed for me,
and that thou bidst me come to thee
O Lamb of God, I come, I come.

Just as I am and waiting not
to rid my soul of one dark blot,
to thee whose blood can cleanse each spot
O Lamb of God, I come, I come

Just as I am thou wilt receive,
Wilt welcome, pardon, cleanse, relieve
Because thy promise I believe
O Lamb of God, I come, I come.
Charlotte Elliott

We live in a throw-away society. There was a day and time when, instead of throwing something in the garbage we would have it repaired, but that day is long past. Take a drive down to your local garbage dump and look around. There will be old appliances – washing machines, dishwashers, refrigerators – and old electronics – televisions, stereos, home theater systems – that have been thrown away rather than repaired.

And then there are bigger items that are thrown away. On occasion I have passed by salvage yards, or, as my father would say, junk yards. And that is certainly what it appeared to be: junk. Wrecked cars and trucks, and sometimes boats and travel trailers. Each one was damaged in some way. Some had been in such vicious accidents that the make and model were unrecognizable. Others appeared to be in decent shape, but for some reason, perhaps a warped chassis or a blown engine, it had been deemed unusable. And still others were vehicles that had simply been abandoned. Maybe because the vehicle had the need for repairs that would cost more than it was worth, or the owner simply didn't want to spend that much on repairs, so he abandoned the vehicle and bought a new one.

There are other types of junk. We all probably have some junk around our homes. You might see some homes with junked cars parked in the yard. They're not drivable, not usable. But instead of taking them to a vehicle graveyard they are left sitting in the yard. Most, though, don't have junked cars in their yards, but they still have junk. For some, it may be something they think could be salvageable, so they don't throw it away, but it just lays there, day after day, week after week. Junk. Or it may be something with some sort of sentimental value, and they can't bear the thought of throwing it away. So, there it is, collecting dust in that corner where it has been for years.

Then, there are those certain individuals who can take what appears to be junk, and through tedious labor, and uncountable hours of painstaking work, transform that piece of junk into a masterpiece. I have a friend, Dwayne Dassaro, who has done that with several automobiles. His accomplishments of restoration include a 1970 Trans Am, a 1968, '70, and '72 Chevrolet truck, and a 1969 Chevelle. He is presently restoring another 1970 Chevrolet truck. Believe me when I say that the finished product looks like the vehicle was just pulled off the showroom floor. Junk turned into treasure.

In the matter of grace, we see this principle at work all through the Bible. God takes something that has been damaged by sin and restores that one to a pristine state. Sometimes the process appears to be rather simple, while at other times it is only accomplished after much pain and struggle.

In this chapter we are now turning our attention to believers who have already entered into a relationship with God through the sacrificial death of Jesus Christ. They have received the effectual call of God unto salvation, and they now have their names written in the Lamb's Book of Life.

There are times when a child of God will give in to the temptation to engage in sin. It may be a one-time act of sin, or it could be an ongoing sinful behavior. The passage on the title page of this chapter is a graphic example of this possibility. It is a prayer of King David, after he has committed adultery with Bathsheba. He learns after their sexual liaison that she is expecting a child, so David further deepens his sin by having her husband, Uriah, placed on the very front line of a heated battle, knowing that this would result in his death. David didn't shoot the arrow, or throw the spear, but he was guilty of the murder of Uriah none-the-less.

Then, further widening the wedge between himself and God, he tries to hide his sin from everyone. For a full year he does everything within his power to keep the facts of his sinful acts hidden. However, God revealed to the prophet Nathan what David had done. Nathan goes to David, following the sovereign guidance of God, to confront him over this entire sordid affair.

> Then the Lord sent Nathan to David. And he came
> to him and said to him: "There were two men in

one city, one rich and the other poor. The rich man had exceedingly many flocks and herds. But the poor man had nothing, except one little ewe lamb, which he had bought and nourished; and it grew up with him and with his children. It ate of his own food and drank from his own cup and lay in his bosom. And it was like a daughter to him. And a traveler came to the rich man, who refused to take from his won flock and from his own herd to prepare one for the wayfaring man who had come to him; but he took the poor man's lamb and prepared it for the man who had come to him.

(2 Samuel 12:1–4)

Nathan begins by reporting an incident to David. As far as David knew Nathan was telling him about an incident that had recently taken place. It was a story of insensitivity and abuse. It is a graphic portrayal of ruthless and selfish behavior. He tells of a rich man who had herds and flocks from which he could have easily taken a lamb or calf to prepare for his visiting traveler. Instead, he takes the only lamb of a poor man for the purpose of feeding his guest. This lamb was more than an animal to this man and his family. It was a cherished family pet.

So, what does David do in light of this information? The text continues:

So David's anger was greatly aroused against the man, and he said to Nathan, "As the Lord lives, the man who has done this shall surely die! And he shall restore fourfold for the lamb, because he did this thing and because he had no pity!"

(2 Samuel 12:5–6)

Picture the scene: David is blinded by his anger. Without hesitation, in a moment of heated rage against a man who could be so heartless and cruel, he pronounces the death penalty. David's rage seems to be completely uncontrollable. Picture it in your mind. The veins are probably bulging in his neck and forehead. His eyes are popping in their sockets. His fists are clenched by his side, his hands beating on his thighs. He is pacing back and forth across the room, unable to contain his emotions.

Perhaps he finally grows quiet, maybe from his emotions crashing, or simply because of his sheer exhaustion. He is quiet enough now for Nathan to speak once again. How will he respond to this explosion from the king? He has just witnessed an emotional meltdown of the most powerful man in Israel. He knows that this man holds sovereign rule over the nation. He is perhaps thinking that he needs to guard his next words carefully, or he could very well be the recipient of David's next emotional outburst.

But instead of cowering before this most powerful man, Nathan says:

> You are the man!
>
> (2 Samuel 12:7)

This must have been a most dramatic moment. Nathan, the prophet of God, is standing face to face with David, the king of the nation. How do you picture this stand-off? Is Nathan shuffling backward away from David as he utters these words? Is he speaking in such hushed tones that David must strain to hear? Is Nathan cowering in fear before this most powerful man? Has he positioned himself strategically close to the exit so he can make a speedy escape if David's uncontrollable anger is thrust at him?

Or is Nathan standing steel-toed and steely-eyed, with his face no more than six inches from the face of David? Is he standing in the power of the flesh, or in the power of the Spirit? The text gives us no details, but I believe that Nathan, empowered by God to deliver His message of conviction to His anointed leader,

David, was standing strong, and speaking even more strongly. Not fearing what David might do, he announces the message.

Regardless of how Nathan spoke, we know how David responded.

> So David said to Nathan, "I have sinned against
> the Lord."
>
> (2 Samuel 12:13)

It is at some point after this confrontation and subsequent confession to Nathan, that David lifts a prayer of sincere contrition and confession directly to God.

> Have mercy upon me, O God, according to Your
> lovingkindness; according to the multitude of Your
> tender mercies, blot out my transgressions. Wash
> me thoroughly from my iniquity, and cleanse me
> from my sin. For I acknowledge my transgressions,
> and my sin is always before me. Against You, You
> only, have I sinned, and done this evil in Your
> sight-that You may be found just when You speak,
> and blameless when You judge.
> Create in me a clean heart, O God, and renew
> a steadfast spirit within me. Do not cast me away
> from Your presence, and do not take Your Holy
> Spirit from me. Restore to me the joy of Your
> salvation, and uphold me by Your generous Spirit.
> Then I will teach transgressors Your ways, and
> sinners shall be converted to You.
>
> (Psalm 51:1–4; 10–13)

In this prayer of repentance David pleads with God to have his sinful heart cleansed, and his spirit renewed. Heart here is to be understood as the center of emotional and spiritual well-being. David has been living in spiritual misery for approximately one year, refusing to repent of his sinful actions. He has become such a horribly miserable human being because of trying to hide his sinful actions. His misery is actually captured even more graphically in another Psalm. Read these painful words slowly, taking time to think of the horror David is experiencing.

> When I kept silent, my bones grew old through my groaning all the day long. For day and night Your hand was heavy upon me; my vitality was turned into the drought of summer.
>
> (Psalm 32:3–4)

It isn't difficult to hear the pain and anguish in David's cries. It is in his day and night groanings that he lifts his pleas to God. Add to this a reference David makes in Psalm 51 about feeling as if his bones were being crushed in his body by the heavy hand of God and the intensity of his constant struggle is clearly in view. David's attempts to keep his sinful actions a well-kept secret have taken their toll. But, even more serious than that, the Holy Spirit's heavy hand of conviction was a never-ending source of grief for the king.

This may make one wonder exactly where the grace of God is in these painful descriptions David gives to his misery. But we must remember that David has brought all this suffering upon himself. First, he has turned his back on God's instruction by committing his atrocious acts of sin, knowing that his actions were not within the parameters of God's demands for holiness. Then, second, his suffering was even more exacerbated by trying to hide it for all those months.

But now he has been confronted by Nathan, he has confessed his sin against God, and he has heard Nathan report that God, in response to his confession and repentance, has put his sin away from him. Truly, this is salvaging grace. David's life that has been like a shipwreck, with the broken pieces left reeling on the jagged rocks of destruction, is now pieced back together by the forgiving, healing hand of God.

David, like one of Dwayne Dassaro's restored vehicles, is restored by God's salvaging grace. He is taken out of the junkyard of sin and salvaged by the grace of God. It would be wise for us to go back to the verse quoted earlier in this chapter. This passage shows clearly what it is the believer needs to do once he has responded in obedience to the prompting of the Holy Spirit's conviction. Please read it again now to gain a better understand of the amazing grace of God in giving believers who allow themselves to fall into sin a means of being restored.

> Create in me a clean heart, O God, and renew a steadfast spirit within me. Do not cast me away from Your presence, and do not take Your Holy Spirit from me. Restore to me the joy of Your salvation, and uphold me by Your generous Spirit. Then I will teach transgressors Your ways, and sinners shall be converted to You.
>
> (Psalm 51:10–13)

Give special attention to an extremely important phrase in this passage: "Do not take your Holy Spirit away from me." This phrase must be understood in light of the progressive self-revelation of God in the Old Testament. The teachings relative to the Person and work of the Holy Spirit are undeveloped in the Old Testament. It is not until we come to the New Testament that we see the clear teaching that the believer in Jesus Christ is actually indwelt by the Holy Spirit. It is obvious as one studies the role of the Holy Spirit in the Old Testament that His operation in the lives of individuals was vastly different. He would come upon individuals but did not indwell individuals. David was responding to God with the limited knowledge that had been revealed up to that point in time. He was fearful of having the Holy Spirit withdraw from him. What a terrifying thought!

And then, he further prays that God would restore to him the joy of God's salvation. Note carefully that he does not ask God to restore salvation, but the joy of salvation. He had not lost his relationship with God: God was still his Father, and he was still God's child. But he had lost the joy of being saved. Anyone who has backslidden on God has experienced the loss of salvation's joy. Being in fellowship with God is the most joyful life imaginable! There is true joy in one's intimate walk with God. But when the intimacy of our fellowship with God is broken because we have engaged in sin, then we no longer experience that joy. Rather, we experience the drought of summer in our spiritual walk. The only thing that will restore the joy is the restoration of the intimacy, and this comes about through confession and repentance.

Also note that he doesn't claim this salvation as something belonging to him, but rather he pleads with God to restore the joy of God's salvation. David understood that salvation is an amazing gift from God. It is His from beginning to end.

The greatest of all the kings of Israel, a man described by God as being a man after God's heart, is a graphic example of the work of salvaging grace. It lets us know that none of us, not one of us, is above falling prey to temptation, and losing the joy of our salvation along with the intimacy of our fellowship with God. How wonderful it would be if we could learn from the mistakes of others!

But we need to note that this matter of backsliding is not just an Old Testament reality. It is also taught clearly in the New Testament. One example from the pages of the New Testament books is the apostle Peter. Jesus called four fishermen – Peter, Andrew, James, and John – as Jesus walked along the shore. Three of these four – Peter, James, and John – became the inner circle of the twelve apostles as they were given the privilege of being with Jesus on special occasions from which the others were excluded.

The apostles had been with Jesus for over three years. They had watched Him as He ministered to the multitudes, and as He ministered to individuals. They had heard His teachings and had been given private instructions as Jesus spent time with them personally. They had witnessed His amazing power as He had healed the sick, raised the dead, calmed the storms, walked on water, restored sight to the blind, and made the lame to walk again. They have plenty of evidence that would validate Jesus' claim to be the Messiah.

On the last night of Jesus' life on earth, He is with the apostles in an upper room that has been prepared for the celebration of the feast of Passover. It is there that He reveals to them some horrible news:

> When evening had come, He sat down with the twelve. Now as they were eating, He said, "Asssuredly, I say to you, one of you will betray Me." And they were exceedingly sorrowful, and each of them began to say to Him, "Lord, is it I?"
>   (Matthew 26:20–22)

It is interesting to note that each of them asked, "Is it I?" Judas Iscariot had hidden his secrets so well that no one was able to accuse him of being the one who would do such an awful deed. As a matter of fact, no one was pointing a finger at anyone. They seem to all be baffled about this statement from Jesus.

Jesus doesn't specifically point the finger at anyone. He simply says that the one who had dipped his hand with Jesus in the dish would be the betrayer. But they had all dipped their hand with Jesus. It could, literally, be any one of them. So, they are left in a state of bewilderment as to whom Jesus might be referring.

After Jesus makes this startling revelation to His apostles things quickly move ahead. They finish the Passover meal, at the conclusion of which Jesus institutes Communion, or the Lord's Supper. He reveals to them that it will be through the sacrifice of His body, and the shedding of His blood, that redemption will come. Finally, they sing a hymn and go out to the Mount of Olives. Jesus then makes some more most startling revelations to the twelve.

> Then Jesus said to them, "All of you will be made to stumble because of Me this night, for it is written: I will strike the Shepherd, and the sheep of the flock will be scattered. But after I have been raised, I will go before you to Galilee."
>
> (Matthew 26:31–32)

What a horrible thing to hear! The apostles must have been completely petrified as they hear this declaration. They had been faithfully following Jesus for a long time. They had placed their faith in the fact that He was the long-awaited, long-anticipated Messiah that the prophets of antiquity had promised would come to deliver Israel. They had set their hopes on the reestablishment of Israel as a world power, with Jesus as their king. And now they hear Jesus say that He is going to be struck down and they will be scattered!

Peter blurts out his response to the Lord's declaration. He refuses to accept the fact of Jesus' assertion. Peter was announcing his complete commitment to the Lord, and further clarifying his stance by saying that no matter what everyone else did, he would never, under any circumstances, be made to stumble.

There may have been a long, uneasy, awkward period of silence as the apostles tried to make sense of what they have just heard. Or there may have been no silence at all between Jesus' statement and Peter's response. Regardless of the time lapse after Jesus makes His declaration, Peter is the first to speak:

> Peter answered and said to Him, "Even if all are made to stumble because of You, I will never be made to stumble." Jesus said to him, "Assuredly, I say to you that this night, before the roosted crows, you will deny Me three times." Peter said to Him, "Even if I have to die with You, I will not deny You!" And so said all the disciples.
>
> (Matthew 26:33–35)

Peter blurts out his response to the Lord's declaration. He refuses to accept the fact of Jesus' assertion. Peter was announcing his complete commitment to the Lord, and further clarifying his stance by saying that no matter what everyone else did, he would never be made, under any circumstances, to stumble.

I'm sure that Peter meant exactly what he said. He will just a little later put his commitment on display as he tries to protect Jesus in the Garden of Gethsemane when the soldiers come to arrest the Lord. Peter drew a sword, swinging it wildly at one of the soldiers, cutting off his ear. He truly was willing to die for Jesus. Peter was backing his words up with actions. He was willing to fight to the end for his Lord.

This action of Peter may have been an indicator that he still believed Jesus had come to establish and earthly kingdom. He may have further been convinced that the way to usher in that kingdom was to start a revolt that would result in a battle at which Jesus would exert His authority. Perhaps Peter felt that by his act of violence in the garden would be the stimulus Jesus needed to get things moving in that direction. But, regardless of his motive for his actions in the garden, he showed beyond doubt that he was willing to die with and for Jesus.

But just a short while later, Jesus is taken into custody and escorted by the soldiers to the home of Caiaphas, the high priest. It is there that he will face the first of six trials. Things begin to unravel for Peter and the rest of the apostles. They are witnessing things they never thought they would see. They watch as Jesus is led away under guard, and it is then that Jesus' prophetic words to Peter come true.

As Jesus arrives at the home of Caiaphas, it becomes obvious that things have already been set in motion to have Jesus condemned in the cover of darkness. The plans begin to unfold, as is clearly seen in Matthew's record.

> And those who had laid hold of Jesus led Him
> away to Caiaphas the high priest, where the scribes

and the elders were assembled. But Peter followed Him at a distance to the high priest's courtyard. And he went in and sat with the servants to see the end.

(Matthew 26:57–58)

It becomes obvious that the events of the next few hours had been planned in detail. There are far too many things happening all at once for them to have happened with much forethought and organizing. Why were the scribes and elders already there? What would have prompted them to gather at the home of the high priest under the cover of darkness? Actually, the plan had been set in motion when Judas Iscariot had earlier agreed to a plan to have Jesus arrested. And, it had been a little earlier this same evening that Judas had gone out into the darkness of the evening, while Jesus was leading in the celebration of Passover, to lead the soldiers to the garden where they would arrest Jesus. The wheels of injustice were turning, the evil plot of the religious leaders was playing out, and Jesus is the center of all attention.

The text above also relates to us that Peter had followed Jesus at a distance and had gone into the high priest's courtyard. He hasn't abandoned Jesus altogether, but he isn't present to come to his defense either. Matthew records that he was there, among the servants of the high priest, *to see the end*. Just how, exactly, is all this going to play out must have been the thought motivating Peter to follow. He was probably hoping beyond hope that somehow, in some inconceivable way, Jesus would be threatened, punished, and released. How could it be any other way? After all, Jesus is the Messiah! Surely nothing of any major consequence could possibly happen to Him.

But things begin to happen that Peter was not expecting. He was probably sitting there, warming himself by the fire, straining to hear what was being said, and to see what was being done. He was there, after all, with a purpose: *to see the end*. But as he sits there, listening and watching, someone walks up to him. His concentration is shattered. His intent stare is interrupted.

> Now Peter sat outside in the courtyard. And a servant girl came to him, saying, "You also were with Jesus of Galilee." But he denied it before them all, saying, "I do not know what you are saying." And when he had gone out to the gateway, another girl saw him and said to those who were there, "This fellow also was with Jesus of Nazareth." But again he denied with an oath, "I do not know the Man!" And a little later those who stood by came up and said to Peter, "Surely you also are one of them, for your speech betrays you."
> Then he began to curse and swear, saying, "I do not know the Man!"
>
> (Matthew 26:69–74a)

The intensity of Peter straining to hear and see probably had him almost mesmerized. He had perhaps become almost oblivious to what was happening around him until he hears the voice of a servant girl. It shatters his tunnel-vision. It crashes his concentration. Perhaps he sat in stunned silence for a few moments before responding. But when he did respond it was not a pretty sight. He denied the allegation and blurted out, "I do not know what you are saying."

He then gets up and moves to a different location. He is probably just simply trying to get to a place where it is less likely that he will be recognized. He moves out to the gateway leading into the garden, where he is met with another servant girl who identifies him as one who had been with Jesus. Peter again denies the statement, and to make his assertion a little more believable, he makes this denial with an oath. An oath would carry the ring of authority.

Peter still seems to be unaware of the seriousness of his

denials. The words of Jesus earlier in the evening seem to have been forgotten. He is still in the courtyard of the high priest, and the third accusation is about to be brought against him. This time some others identified him as having been with Jesus because his speech gave him away. This leads to Peter's third and final denial. It may have been out of his desperation to get his point across, or it may have been out of his frustration with these who were identifying him as having been with Jesus, but this time Peter curses and swears that he does not know Jesus.

Maybe the word "man" was still coming from Peter's mouth. Perhaps the reverberation of the loud shout was still echoing around the courtyard. Luke's record says that the rooster crowed while Peter was still speaking. And Luke adds an even more serious note to the third crow of the rooster.

> But Peter said, "Man, I do not know what you are saying!" Immediately, while he was still speaking, the rooster crowed. And the Lord turned and looked at Peter. Then Peter remembered the word of the Lord, how He had said to him, "Before the roosted crows, you will deny Me three times." So Peter went out and wept bitterly.
>
> (Luke 22:60–62)

Jesus turned and looked directly at Peter. All this time Peter has been straining to see and hear. He has probably been moving from one position to another, trying to find a spot where his line of sight would be unhindered. He wants to see it all; to hear it all. But now, all he hears is a rooster's crow echoing through his ears. All he sees is the steely stare of the Lord, looking deeply into the depths of his soul as he has just shouted his third and final denial with swearing and cursing. If he could have just disappeared Peter probably would have done so.

That stare of the Lord must have stayed with him. Every time he closed his eyes, he probably saw those eyes. In a state of deep regret and remorse Peter went out from the courtyard of the high priest and wept. Bitterly. Uncontrollably. Unconsolably. Crushed from without by those piercing eyes of the Lord. Crushed from within by those memories that now haunted him.

But before we come down too terribly hard on Peter, we need to consider another enlightening verse. Earlier that evening, when Jesus reveals to the apostles that they will all be scattered and that Peter would deny Him three times, they all say the same thing: I will not deny you, even if I must die with you. Granted, the others did not deny in the same manner as Peter, but they still denied. They denied Jesus their presence. They could have been by His side through the most horrible ordeal of His life, but Jesus was abandoned by them all. So, in a very real sense, they were all guilty.

But Peter's guilt stands out due to the circumstances. He was the one who boisterously exclaimed his all-out commitment to go with Jesus, even to death.

And let's not come down too hard on all the apostles because, if we are honest with ourselves, we have all probably been guilty of the sin of denial at some time in our Christian lives. It may have been an outright verbal denial, where we felt backed into a corner, and to admit our relationship with Jesus could have major repercussions. Perhaps we kept our relationship with the Lord a top secret on our job for fear that we would be passed over for that coveted promotion. Or perhaps we kept silent simply because of peer pressure on the job or in the classroom, not wanting our friends and co-workers to stereotype us or worse, to ostracize us. Maybe we would rather be part of the fun crowd than to take a stand for Jesus.

Paul Harvey, radio personality from a bygone day, used to come to a point in his daily broadcast where he would exhort: "Now, for the rest of the story." We have now reached that point in this chapter. We are ready for the rest of the story, and how thankful we should be that it did not end with Peter weeping bitterly at his denial of the Lord.

The next three days must have been the most miserable days ever in the lives of the followers of Jesus. He had spoken to them on several occasions about the fact that He was going to be put to death at the hands of wicked men, but that He would come forth from the grave on the third day. Their minds had not been able to comprehend those words of the Lord, because none of them remember them after Jesus' death. They are bewildered at what has transpired and are probably spending most of their time trying to figure out how they could have been so deceived by Jesus. After all, had He not insisted that He was the Messiah, who would establish the kingdom? Had they not forsaken all to follow Him? What would become of them now that their Leader was dead and buried? A spirit of sheer hopelessness must have been the course of the day.

Not much is known about what actually happened over those next 48-72 hours. The Gospels skip abruptly from the burial to the morning of the resurrection. It is merely a matter of speculation as to what they may have been doing. They may have resigned themselves to the fact that the same fate that had now befallen Jesus would soon be theirs as well. After all, they were known to be His disciples. They were part of His band of followers. If He was thought to have been an insurrectionist, then they would probably be identified as such and be executed as He had been. The conversations must have been animated as they all shared their thoughts and ideas as to how they could have been so blinded and brainwashed by Jesus.

Sunday morning comes and some women go to the tomb in which Jesus had been buried. They go there with no hope of seeing a risen, living Lord. They are go there to anoint a cold, lifeless body in preparation for permanent burial. This is certainly to be understood as the normal response. After all, no one has died and come back to life on their own. Granted, Jesus has raised certain individuals back to life after experiencing physical death, but how could He possibly raise Himself up from the dead? That thought was sheer nonsense!

So instead of going to the tomb expecting to see Jesus, alive and well, considering His predictions about Himself, they go to anoint His body. Imagine their consternation when they arrive at the tomb to find the huge stone that had been placed in front of the tomb's entrance rolled away. And then, to be given a most amazing and unbelievable message. They are met at the tomb by an individual dressed in a flowing white robe, who has a most unexpected and unbelievable message for them. Allow the text to paint the picture for us:

> Now when the Sabbath was past, Mary Magdalene, Mary the mother of James, and Salome bought spices, that they might come and anoint Him. Very early in the morning, on the first day of the week, they came to the tomb when the sun had risen. And they said among themselves, "Who will roll away the stone from the door of the tomb for us?" But when they looked up, they saw that the stone had been rolled away – for it was very large. And entering the tomb, they saw a young mad clothed in a long while robe sitting on the right side; and they were alarmed. But he said to them, "Do not be alarmed. You seek Jesus of Nazareth, who was crucified. HE is risen! He is not here. See the place where they laid Him. But go, tell His disciples – and Peter – that He is going before you into Galilee; there you will see Him, as He said to you."
>
> (Mark 16:1–7)

After three days of waiting behind closed doors, talking about who knows what, striving to figure out what their next plan of action should be, they finally come to the day after the Sabbath. There was nothing they could have done on the Sabbath day as that would have broken the law. So, with broken spirits and shattered hopes some women make their way to the tomb.

Dreams are destroyed. Hope is gone. Their leader is dead, and with Him so is any hope for the future.

But when they arrive, they are met with the most unbelievable sight they could have ever imagined. The stone has been moved, the body of the Lord is not there, and a messenger is waiting to give them the news: Jesus is alive!

He invites them to investigate, instructing them to look at the place where Jesus' body had been laid. It was now vacant! No body. No Jesus. No stench of death. No vestige of decay. Jesus is alive!

And then he instructs them as to what to do next: go, tell the disciples that Jesus will meet them in Galilee. Oh, yes, by the way, be sure to tell Peter.

But why give Peter a special, personal invitation? He is, after all, one of the disciples. The angel didn't single out anyone else. He didn't mention James, or John, or Andrew, or Bartholomew, or any of the others. Why Peter?

I'm sure the answer to that goes much, much deeper than could ever be understood, but one thing for sure: the angel singled out Peter because Peter probably thought that even if Jesus was alive He surely wouldn't want anything to do with him! He was probably remembering the denials, the curses, the swearing. He was probably once again crushed in his spirit remembering how low he had fallen just three days earlier, at the moment Jesus needed him most.

We should be ever so thankful for this story, not because we are glad Peter made the mistake of denying the Lord, but because of the hope it gives us when we deny the Lord. Peter was salvaged by grace. Oh, he didn't lose his salvation, just as we noted in the life of David. But he did lose the joy of his salvation. He wept bitterly as he was brought under conviction for this sin, but he was given a special message that all was not lost: Jesus wanted to see him again.

And that is the rest of the story. Once we have allowed ourselves to become wrecked by our own wayward sinfulness, and we find ourselves in the spiritual junkyard, remember that God's salvaging grace is available, and more than sufficient, to pick us up, clean us up, stand us up, and send us forth once again walking in the joy of His salvation.

Perhaps someone reading these words can identify with Peter or David. Perhaps you can remember an occasion when you did as they did: you turned your back on the things of God and engaged in sinful behavior that caused a break in your fellowship with God. Perhaps you remember how God's heavy hand of conviction came crashing down on you as He brought your sin to your attention. And now you can rejoice in the fact that you have been forgiven and restored by the grace of God.

But perhaps there are some reading these words who can relate more to David and Peter in their pre-repentant state. Perhaps the hand of God is heavy against you, and yet you still haven't come to the place of confession and repentance. You may even be thinking that what you have done is so horrible that you are beyond the grace of forgiveness and restoration. The good news is that no one is beyond the forgiving grace of God. If you are His child, and you have allowed yourself to engage in some sinful behavior that has caused you to lose the joy of your salvation, please know that God's forgiveness is available to you.

All you need to do is to respond to the convicting power of God bringing your sinful behavior to your attention. Agree with God that you have fallen away by rebelling against Him. Ask Him to forgive you of your sin. And accept His gift of forgiving grace. Once again you will experience the overwhelming power of His love and forgiveness. Then, follow Him. Allow Him to once again be your source of fulfillment, contentment, and joy.

POINTS TO PONDER

1. How do you understand the author's statement about this being a "throw-away society?"

2. Have you ever thrown something away instead of having it repaired? Why did you decide to do so?

3. How do you reconcile the fact that David committed the horrific sins of adultery and murder, but yet be referred to as "a man after God's own heart"?

4. What was the difference between the actions of Judas Iscariot and the Apostle Peter?

5. Is there any sin God will not forgive? If so, name it and explain why it is unforgivable.

6. Have you ever experienced the reality of God's salvaging grace? If so, allow God to use it as a testimony to His amazing grace.

7. Explain what the angel meant when he instructed the women to "go tell the disciples – and Peter..."

CHAPTER 5

Sanctifying Grace

"And such were some of you. But you were washed,
but you were sanctified, but you were justified in
the name of the Lord Jesus and by the Spirit of
our God."

(1 Corinthians 6:11)

His Blood is on My Soul
Dear Jesus all my sins forgave,
And washed and made me whole,
I have sweet peace and joy within,
His blood is on my soul.

His blood is on my soul,
His blood is on my soul,
I rest securely in His hand,
His blood is on my soul.

The tempter cannot overcome,
Or gain the least control,
I have God's everlasting seal,
Christ's blood is on my soul.
R.E. Winsett

95

I had recently moved to a new town where I would serve as pastor of one of the local, rural congregations. I was beginning to learn my way around the rugged country roads in the community in which the church was located. Stopping at convenience stores, grocery marts, and gas stations kept me busy for the first few weeks after my arrival. My hair had grown quite long since moving into the neighborhood, so I began to inquire where I might find a barber shop.

After getting directions to several, I chose one and stopped by, where I was greeted by an old-fashioned barber pole and a large sign on the outside of the shop with the words, "Walk-ins Welcome," painted in bright red. So, I took that as my personal invitation to walk in, sit down, and wait my turn in the barber's chair.

There were several others ahead of me, so I picked up a magazine, sat back, and began listening to the conversation. Every time there was a change of customer in the barber's chair there would come a change of subject matter being discussed. One customer talked about his hunting dogs, while another spoke about his family coming home for a visit for the holidays. Another wanted to share all the details of an upcoming family vacation when the whole family was going to be together for the first time in several years.

The topics were different customer to customer. They all wanted to talk about things of interest to them. But as I sat and listened to each of them, one common thread ran through every conversation: the barber's vocabulary. Every comment he made was sprinkled with profanity. Several times it was not a sentence, but just a one-word expletive he would say in response to a remark made by one of his customers. They must have all been regulars because his use of so many profane words did not seem to catch them off-guard, and they did not seem to be offended by his vulgarity.

The customers came and went, and finally it was my turn to get in the chair. I sat there as the barber tied the covering around my neck and draped it across my body to catch the falling hair. Being the extreme introvert that I am I waited for him to engage the conversation, and it wasn't long in coming. It began with a simple observation: "Don't think I've seen you in here before. You new to these parts, are you?" My reply must have taken him a bit by surprise as I remember that he seemed to choke a little before speaking again. I said, "I'm the new pastor at one of the local churches. Do you attend church anywhere?"

It was obvious he was struggling for words. I'm sure it had something to do with the language he had been using the entire time I had been waiting my turn. After clearing his throat a couple of times, he finally managed to say, "Oh, yes, I'm a member of the First Baptist Church here in town. I really love my church." He paused for a moment before he made his next statement. Finally, he said, "And I'll tell you what, preacher, I'm totally satisfied with Jesus."

This is the point at which I almost choked! After sitting there for well over an hour, listening to this man use every word of profanity I had ever heard, and using the Lord's name in vain quite a few times, I must admit my utter shock to hear him say that he was a member of a church, and, even more that he would speak of his satisfaction with Jesus. I realize that some reading this account are thinking that I had no right to judge this man simply on the basis of his vocabulary, and that is true. I have no right to judge anyone for anything. But Jesus did say that we could be fruit inspectors. I simply listened to him, and made an assessment based on what I heard. That assessment led me to reach a conclusion that may or may not have been true. My assessment also prompted me to respond to his statement.

So, what was my response? I looked him straight in the eye and said, "But is Jesus satisfied with you?" That may not have been the most tactful or diplomatic thing to say considering we had just met, but I said it none-the-less.

It led into a conversation about the importance of being set apart for the things of God, and to live our lives to the glory of

God. That is the subject of this chapter: sanctifying grace. This is such an important matter for professing believers to consider.

The word 'sanctify' literally means to be set apart. In the Old Testament the concept is seen mostly in the use of the word 'holy.' This concept is also seen quite often in the New Testament, where the word is 'sanctify,' or 'sanctification.' Each of these words means to be set apart.

In the Old Testament, for example, the utensils used in the Temple were said to be holy, set apart for use in the worship of God. The priest was said to be holy, as he was set apart for the service of God. In an orthodox Jewish home, there would be two complete sets of dishes, one for common, everyday use, and the other for use only on special days of worship and celebration. This set was referred to as holy: set apart for the things of God, and never to be used for the purpose of serving meals on a day-to-day basis.

This concept is carried over into the New Testament as believers are referred to by the word sanctified – those who are set apart. The New Testament further describes sanctification in two distinct ways: positional sanctification, and practical sanctification.

POSITIONAL SANCTIFICATION

Consider first the matter of positional sanctification. When an individual becomes a child of God through faith in the sacrificial death of Jesus Christ, he is immediately in a position of sanctification: he has been set apart by God and is now in a position of complete sanctification. In the eyes of God, this is a completed action. God the Father now looks at the believer as being in Christ, and when He looks at Christ, He sees nothing but absolute perfection. Thus, as a child of God, the believer is positionally sanctified.

This is something for which we should be extremely and

eternally grateful. There is nothing that we have done, or ever could do, to earn this standing with God. When He looks at us, He sees nothing that would warrant His setting us apart for Himself. We are all under the curse of God because of our sinfulness, and we deserve His pronounced wrath against those who sin against Him. So, when He proclaims that we are now in a position of sanctification, it is a gift that is given totally by His amazing grace.

There is biblical testimony that shows clearly fact of the positional sanctification of believers. One such passage is found in Paul's correspondence with the believers in Corinth.

> Paul, called to be an apostle of Jesus Christ through the will of God, and Sosthenes or brother, to the church of God which is at Corinth, *to those who are sanctified in Christ Jesus, called to be saints...*
> (1 Corinthians 1:1–2a; emphasis added)

Paul refers to the believers as being sanctified in Christ Jesus and called to be saints. This is a statement referring to positional sanctification. Note the phrase "who are sanctified." This is clearly and unmistakably an assertion that the people to whom Paul addresses this letter are in a position of sainthood. It certainly does not mean that they have reached sanctified perfection – the remainder of 1 Corinthians shows that the believers in Corinth have some serious problems with sinful behavior and practice, but in relation to the matter of sanctification Paul refers to them as being positionally sanctified.

However, in the arena of this earthly existence, the believer is still in the process of practical sanctification. Read the words of Paul carefully as consideration is given to this important topic.

> Do you not know that the unrighteous will not inherit the kingdom of God? Do not be deceived. Neither fornicators, nor idolater, nor adulterers,

nor homosexuals, nor sodomites, nor thieves,
nor covetous, nor drunkards, nor revilers, nor
extortioners will inherit the kingdom of God.
And such were some of you. But you were washed,
but you were sanctified, but you were justified in
the name of the Lord Jesus and by the Spirit of
our God.

(1 Corinthians 6:9–11)

Paul gives a list of sinful lifestyles and activities for the purpose of illustration. This is certainly not to be thought of as an all-inclusive list, as there are multitudes of others that could be added, but for the sake of clarity Paul lists these to make his point.

And what exactly is his point? Simply this: *Such were some of you*. So, in the Corinthian congregation there were some former fornicators, and idolaters, and adulterers, and homosexuals, and drunkards, and extortioners. But they are no longer living these lifestyles and habitually committing these acts of rebellion against God's Word. Why? Because they have been washed, sanctified, and justified.

First Paul says they have been washed. There is a beautiful Christian hymn that speaks powerfully to this matter of being washed by asking the question, "Have you been to Jesus for the cleansing power? Are you washed in the blood of the Lamb?" What does it mean to be washed in the blood of Jesus? And, more importantly, is this a Biblical teaching, or simply a poetic way of describing the power of Jesus' blood?

Blood plays a significant role in the Bible. In the Old Testament we are taught that life is in the blood. God prohibited eating meat unless the blood had been drained because the life of the animal was in the blood. God also required animal sacrifices, because, as He instructed Moses, there must be the shedding of blood to make atonement for sin. Because of this, Moses was given instructions on an elaborate sacrificial system where animals were sacrificed as different types of offering: sin offering, trespass offering, burnt offering, and peace offering. This was a powerful testimony to the people that God required the shedding of blood to pay the penalty for the sins of the people.

The New Testament continues this emphasis on the shedding of blood. However, it is not now the shedding of the blood of animals, but rather the shedding of Jesus' blood. Understood correctly, it teaches that the sacrificial system of the Old Testament was pointing prophetically to the ultimate sacrifice Jesus made on the cross.

The author of the Epistle to the Hebrews says clearly, "And according to the law almost all things are purified with blood, and without shedding of blood there is no remission" (Hebrews 9:22). This same author also states, "For it is impossible that the blood of bulls and goats could take away sins" (Hebrews 10:4). The Apostle Peter also has something to say about this matter of the importance of blood sacrifice. In his first epistle he said:

> Knowing that you were not redeemed with corruptible things, like silver or gold, from your aimless conduct received by tradition from your fathers, but the with precious blood of Christ, as of a lamb without blemish and without spot.
> (1 Peter 1:18–19)

These verses teach beyond doubt that the blood of Jesus Christ is the only means of salvation, and that the individual believer has been washed in that blood, ensuring his eternal security. It is through this sacrificial death that God's wrath has been appeased, and the believer has passed out of darkness into the light of Jesus Christ.

The second thing Paul states as being true in the life of the believer is that they had been sanctified. We are to understand from this that Paul is referring to positional sanctification, and this is something that has happened in the past. The individual who responds to the effectual call of God and professes with his mouth that Jesus Christ is Lord is saved, and thereby set apart to the glory of God (see Romans 10:13). So, the individual believer is in a position of total sanctification through the righteousness of Jesus Christ which has been imputed to him. This position of sanctification will begin the process of practical sanctification which will be discussed a little later in this chapter.

The third thing Paul speaks about in the believer's life is their justification. He states that, even though their lives before being washed in the blood of Jesus had been characterized by sinful lifestyles and actions, they are now positionally sanctified and perfectly justified. Even though we were dead in trespasses and sins, we have now been brought to life by the sovereign grace of God. Listen to how Paul describes this miraculous work.

> And you He made alive, who were dead in trespasses and sins, in which you once walked according to the course of this world, according to the prince of the power of the air, the spirit who now works in the sons of disobedience.
>
> (Ephesians 2:1–2)

God brings death into life by His grace and according to His will. This act of God puts the individual in a position of total justification before God. Thus, by God's amazing grace the individual, whose life has been characterized by sin, has been pronounced just by the only One who has the authority to do so.

To clarify this even further Paul speaks of how God accomplishes this amazing work. A little later in this same chapter of Ephesians, Paul says:

> For by grace you have been saved through faith, and that not of yourselves; it is the gift of God, not of works, lest anyone should boast. For we are His workmanship, created in Christ Jesus for good

works, which God prepared beforehand that we should walk in them.

(Ephesians 2:8–10)

The entire work of justification is produced by God – from beginning to end. Remember, it was while we were dead in trespasses and sins that God made us alive. Before being made spiritually alive by a sovereign act of God we were unable to comprehend the things of God, because those things are spiritually discerned. Having no spiritual ability to discern the things of God, we were hopelessly and helplessly lost, dead in sin, and in desperate need of God's gracious intervention.

Thankfully He did intervene, and in His intervention, He made us alive, He washed us in the blood of His Son, He set us apart, and He pronounced us justified! What an truly astounding thing to consider.

PRACTICAL SANCTIFICATION

Once we are positionally sanctified, the process of practical sanctification begins. This process will continue for the remainder of the physical life of the follower of Jesus Christ. The sovereign act of positional sanctification is accomplished instantaneously by the hand of God. The matter of practical sanctification takes place incrementally over the span of a lifetime as a joint effort between God and the individual believer. Paul speaks of this reality in his correspondence with his friends in Philippi.

...being confident of this very thing, that He who has begun a good work in you will complete it until the day of Jesus Christ...

(Philippians 1:6)

The work to which Paul refers is the work of sanctification. Practical sanctification begins the moment an individual responds to the effectual call of God. However, it is not something that we are left to accomplish on our own, with no assistance. God does not make this demand of His children and then expect them to be able to accomplish the work of practical sanctification without divine help. There are different means of growing toward our fullness in Christ. Paul further elaborates on this subject in the next chapter of Philippians:

> Therefore, my beloved, as you have always obeyed, not as in my presence only, but now much more in my absence, work out your own salvation with fear and trembling; for it is God who works in you both to will and to do for His good pleasure.
>
> (Philippians 2:12–13)

It is crucial that we understand this passage correctly. Paul does not say here that we are to work *for* our salvation. The Bible makes it clear beyond all question that salvation is a gift of God. We are saved by the sovereign grace of God. The work of salvation was accomplished by Jesus Christ when He gave Himself as the substitutionary sacrifice, paying the penalty for sin. When Jesus cried out on the cross, "It is finished," one of the many things He meant by that statement was the work of salvation was completely done. He had accomplished the plan of God assigned to Him from eternity past.

So, when Paul says here that we are to work out our own salvation, he means something different. Working out our salvation is to be thought of in terms of sanctification. Our salvation calls for us to begin the process of becoming conformed to the image of Jesus Christ. This is the work assigned to each and every individual believer in Jesus Christ.

And yet, again, we are not left to ourselves to accomplish this daunting task on our own. Paul goes on to say that it is God who works in us both to will and to do for His good pleasure. What an encouragement it is to know that God Himself is working on our behalf, supplying what we need to be consistent in making progress in our personal, practical sanctification.

But what exactly does sanctification look like? How are we to engage in this important life-long task? The Bible sheds much needed insight and instruction into this matter. To begin striving to gain a fuller understanding of this major Biblical mandate it would be wise to observe the Bible's emphasis on the subject. Once again turning to the writings of the apostle Paul, we hear this word of admonition:

> For this is the will of God, your sanctification: that you should abstain from sexual immorality; that each of you should know how to possess his own vessel in sanctification and honor, not in passion or lust, like the Gentiles who do not know God.
>
> (1 Thessalonians 4:3–5)

God's will for every believer in Jesus Christ is their sanctification. This verse leaves no room for debate or discussion, only for obedience or disobedience. It is to be thought of as a type of springboard, not as an end in itself. It is extremely limited in scope. The process of sanctification is so much broader in scope than the very narrow definition seen here. The process of practical sanctification touches every area and aspect of life. Salvation begins a journey through which believers are to become more and more like Jesus as we go through life. But the foundation for it all is the understanding that this is the will of God.

There are many passages of Scripture which give further clarification on the subject. Paul speaks quite often about being sanctified, giving examples of how it looks in the life of the individual. The following passage from his letter to the Ephesians is one that displays the mandate for sanctification as well as several specific examples of how it would look in the life of the individual.

This I say, therefore, and testify in the Lord, that you should no longer walk as the rest of the Gentiles walk, in the futility of their mind, having their understanding darkened, being alienated from the life of God, because of the ignorance that is in them, because of the blindness of their heart; who, being past feeling, have given themselves over to lewdness, to work all uncleanness with greediness.

But you have not so learned Christ, if indeed you have heard Him and have been taught by Him, as the truth is in Jesus: that you put off, concerning your former conduct, the old man which grows corrupt according to the deceitful lusts, and be renewed in the spirit of your mind, and that you put on the new man which was created according to God, in true righteousness and holiness.

(Ephesians 4:17–24)

Once again, it is important to note that this passage is made up of examples of sanctification and is not to be thought of as exhaustive. The individual follower of Jesus Christ is to study Scripture and strive to follow His teachings as well as His actions.

Paul describes the process of sanctification as putting off and putting on. It would be discarding something old and replacing it with something new. This is actually a description of Biblical repentance. True and sincere repentance can be thought of as taking an about face. Repentance is a change of mind that leads to a change of action. It cannot be one or the other, but it requires both. For instance, think of someone who has been engaged in an adulterous relationship. This individual then reads the Bible's prohibition against adultery, and the Holy Spirit brings about conviction in his life. He then changes his mind about his sinful action to agree with the Bible's prohibition against this sexual sin. However, even though he now agrees with God about his sin, he continues to engage in the sinful relationship. This is a change of mind without an accompanying change of action.

On the other hand, this same individual may read the prohibition, and immediately change his behavior by getting out of the adulterous relationship but continue to lust in his heart for the individual with whom he was committing adultery. He is still committing adultery in his heart, as Jesus taught in the Sermon on the Mount. True repentance requires both the mind and the will. It requires a change of mind to come to alignment with Biblical instruction, and a change of behavior to align with the change of mind.

Paul gives a couple of specific examples to help his readers better understand.

> Therefore, putting away all lying, 'Let each one of you speak the truth with his neighbor...
>
> Let him who stole steal no more, but rather let him labor, working with his own hands what is good...
>
> Let all bitterness, wrath, anger, clamor, and evil speaking be put away from you, with all malice. And be kind to one another, tenderhearted, forgiving one another, even as God in Christ forgave you.
>
> (Ephesians 4:25, 28, 31, 32)

These examples clearly show the process of putting off the old and replacing it with the new. The process of sanctification is the continual, consistent work of each individual believer in Christ.

Back to the barber mentioned at the beginning of this chapter. It was quite obvious that when I sat down in the barber's chair and shared with him that I was the new pastor of a local church, he was convicted over his choice of words, especially using the Lord's name in vain. Was he convicted because I announced my status in the community? If so, there would have been no sincere repentance, even though he refrained from using profanity for the rest of our conversation. It was nothing more than embarrassment because he got "caught".

If, however, he was convicted by the Holy Spirit's work in his life, and he quit using profanity from that point on, then his repentance would have been sincere, as he put off the old and replaced it with the new.

Sanctification should be the goal of every believer in Jesus Christ. We should never settle for anything less. God requires it of us, expects it from us, and works in us to bring it about. As we learned in the chapter on salvaging grace, when we do fall to temptation, God is quick to bring us under conviction, calling us to confession and repentance. As we allow Him to do His work in us, He further assists us in making incremental progress in our ongoing personal process of practical sanctification.

It is always wonderful to see an individual who has placed his faith in Jesus Christ as Savior. It is also wonderful when we see that same person a while later and notice obvious growth and development in their relationship with God. On the other hand, it is distressingly sad to see a professing believer who remains a spiritual baby. They are still in spiritual infancy, needing to be constantly nurtured by others and never able to nurture others.

We are all called to be followers of the Lord, not only as observers, but also as those who take seriously the admonitions and exhortations in the Bible about becoming more like Him.

I came across a story years ago that illustrates the process of sanctification in a simple yet beautiful and profound way. There was once a sculptor who purchased a large piece of marble and had it delivered to his studio. The marble sat there for a few days, and passers-by would ask the sculptor what exactly he was going to make out of it. His answer was always the same: "I'm not going to make anything out of it. I'm going to find something in it." Those making the inquisition were a bit confused and asked for explanation. The sculptor then replied, "There is an angel inside that slab of marble. I'm going to take my hammer and chisel, and I'm going to chip away everything that doesn't look like an angel."

God is the sculptor, and each individual believer in Jesus Christ is like that slab of marble. God graciously takes His chisel in hand and begins the process of chipping away, carefully removing anything that doesn't look like Jesus. Sometimes the process is easy and relatively pain-free as those pre-conversion habits, mannerisms, vocabulary, and behaviors are chipped at with the chisel. The individual reads in Scripture that a certain character trait in his life is not in alignment with the Bible's description of how a true believer should live, so by the grace of God they put away the old and replace it with the new.

However, there are other times in which the believer has a stronghold in his life. It is an entrenched, habitual part of his life which he has been engaged in for years, perhaps decades. The Holy Spirit brings this matter to the attention of the believer, convicting him of God's desire that he change his mind and his behavior to align with scripture. But he doesn't do it. He enjoys this sinful activity so much that he decides he will hold on to it for the sheer pleasure it brings. However, for the sincere believer in Jesus Christ there will be no pleasure in those sinful activities because the Holy Spirit immediately brings the sinner under conviction. If he refuses to repent, the conviction will become more severe and painful. The Holy Spirit will not allow a true child of God to draw pleasure from behaviors and actions that are clearly forbidden in the word of God.

This continual and consistent conviction by the Holy Spirit ultimately leads the believer into a state of spiritual misery, as we saw in the lives of David and Peter in an earlier chapter. God relentlessly chisels away at the believer, working according to His good pleasure.

It should be the desire of every believer in Jesus Christ to obey the admonitions and exhortations in the Bible to become more like Jesus as time presses on. It should be our personal goal to decrease in our own personal desires, and to increase in the desire to be more like Jesus. May it be so with everyone who reads the words of this chapter.

POINTS TO PONDER

1. What is your definition of the word "sanctification"?
2. How do you explain the process of sanctification?
3. What is the purpose of sanctification?
4. Does anyone ever achieve absolute sanctification in this life?
5. When does sanctification begin in the life of a believer?
6. When does sanctification end in the life of a believer?
7. What should be the ultimate goal of the believer as he strives to be sanctified?
8. How do you understand the admonition, "work out your own salvation with fear and trembling"?

CHAPTER 6

Sin-defeating Grace

What shall we say then? Shall we continue in sin that grace may about? Certainly not! How shall we who died to sin live any longer in it?

(Romans 6:1)

There's Power in the Blood
Would you be free from the burden of sin?
There is power in the blood, power in the blood;
Would you o'er evil the victory win?
There is wonder-working power in the blood.

There is power, power, wonder-working power
In the blood of the Lamb;
There is power, power, wonder-working power
In the precious blood of the Lamb.
Lewis E. Jones

As we learned in the previous chapter, at the moment of salvation the believer is instantaneously positionally sanctified, set apart, for God and to God. However, practical sanctification begins at that moment and progresses incrementally for the remainder of the believer's life. In this process the believer systematically and progressively becomes more and more like Jesus.

Part of that process is the putting off of old sinful habits and behaviors, replacing them with godly lifestyles that glorify Jesus Christ. Through the ensuing years the life of the believer should be one of less sin and more holiness. The ultimate goal of every believer is to be conformed to the likeness of Jesus Christ. But there is something that seems to always get in the way of reaching that goal: self and sin.

A BIBLICAL OVERVIEW OF SIN

The Bible has much to say about the matter of sin. For the sake of discussion, we will give consideration to three important matters pertaining to this subject: Inherent sin, imputed sin, and personal sin.

INHERENT SIN

First is the subject of inherent sin. To understand this, we need to revisit the garden of Eden once again. God created Adam and Eve and placed them in a perfect paradise. Everything they could ever possibly need was provided by the gracious hand of God. The majesty of the garden can only be imagined, as it was far different from anything we could ever experience in our sin-cursed world. The earth bore fruit without the labor and toil of tilling, planting, weeding, and watering. There were trees bearing all manner of delicious fruit which provided food for Adam and Eve. There was no such thing as thorns and weeds, which would be part of the curse of God on the planet.

Adam and Eve enjoyed fellowship with God in the garden in the most intimate of ways. It was truly heaven on earth. This is far beyond our comprehension, even beyond our most vivid and creative imagination. To think about a perfect paradise in which they were able to actually walk and talk with God in the coolness of the garden is a blessing that we cannot begin to envision.

My wife and I have always enjoyed visiting gardens. We have visited beautiful gardens in several different states. During the spring of the year these gardens burst with color and aromatic fragrances as countless varieties of flowers bloom in all their brilliance. In my mind, I can't picture anything more beautiful than these beautifully manicured botanical masterpieces. But I am convinced that they are nothing in comparison to the garden of Eden.

But once Adam and Eve disobeyed God, thereby committing the very first act of sin, everything changed. The earth would now only bear fruit through much toil and labor. Thorns and weeds were now a common part of the landscape. God no longer shared in close, intimate fellowship with Adam in the garden. Adam and Eve are driven from the perfect garden paradise. There would now be pain and suffering and death – all a result of God's curse on the earth.

Why did God place this curse on the earth? Because of sin! God had warned the first couple of the dire consequences that would result from their disobedience. Their act of sin would change everything and would affect everyone. Paul says it this way in his letter to the Romans:

> Therefore, just as through one man sin entered the world, and death through sin, and thus death spread to all men, because all sinned – (For until the law sin was in the world, but sin is not imputed when there is no law...).
>
> (Romans 5:12–13)

Through Adam sin entered the world and has passed to all men. The sin nature has been passed down to all generations since Adam. Man is born in sin, and thus are sinners by birth. It is important to remember that we do not become sinners when we sin, but rather we sin because we are sinners. We are all born sinners. Inherently sinful. We have no choice in the matter. Through the first human parents came sin, and it has passed to all humankind.

IMPUTED SIN

The second thing to note in the passage quoted above is Paul's reference to imputed sin. He makes mention of the law, which is a reference to the law given to Moses. Note carefully that he says sin was in the world before the law was given, but it was not imputed until the law was given. This is crucial for our proper understanding of the law of sin and death. Sin was in the world from Adam to Moses, and man was accountable for sin because they were inherently sinful due to the sin nature. But sin was not imputed to man until the giving of the law, as sin was now viewed as lawlessness, or rebellion against the law, which was the vehicle God used to make man aware of his sin.

This is a very important truth that we need to make sure we understand before moving on. Oftentimes we think of the breaking of the law of God revealed in the pages of scripture as that which causes us to be separated from God. But that is not the case at all. It was the law that revealed to man his sinfulness. Paul speaks to this matter in his letter to the Galatians, where he tells us why the law of God is so vitally important.

> Therefore the law was our tutor to bring us to Christ, that we might be justified by faith. But after faith has come, we are no longer under a tutor.
>
> (Galatians 3:24–25)

The picture Paul is painting for us would have been quickly, easily, and completely understood by the people in his lifetime. In the Roman empire boys would be taken to school each day to be tutored in their studies. The child would be taken to the door of the classroom by a household servant. The servant could walk the child to the door of the classroom, but, being a servant, could not go in. The picture is one that gives the reader a graphic image of the function of the law.

The law is like the household servant who could take the child to the tutor. The law can take us to the place where we can, by faith, enter into a relationship with God through Jesus Christ. The law can take us to the door, but it cannot take us through the door. The purpose of the law, then, was to show us that we are sinners in desperate need of salvation but cannot provide the salvation we so desperately need. This is the reason it is important to note that man was accountable to God for sin even before the law was given. To reiterate, the law was given to show man his sinfulness. We are not guilty of sin because we break the law of God – we are guilty of breaking the law of God because we are sinners.

Now, back to the matter of imputed sin. Sin is imputed to man through the law because we are lawbreakers. It is in understanding this biblical truth that the grace of God in providing salvation through Jesus Christ is all the more amazing. In giving His life as the propitiatory sacrifice for sin, thereby paying the penalty of sin that we all rightfully deserve, our sin was imputed to Christ. Read carefully the following assertion from the apostle Paul:

> For He [God] made Him [Jesus Christ] who knew
> no sin to be sin for us, that we might become the
> righteousness of God in Him.
>
> (2 Corinthians 5:21)

Man should be grateful to God for imputed sin as it was through the imputation of our sin to Jesus on the cross that our death penalty was paid in full by Him. Our sin was imputed to Him, and His righteousness was imputed to us.

So, all men are inherently sinful due to the sin nature passed down from Adam and Eve. Through the law sin has been imputed to us because the law has revealed to us our sinfulness. And our sin has been imputed to Christ on the cross so that we might be made righteous in Him.

PERSONAL SIN

And now to a third and final observation about sin before we begin looking at the power of sin-defeating grace. The sin nature has been passed down to all humanity, bringing each of us under the penalty of death. This is yet another crucial truth for us to grasp. I am not guilty because of Adam's sin. You are not guilty because of his sin. Yes, Adam is the federal head of the human family, and it is through his act of rebellion against God that the sin nature has been inherited by humankind. But we are not guilty of Adam's sin. God is not holding us personally responsible and accountable for anything done by Adam or anyone else. Each of us is guilty of personal sin.

Personal, individual sin. I am guilty. You are guilty. All are guilty. We are all under the penalty of sin, and to a very large degree under the power of sin, because of personal sin.

To review, we are inherently sinful because we have inherited the sin nature from the first human couple. Through the law of God given to Moses, we have now experienced the imputation of sin. The law of God reveals to us our sinfulness and shows us our desperate need of a Savior. God has now imputed our sin to Jesus on the cross, where He paid the penalty for sin that each of us rightly deserved. We are not being held accountable for Adam's sin. As head of the human family, sin did enter the world through him and the sin nature has now been passed down to each of us, but we are guilty and accountable for our personal sin.

For all have sinned and fall short of the glory
of God.
For the wages of sin is death.

(Romans 3:23; 6:23)

We will now turn our attention to the power of sin. An understanding of this subject is essential in large part due to the fact that in the modern church, the subject of sin seems to be conspicuously missing. Sinful behaviors and lifestyles that are clearly denounced in scripture are now being embraced and accepted in many churches in our current cultural climate. In an attempt to be less offensive, many contemporary pastors are focusing more on the positive aspects of God's nature and attributes, such as love, grace, and mercy. These are extremely important aspects of the Gospel message, but they present only one side of the biblical portrait of God. It is important for us to understand the seriousness of sin in the life of the individual, or we will never be able to understand the need for sin-defeating grace.

THE POWER OF SIN

Due to the fact that we have a sin nature, we are, to a large degree, under the power of that nature. Have you ever heard a parent speak of having to teach his child to sin? Temper tantrums, selfishness, anger, lying, stealing and so many other acts of sinful behavior are committed by our children. Who taught them to do those things? Short answer: no one! They do them because of their fallen sinful nature. The responsibility of the parent is to teach the child to not sin, because they already know how to sin. Remember, we sin because we are sinners, and sin has power over us.

We have already learned in a previous chapter that all have gone astray and that none are seeking after God. Sin is the natural tendency of the human spirit.

Turning once again to the writings of the apostle Paul, he gives a graphic depiction of the struggle we have with the overwhelming power of sin. In the sixth chapter of Romans, he begins a discourse on this subject that will continue all the way through the eighth chapter. It is a long passage dealing with Paul's personal struggle with the power of sin in his own life, and how he came to have victory in this exhausting fight. He begins chapter six with a thought-provoking question:

> What shall we say then? Shall we continue in sin
> that grace may abound?
>
> (Romans 6:1)

There were obviously some in Rome who thought grace would abound more, and the testimony of grace would be more clearly seen, in the life of one who constantly sinned and then sought forgiveness. Would this not show more powerfully and profoundly just how amazing God's grace is? The more we sin, the more His grace abounds in our lives!

Just think about what a powerful testimony to God's grace it would be for the drunkard to regularly get intoxicated every Saturday night, then go to church on Sunday, make confession of his sin, and receive God's forgiving grace. What a powerful witness that would be to a loving, merciful, forgiving, gracious God. Would that not draw the drunkard's drinking buddies to repentance as they see that they could live their life of sinfulness and still receive God's forgiving grace? Powerful testimony, right?

Wrong. It is a testimony, not to God's grace, but to man's self-centered sinfulness. So how does Paul answer the question?

> Certainly not! How shall we who died to sin live
> any longer in it? Or do you not know that as many
> as were baptized into Christ Jesus were baptized
> into His death? Therefore, we were buried with
> Him through baptism unto death, that just as

> Christ was raised from the dead by the glory of
> the Father, even so we also should walk in newness
> of life.
>
> > (Romans 6:2-4)

Paul teaches that we have now been baptized into the death of Jesus Christ. But, just as Jesus was raised from the dead, even so have we been raised to live new lives in the power of the resurrection. This is a profound truth that needs to be embraced by everyone who is born into the family of God.

To once again use the same terminology used in discussing positional sanctification, the salvation of a lost sinner is a one-time, instantaneous experience. We die to our old self and are made new in Christ. But the struggle against sin continues until the day we die. This struggle is intense and calls for us to be on guard at every moment. Paul describes his own personal struggle in his letter to the Romans.

> For what I am doing I do not understand. For what
> I will to do, that I do not practice; but what I hate,
> that I do.
> For the good that I will to do, I do not do; but the
> evil I will not do, that I practice.
>
> > (Romans 7:15, 19)

Paul is describing what we might refer to as a spiritual tug-of-war. He is being pulled in two different directions. The sinful nature that is alive and well in Paul is enticing him to do the things he knows he should not do. He knows the law of God, and more importantly, as a born-again believer, he knows the will of God. He has the Spirit of God living in him, and the Spirit is leading him to follow the will of God, to walk away from sin's appeal, and to reckon his body to be dead to sin and alive to righteousness. It is a very real struggle between the old, sinful, Adamic nature and the new nature he has in Christ.

When I was a teenager, I was a member of Boy Scout Troop 180. Every summer we would go to summer camp at Camp Palmetto in the beautiful foothills of South Carolina. Field day was one of the highlights of the week at camp. Relay races, three-legged races, wheel-barrel races, campfire building contests, and log-chopping contests were the course for the day. One of my personal favorite competitive contests was the tug-of-war. A rope would be stretched out on the ground with a handkerchief tied in the middle. Each scout troop attending camp would choose ten troop members to compete. They would take the rope in hand, and when the whistle sounded, they would pull with all their combined energies trying to get the rope across the line on their side. It was an intense competition, sometimes lasting several minutes before one troop succeeded in pulling the other troop over the line.

Paul is describing a tug-of-war of sorts in this passage. However, it is not a team effort but a personal struggle. Paul is describing in graphic terms how much of a struggle it is for the individual believer to fight off the temptation to engage in sinful behavior. You can almost feel the intensity of Paul's battle as he states that what he knows he should not be doing are the very things he does, while the things he knows he should be doing he cannot find the will to do.

The struggle is real. The intensity is extreme. The individual believer engaged in this spiritual warfare oftentimes feels that he is in the arena fighting all alone against his formidable enemy. And please understand, he is indeed formidable, sometimes so much so that he seems to be insurmountable.

Paul gives some very enlightening insights into this personal struggle. Back in chapter six of Romans he makes the following observations:

> Now if we died with Christ, we believe that we shall also live with Him, knowing that Christ, having been raised from the dead, dies not more.

Death no longer has dominion over Him. For the death that He died, He died to sin once for all; but the life that He lives, He lives to God. Likewise you also, *reckon yourselves to be dead indeed to sin, but alive to God in Christ Jesus our Lord.*

(Romans 6:8–11; emphasis added)

The believer is to reckon himself dead to sin. This is a continuation of the thought Paul has already shared earlier in this same chapter: That the believer has been buried with Christ and raised to new life in Christ. Since Christ died, and the believer is now identified with Christ in His death, so is the believer identified with Christ in His resurrection. And, since death no longer has dominion over Christ, it no longer has dominion over us. Therefore, reckon, believe in the fact, that you are dead to sin and alive to God. We are simply to agree with God that we have died with Christ. Paul makes this even clearer in his letter to the Galatians.

I have been crucified with Christ; it is no longer I who live, but Christ lives in me; and the life which I now live in the flesh I live by faith in the Son of God, who loved me and gave Himself for me.

(Galatians 2:20)

This is an action that has taken place in the past. When an individual accepts the call of God unto salvation, then at that very moment he is crucified with Christ. This signifies that he is identified with Christ in His death. But it also signifies that he is alive in Christ. Or, as Paul says, Christ is alive in him. From the moment of the individual's salvation to the moment of his physical death the believer lives by faith in Jesus Christ.

The believer now has the ability to live a life of holiness and righteousness, not because of his own abilities but because of the fact that he is indwelt by Christ. This goes back to our earlier observation from the book of Romans that we are to reckon our bodies to be dead to sin and alive to righteousness. This is an act of faith, and it is displayed in our faithfulness to God.

But this is not something we can do in our own strength. So, having now given a brief overview of the principle of sin and the power of sin, we will now give attention to the believer's power over sin.

THE POWER OVER SIN

Sometimes temptation seems to be irresistible and insurmountable. The grip of sin on us, and the power of sin over us, is oftentimes overwhelming. In the life of a non-believer, the will to sin is left unchecked due to the fact that there is no desire to live lives of holiness that will ultimately bring glory to God. Non-believers, even though they have good traits and do good things, are for the most part self-centered and do the things they do for self-gratification. The believer, however, has a different purpose in life. As we are admonished in Scripture, we are to do all that we do for the glory of God. That should be the desire of every child of God.

> And whatever you do, do it heartily, as unto the Lord and not to men, knowing that from the Lord you will receive the reward of the inheritance; for you serve the Lord Christ.
>
> (Colossians 3:23–24)

But, as Paul says, sin and self very often get in the way of making that a reality. Even our service to others is sometimes an act of selfishness. As I look back on my forty years of pastoral ministry, I must admit that there were times – more than I would like to admit – that I did "works of ministry" motivated, not by my desire to serve people or even to bring glory to God, but to make me look good. There were times I did things out of a sense of duty rather than out of a sincere desire to glorify Jesus Christ. We don't have to do "bad things" to involve ourselves in sinful behavior. Even the "good things" we do, if done for the wrong reasons and to serve self rather than to serve others are acts of sinful behavior. Jesus makes this vividly and painfully clear in these words:

> Not everyone who says to Me, "Lord, Lord," shall enter the kingdom of heaven, but he who does the will of My Father in heaven. Many will say to Me in that day, "Lord, Lord, have we not prophesied in Your name, cast out demons in Your name, and done many wonders in Your name?" And then I will declare to them, "I never knew you; depart from Me, you who practice lawlessness."
> (Matthew 7:21–23)

These people come before Jesus and recount to Him the things they have done. They have prophesied, cast out demons, and performed many wonders. This sounds wonderful. These are good works they have done. And they even performed these works in Jesus' name! What a commendable testimony.

Yet, note carefully how Jesus identifies these works: Lawlessness. What appears to be works of righteousness is in reality works of lawlessness. How could this be? Simple: the motivation behind them. Jesus doesn't specify exactly what their motivation was, but it obviously was not to glorify God.

What is the motivation behind the things we do? Often, the motivation is sincere and pure. It is in those times that we do things in service to others out of a genuine desire to do good with no thought of what I might get in return. There are times we see a need and use our own resources to meet that need with no thought of "what will I get out of this?" Sometimes we even do things anonymously, with no desire to even be recognized for the deed we have done. Those are acts of kindness that are motivated by a pure heart and with pure motives. But sadly, many times we do things to serve self, to bring recognition to self, to get something out of if for self.

At still other times, we do things solely for self. We engage in business deals with selfish ends in mind. We initiate personal relationships with self-gratification in mind. We volunteer for community, church or civic duties with self-recognition in mind. We engage in sinful behavior for the pleasure we will get out of the experience. Self. Self-fulfillment. Self-gratification. Self-recognition. Self-serving. We often make it all about self.

So, how are we to gain victory over sin? Where do we attain power to overcome? We turn once again to Paul's letter to the Romans for instructions in this matter.

> There is therefore now no condemnation to those who are in Christ Jesus, who do not walk according to the flesh, but according to the Spirit. For the law of the Spirit of life in Christ Jesus has made me free from the law of sin and death. For what the law could not do in that it was weak through the flesh, God did by sending His own Son in the likeness of sinful flesh, that the righteous requirement of the law might be fulfilled in us who do not walk according to the flesh but according to the Spirit. For those who live according to the flesh set their minds on the things of the flesh, but those who live according to the Spirit, the things of the Spirit.
>
> (Romans 8:1–5)

This may sound like an overly simplified way of looking at this matter, but in actuality it is a profound biblical truth. To boil it down to one simple statement, it asserts that in order to have power over sin we need to walk in the Spirit. Simple statement: Profound truth!

Paul contrasts walking according to the flesh with walking according to the Spirit. Walking refers to our conduct, our behavior, our manner of life. How do we conduct ourselves? Does our behavior look more like the world, or more like Christ? Do our decisions reflect the world's way of life, or do they reflect principles gleaned from Scripture? Do our attitudes display a worldly mentality, or a Wordly mentality? Are we living by the dictates of our sinful, fallen world, or are we living the declarations of Holy Scripture?

Paul says that those who live according to the flesh set their minds on the things of the flesh, but those who live according to the Spirit, the things of the Spirit. What do we think about? What do we fill our minds with? We should have the desire to fill our minds with God's Word, and then let that Word be the controlling force in our lives. If we do, then we will stand a far greater chance of experiencing power over sin instead of succumbing to the power of sin.

What have you filled your mind with lately? Our minds are inundated with verbal stimulation and visual stimulation. Different forms of media fill our minds with suggestive thoughts and ideas that cause us to think certain ways, to have certain desires. Marketing experts know how to use these visual and verbal expressions to appeal to our senses. Through research they determine what colors are most appealing to the majority of consumers and suggest these to manufacturers as they design packaging for their products. Television commercials are designed to appeal to the senses, and therefore are filled with images and backgrounds that attract the attention of the viewer. These are all designed to appeal to our senses and motivate us to respond in positive ways to their messages.

We also fill our minds with subliminal messages that are presented to us in television programs, movies, magazines, newspapers, on-line news sources, and other forms of media and entertainment. We would all probably be amazed at how much our way of thinking is affected by the things we watch and hear.

We are sometimes motivated to purchase something because our minds have been motivated by "messages" our brains have received, but not in a recognizable way. For example, we may be watching a movie, and in an action scene there is a billboard that momentarily fills the screen with the name of a brand of clothing. It isn't part of the plot of the movie. It doesn't even have any real reason for being in the movie. But, there it is. It comes and goes so quickly that we don't even acknowledge it was there. It plants a thought, sub-consciously, in our minds that could possibly cause us to think about that product a little later, and, without realizing why, we find ourselves going to the clothing store to look for that particular brand.

This, of course, is in reference to those things that enter our minds without our conscious knowledge. But what about those things we purposefully fill our minds with? What about the things we read, the television programs and movies we watch, the particular news outlet we get most of our information from, even the places we frequently visit? What are they filling our minds with, both consciously and subconsciously? Paul gives a word of admonition and encouragement about this in his letter to the Philippians.

> Finally, brethren, whatever things are true, whatever things are noble, whatever things are just, whatever things are pure, whatever things are lovely, whatever things are of good report, if there is any virtue and if there is anything praiseworthy – meditate on these things. The things which you learned and received and heard and saw in me, these do, and the God of peace will be with you.
>
> (Philippians 4:8)

Someone has said that an idle mind is the devil's playground. This may be true, but from the foregoing observations an active mind can also be the playground of the devil, or simply the feeding of the self-indulgent flesh. It provides us with ample warning that our minds are very vulnerable to what we feed them, and what we feed them will motivate us to do certain things, to buy certain products, or to embrace a philosophical approach to life that takes us down a path far different than the one we have been traveling through life.

It is, therefore, incumbent on the life of every disciple of the Lord Jesus Christ that we understand the seriousness of doing as Paul instructs: walk in the Spirit so that we do not fulfill the lusts of the flesh. The power of the flesh, and appeal of the world, and the wiles of the devil are all working against us. Any one of them can affect the way we think, the way we view world events, and the way we interpret those events in light of our philosophical worldview.

Therefore, we must develop a solid, biblically based world-view that will help us stand against the onslaught of those things that would pull us into a worldly world-view. We should always strive to view world events through the lens of biblical truth. Cultural winds of change should be viewed through the lens of scripture so that we interpret that shift against the backdrop of the Bible. When culture, for example, begins to embrace a behavioral pattern that is clearly forbidden in scripture, then when we view it through those Biblical lenses we are able to see it for what it is: an affront to the teachings of God's Word.

There are many passages of scripture that would prove to be extremely helpful in understanding the seriousness of this subject and would also provide us with much-needed instructions on how to be victorious in this area of life.

> For the weapons of our warfare are not carnal
> but mighty in god for pulling down strongholds,
> casting down arguments and every high thing that
> exalts itself against the knowledge of God, bringing
> every thought into captivity to the obedience of

Christ, and being ready to punish all disobedience when your obedience is fulfilled.

(2 Corinthians 10:4–6)

...let us lay aside every weight, and the sin which so easily ensnares us, and let us run with endurance the race that is set before us, looking unto Jesus, the author and finisher of our faith, who for the joy that was set before Him endured the cross, despising the same, and has sat down at the right hand of the throne of God.

(Hebrews 12:1b–2)

I say then: Walk in the Spirit, and you shall not fulfill the lust of the flesh. For the flesh lusts against the Spirit, and the Spirit against the flesh; and these are contrary to one another, so that you do not do the things that you wish. But if you are led by the Spirit, you are not under the law.

(Galatians 5:16–18)

These all teach truths that give guiding principles to living life in victory over the power of sin. First, they teach us that attaining power over sin is not a matter of self-will, or self-discipline. Yes, it does involve the will, and it is reliant on discipline, but not in the way we usually think of those terms. The fact of the matter is that I cannot "will" myself to do good, to ward off temptation, or to discipline myself by sheer brute strength. I am not able, in and of myself, to accomplish this task. Let's be reminded of the intense battle Paul described in Romans about his own personal struggle. He oftentimes found himself doing what he knew he should not do, while not doing the things he should. If were a simple matter of the will, Paul would certainly have been one who could pull it off. But even the great apostle needed help from some source other than himself.

A second principle we can learn from these passages is that there is a source of help beyond self. We have already heard Paul speak of having been crucified with Christ, and now living by faith in Christ. We now live in the power of the resurrected Lord, and accordingly should reckon our bodies to be dead to sin and alive unto righteousness. We are to walk in the Spirit, and not according to the spirit of the world. And our ever-present help is none other than the Holy Spirit Himself. He indwells us; He empowers us; He enables us; He assists us; He guides us into truth. Walking in the Spirit does involve discipline in the life of the believer, but not in the sense of imitating Godly behavior. It is much more than that: It is actually being empowered by Him to live according to God's standards of righteousness and holiness.

The third principle we must understand is that this is a joint effort between the individual and God. In a previous chapter we heard the apostle Paul speak of working out our own salvation with fear and trembling, and that God was working through us to bring about His good pleasure. Therefore, as we walk in the Spirit, and as He guides us into all truth, we are then to submit ourselves to the truth He reveals, putting into practice the things of the Spirit while at the same time discarding the things of the flesh. We are to lay aside those sins that so easily and so often ensnare us and take every thought captive that does not honor and glorify Christ. We are to reckon our bodies to be dead to sin and alive to righteousness.

The power to overcome sin in our lives is the power of the Spirit indwelling us and empowering us to be overcomers instead of being overcome. This is all possible because of the grace of God working through us to mold us into the image of Christ.

We do not have to succumb to the power of temptation. Let's claim, by faith, the power that overcomes!

POINTS TO PONDER

1. What do the lyrics of "There's Power in the Blood" mean to you?
2. In your estimation, is it possible for a true believer to continue a lifestyle of sin after his/her salvation? Why or why not?
3. How do you think we should understand the phrase, "reckon yourselves to be dead to sin and alive to righteousness"?
4. How would you explain the law being our tutor, bringing us to Christ?
5. What is meant by statement that Adam is the federal head of the human race?
6. Are we held accountable for Adam's sin? Why or why not?
7. God had pronounced to Adam and Eve that if they disobeyed they would die that day. How do you explain the fact that they lived hundreds of years after their act of disobedience?
8. Will we be judged for our sin when we stand before the Lord?
9. How are we to have victory over the temptation to sin?

CHAPTER 7

Supplying Grace

"And my God shall supply all your need according to His riches in glory by Christ Jesus. Now to our God and Father be glory forever and ever. Amen."
(Philippians 4:19-20)

Great is Thy Faithfulness
Great is Thy faithfulness, O God my Father
There is no shadow of turning with Thee
Thou changest not, Thy compassions, they fail not
As Thou hast been, Thou forever will be.
Refrain:
Great is Thy faithfulness!
Great is Thy faithfulness!
Morning by morning new mercies I see:
All I have needed Thy hand hat provided-
Great is Thy faithfulness, Lord, unto me!

Summer and winter, springtime and harvest
Sun, moon, and stars in their courses above
Join with all nature in manifold witness
To Thy great faithfulness, mercy, and love.
Thomas O. Chisholm

S everal years ago, while leading a discipleship group in a study of the provisions of God, the discussion focused on the subject of needs and wants. What is the difference between needs and wants? How do we distinguish the two? We then began looking at a list of things and were asked to determine if they represented a real need, or if it would best be described as simply something we want.

The list contained items that were, for the most part, common, everyday items that we all have around our homes. Washers and dryers, refrigerators, dishwashers, vacuum cleaners, TV's, VCR's (which would now be DVD players), home theater systems, two automobiles, freezers, etc. It was so surprising to see what some identified as needs. One suggested that she really needed her VCR because that was the only way she could record her daytime dramas to watch when she got home later in the day. As hard as I tried to convince her that this was not a genuine need she refused to change her mind.

In reality, each of the things named above are wants. Granted, we have become accustomed to having these around the house, but it is not a necessity to have them. It might be an inconvenience to go without some of them, but we could certainly survive without them.

The verse at the beginning of this chapter speaks of God supplying all our needs. Every child of God should be eternally thankful to Him for this amazing promise. God has given us His assurance that we will the necessities of life. It may not always be everything we want, but we should not be overly concerned about that. As long as we have everything we need we should not complain about the things that are simply wants. Paul's words in this verse are insightful:

> Indeed I have all and abound. I am full, having received from Epaphroditus the things sent from you, a sweet-smelling aroma, an acceptable sacrifice, well-pleasing to God.
>
> (Philippians 4:18)

However, we must be careful in how we interpret this verse as we strive to apply its teaching to our everyday life. When consideration is given to the context of this statement, it is clear that Paul has just been speaking about the wonderful and sacrificial way the Philippians had ministered to him. In the verse immediately before the one quoted above Paul says:

> For even in Thessalonica you sent aid once and
> again for my necessities. Not that I seek the gift,
> but I seek the fruit that abounds to your account.
> (Philippians 4:16–17)

Paul's friends in Philippi had come to his aid by sending him the things he needed in order to continue his ministry. In response to that he tells them that God will supply their needs as they have supplied his. In this statement Paul is telling them that they will receive from God as they have given.

Jesus made a similar statement concerning this matter.

> Give, and it will be given to you: good measure,
> pressed down, shaken together, and running over will
> be put into your bosom. For with the same measure
> that you use, it will be measured back to you.
> (Luke 6:38)

Once again, this verse must be understood in its context. Jesus has been speaking about different topics in Luke's record of His sermon on the plain. In the verse immediately preceding the one quoted above Jesus has been speaking about two topics that are so vitally important in the life of His disciples:

> Judge not, and you shall not be judged. Condemn
> not, and you shall not be condemned. Forgive, and
> you will be forgiven.
> (Luke 6:37)

When consideration is given to the immediate context of Paul's statement in Philippians, and Jesus' statement in Luke, it is obvious that each passage is speaking of reciprocity. Paul is telling the Philippians that just as they have given to him, God will reciprocate. And Jesus is telling His disciples that just as they show mercy, and as they extend forgiveness, and as they give, it will all be reciprocated back to them.

The reason I have started this chapter with these verses is because I don't want anyone reading this book to think that your cupboard will always be full of the best foods, and that you will always be driving the best car, and that you will always be living in the best neighborhood, and that your children will always attend the best schools. God's supplying grace is just as real in the lives of those believers who struggle to make ends meet as it is in the lives of those who are truly rich in the world's resources.

There are certain individuals in Scripture who were abundantly wealthy in the world's goods. But the Bible also speaks of others who were not so wealthy – at least not in terms of material resources. God supplies each individual as He sees fit. The rich should not look down on the poor, and the poor should not be envious of the rich.

So, how are we to understand this matter of God's supplying grace? We strive to understand it by beginning with the distinction between wants and needs. It would be a good exercise to sit down with pen and paper and make two columns. On the top of one of the columns write the word "needs", and on the top of the other write the word "wants". Then, begin making a list of both.

What would you identify as a real need in your life? Write it under the "needs" column. What do you identify as things you want? Write them under the "wants" column. To help you come up with your list, go from room to room in your home, writing down the things you see. Which column would you put them on?

Refrigerator: need or want. Microwave: need or want. Television: need or want. Continue going through the entire house, room by room, identifying everything. Do you really need it, or do you just want it?

To help us understand this distinction correctly we will look briefly at how this specific manifestation of God's grace was fleshed out in the lives of a few people found in the pages of the Bible. As we look at them perhaps we will be able to appreciate God's supply in our lives.

ELIJAH – PHYSICAL NOURISHMENT

> And Elijah the Tishbite, of the inhabitants of Gilead, said to Ahab, "As the Lord God of Israel lives, before whom I stand, there shall not be dew nor rain these years, except at my word."
>
> Then the word of the Lord came to him, saying, "Get away from here and turn eastward, and hide by the Brook Cherith, which flows in the Jordan. And it will be that you shall drink from the brook, and I have commanded the ravens to feed you there."
>
> (1 Kings 17:1–4)

Elijah was a prophet during the reign of King Ahab in Israel. Elijah appears on the scene abruptly in the seventeenth chapter of First Kings. He is sent to Ahab with a message from the Lord. God is going to cause a drought to ravage the land of Israel because of the sins of the people, and specifically because of Ahab's personal wickedness. Ahab, according to the verses preceding those quoted above, was more wicked than any of the kings of Israel who had reigned before him. God sends Elijah to confront him about the wickedness he had committed, as well as that which he had led Israel to commit.

However, after Elijah delivers his message of the impending drought, he has to flee from the wrath of Ahab. It is here that

God gives the instructions to Elijah as to how God would provide for him during this season of drought. He was to go to the Brook Cherith where he would be supplied with everything he had need of to survive while in hiding. Miraculously, God had ravens bring him meat to eat in the morning and evening every day.

This is a remarkable display of God's supplying grace. Elijah, along with the entire nation of Israel, is suffering from the ravages of the drought. It is hard to imagine a drought that lasts three and a half years, isn't it? It is bad enough when it does not rain for perhaps a month, or two, or even for several months in a row. When a drought of this magnitude occurs our weather prognosticators begin telling us how dire the situation is. We may be told that we will have to curtail our water usage so as to safeguard against our water supplies being depleted. We may be told that we cannot water our lawns, or wash our vehicles in an attempt to make our supplies of water last as long as possible.

But can you imagine three and a half years without rain? The land would be baked and cracked open. It would be as hard as brick, nearly impossible to break open with the strongest swing of a pick. So, God supplies Elijah with his need for nourishment by sending him to a brook which would provide his need for water, and supplies his need for food by sending a raven twice daily with a ration of food.

Eventually, however, the brook dried up due to the lack of rain. Once again God reveals a new plan to Elijah. God tells Elijah to move once again to a different place where his needs would be met.

God proves again that He could be trusted in providing Elijah everything he needs to survive during the years of the disastrous drought. The land is languishing from the lack of rain. Crops will not grow. Herds and flocks are all suffering from lack of water. Vegetation is scorched from the arid dryness. There is no water for the livestock, just as there is no water for the people.

> And it happened after a while that the brook dried up, because there had been no rain in the land. Then the word of the Lord came to him, saying, "Arise, go to Zarephath, which belongs to Sidon, and dwell there. See, I have commanded a widow there to provide for you." So he arose and went to Zarephath.
>
> (1 Kings 17:7–10a)

Elijah is experiencing the ravages of the drought just like everyone else. But God supplies him with what he needs to survive. It is important to note that he is not supplied with an abundance, but only with what he needs to survive until the drought is over.

The text goes on to tell us exactly how God continued to supply Elijah with his needs even after the brook had dried up. He sends the prophet to Zarephath, where he is told a widow would provide his needs. However, when he arrives in the town he receives a most distressing message from the widow: she has nothing with which she can provide his needs. The text reveals the sad situation:

> So he arose and went to Zarephath. And when he came to the gate of the city, indeed a widow was there gathering sticks. And he called to her and said, "Please bring my a little water in a cup, that I may drink." And as she was going to get it, he called to her and said, "Please bring me a morsel of bread in your hand." So she said, "As the Lord your God lives, I do not have bread, only a handful of flour in a bin, and a little oil in a jar: and see, I am gathering a couple of sticks that I may go in and prepare it for myself and my son, that we may eat it, and die."
>
> (1 Kings 17:10b–12)

What an unbelievably horrific situation! The widow had been devastated by the drought. Her cupboards are completely bare. She is destitute, having used up everything during the relentless scorching from the savage heat and drought. She has nothing left but a small amount of flour with which she is going to make one last meal of bread and water for herself and her son. Then, in a somber addendum to this sad state of affairs, she announces that she and her son would then die for lack of nourishment. The drought had not only caused the depletion of the water supply, which had in turn destroyed any crops that had been sown, but it also had dried up any hope that the widow had of being able to survive. He declaration about her own impending death was a clear display of distress, with no evidence of any hope of survival.

God, of course, does not allow that to happen, as He miraculously multiplies the widow's supply of flour and oil for the duration of the drought. Through this miracle, God also provides for Elijah until the drought is over. He provided everything Elijah needed to survive. But again, we need to be reminded of the fact that Elijah had to suffer the consequences of the drought, just as the widow and her son. God provided what they needed, but no more.

When we have all that we need to survive we should be grateful to God for His bountiful supply. After all, he promised that we would have the necessities of life. Thanksgiving should be a constant in the life of every believer for God's supply.

DAVID – PHYSICAL PROTECTION

Another example of God's supplying grace can be seen in His providing physical protection for David. There were many times during David's life in which he experienced this protective grace. We will focus on just one example: King Saul attempting to kill David because of his intense jealousy of David's popularity.

During a stand-off between the Israelites and the Philistines, Goliath, the leader of the Philistine army, taunted the armies of Israel. He constantly called for a soldier from Israel to face him one-on-one in hand-to-hand combat. These taunts from the giant went on day after day. Listen to him as he makes light of the army of Israel:

> Then he stood and cried out to the armies of Israel, and said to them, "Why have you come out to line up for battle? Am I not a Philistine, and you the servants of Saul? Choose a man for yourselves, and let him come down to me. If he is able to fight with me and kill me, then we will be your servants. But if I prevail against him and kill him, they you shall be our servants and serve us." And the Philistine said, "I defy the armies of Israel this day; give me a man, that we may fight together." When Saul and all Israel heard these words of the Philistine, they were dismayed and greatly afraid.
>
> (1 Samuel 17:8–11)

The taunts continue day after day. The Israelites cower in fear before this giant of a man. This is an indictment against the soldiers of Israel, and of King Saul himself. They should have had faith in God, even if they had no faith in themselves. God had gone before the Israelites in many battles, striking decisive blows to their enemies. But now, they are all cowering before this one man. Goliath has the entire army of Israel stricken and paralyzed with fear.

Finally, a shepherd boy named David arrives on the scene. His father, Jesse, has sent him to the front line of the battle to check on his brothers, who were serving in Saul's army. David hears the taunts of Goliath and is indignant toward him and the army of the Philistines. So David goes to King Saul and volunteers to face Goliath one-on-one. All he has is a slingshot and a few stones, but that is all it took to defeat the giant and send the Philistine army running in retreat.

This was a time of great celebration for the nation. The army of Israel, led by King Saul, made their victorious entrance into the city to the shouts, cheers, and accolades of the multitudes gathered in the streets to welcome them home. It was a festive occasion, as the soldiers made their way back into the streets of Jerusalem to the sound of victory! King Saul rode triumphantly ahead of the entourage as they responded to the victorious shouts of the throngs of people gathered there to welcome them home.

But something happened on that day of celebration that would change King Saul forever.

> Now it happened as they were coming home, when David was returning from the slaughter of the Philistine, that the women had come out of all the cities of Israel, singing and dancing, to meet King Saul, with tambourines, with joy, and with musical instruments. So the women sang as they danced, and said:
> "Saul has slain his thousands,
> and David his ten thousands."
> Then Saul was very angry, and the saying displeased him; and he said, "They have ascribed to David ten thousands, and to me they have ascribed only thousands. Now what more can he have but the kingdom?" So Saul eyed David from that day forward."
>
> (1 Samuel 18:6–9)

It is here that Saul begins to sense a shift in the confidence of the people. This can be easily understood in one sense as the crowds shout more accolades for David than for Saul. Saul's confidence is probably shaken to the core. He was probably perplexed over the shouts of praise to David when he was the leader of the army and the king of the nation. He was moved with indignation as the people were obviously more enamored with David's military victory over Goliath than they were, at least for the moment, with Saul's leadership as king.

From that day forward Saul looked for an opportunity to kill David. But God provided physical protection for David each time. And finally, God took the kingdom from the family of Saul and established the reign of David. God was watching over him even on occasions when David was totally unaware of God's supplying grace.

Saul became so set on destroying David that it seemed as if he thought of nothing else. He was consumed with his evil intent. He would experience periods of uncontrollable rage as he seethed over the popularity of David. But through it all God provided protection for David.

Have you ever thought about the many times you were protected from harm by God's grace? Of course, it is impossible to know of all the times His protection has kept you from some type of harm, because most times we are completely unaware of His protection. In 1989, my family moved from South Carolina to Texas in order for me to continue my education. It is approximately 1100 miles from where we had lived to where we moved. Over the next eleven years we made the trip back to visit family an average of two times per year.

On all those trips we passed by countless cars, traveling at 70 miles per hour, without once having an accident. There were a few close calls, and after each one my wife and I would always pause to thank God for His protection. Those were obvious moments of God's protection, but we have wondered through the years how many times God kept us out of accidents by our schedule being changed a few minutes one way or the other at the beginning of our journey. We have talked several times about the fact that for two vehicles to be involved in an accident, both of them have to be in exactly the same spot at exactly the same time. Just a few seconds difference could be all that separates you from going on your way safely, or being involved in an automobile crash.

There were times we would come upon the scene of an accident that had occurred only seconds, or minutes at the most before we arrived. Had we been just a few seconds earlier it could have been us involved in the crash. We would pause for a moment and pray for the welfare of those involved, and then we would pray thanking God for His protection over us.

God's supply of protective grace is a reality in our lives so many times and in so many ways. It may not be escaping the hands of an angry king, but He protects us none-the-less.

HEZEKIAH – PHYSICAL HEALING

Another type of God's supplying grace is observed when He supplies physical healing. Hezekiah was king of Judah in the eighth century BC. He proved to be one of the more righteous kings of the southern kingdom. During his reign he led the nation in spiritual reforms as he tried to lead the nation to follow God while rejecting the gods of the nations.

Jerusalem had been besieged by Sennacherib of Assyria. The armies of Assyria had been displaying their power as nations had been falling before them like a series of dominoes. Now the Assyrian forces had encircled the city of Jerusalem and were threatening to destroy it.

To intervene on behalf of Judah, God sent a death angel into the camp of the Assyrian army and in one night 185,000 Assyrian soldiers died. God came to the aid of His chosen people, as He had done so many times before.

Soon after this amazing display of God's protective omnipotence on behalf of Judah, King Hezekiah contracted an illness that was so serious it appeared that he would die. As a matter of fact, God sent the prophet Isaiah to deliver a message to Hezekiah concerning the seriousness of his illness.

In those days Hezekiah was sick and near death. And Isaiah the prophet, the son of Amoz, went to him and said to him, "Thus says the Lord: Set your house in order, for you shall die, and not live." Then he turned his face toward the wall, and prayed to the Lord, saying, "Remember now, O Lord, I pray, how I have walked before You in truth and with a loyal heart, and have done what was good in Your sight." And Hezekiah wept bitterly. And it happened, before Isaiah had gone out into the middle court, that the word of the Lord came to him, "Return and tell Hezekiah the leader of My people, 'Thus says the Lord, the God of David your father: I have heard your prayer, I have seen your tears; surely I will heal you.'"

(2 Kings 20:1–5a)

God graciously healed Hezekiah and extended his life fifteen years. Hezekiah would now be able to continue his work for the Lord. This would all be possible because of the amazing, healing power of God.

God is still in the healing business. Sometimes He chooses to heal by a miraculous touch of His hand, and other times He chooses to do it by the hand of a physician, or with medications or other types of treatments.

My wife and I had a very close and dear friend who was diagnosed with terminal cancer. Her surgeon set a date for her surgery and told her and her husband what they could expect after the procedure was completed. However, not long after the surgery started, the surgeon came into the waiting room with the news that he had discovered there was nothing he could do. The cancer had spread throughout her body, and she would only have six months to live. He did inform the family that another surgery would be performed in two weeks based on the new knowledge he had gained from the first surgery.

When the day of the next surgery arrived, I was sitting in the waiting room with her husband. What happened as we sat there is still an absolute marvel to me. I asked him if I could pray with him, and in the middle of the prayer God spoke so clearly and powerfully to me. He spoke with such clarity that I could not possibly miss the message. The message terrified me. I wasn't terrified because the message revealed terrible news. Rather, the message was one of wonder and amazement. The message I was to give him was simply this: She's going to be alright. That was the entirety of the message: She's going to be alright.

I finished my prayer, and I sat there in silence for a few seconds, trying to decide what I should do. If I were to tell him that his wife was going to be alright and it did not turn out that way I could cause serious spiritual damage to the couple. However, if I did not tell him, then I would be disobedient to what I felt God told me to do.

So, I looked directly into my friend's eyes and told him that God had given me a message for him. I then told him what I had received. He and I sat there in silence for a few minutes before he spoke. Neither of us knew exactly what the message meant. Is she going to be alright because she is saved? Is God trying to give comfort by the fact that she will be with Him when death takes her? Or was she going to be alright physically? Was God going to heal her?

We had no way of knowing the answer to that question, so we chose to believe by faith that God was going to heal her, physically. The next couple of hours seemed like an eternity as we waited for the surgeon to walk into the waiting room. Finally, the door opened, and the surgeon walked in. He made his way across the room, sat down, and said, "I can't explain what I'm about to tell you." He then proceeded to tell us that when he made the incision, and began to inspect her vital organs, looking for the cancer he had just seen two weeks earlier, he found no evidence of the cancerous growth. None! Absolutely none! The cancer was gone, and he had no explanation.

Sometimes God chooses to provide healing, physically, and other times He chooses to heal eternally. But regardless of what He does, and how He does it, God's supplying grace heals. He is the great physician who has all power to heal all manner of sickness when He chooses to do so.

ELISHA'S SERVANT – SPIRITUAL SIGHT

There are two very real realms in which we live: the physical realm and the spiritual realm. We are all very familiar with the physical realm. It consists of that which we experience with our senses. The spiritual realm, on the other hand, is not so easily discernible with the senses. We cannot see it with our physical eyes; we cannot touch it with our hands; we cannot hear it with the physical ears; and we cannot taste or smell it with our mouth and nose. But even though we cannot experience the spiritual realm as we do the physical, it is real none-the-less.

Followers of Jesus Christ are in a constant battle with an enemy they cannot see. Satan, along with his wicked host of fallen angels, are always striving to wreak havoc in the lives of believers, while at the same time striving to put obstacles in the way of non-believers to keep them from seeing their need for a relationship with God.

The reality of the spiritual realm is seen clearly in scripture. Both the Old and New Testaments speak of both realms. It is a subject that is often disregarded in our contemporary cultural climate. I have even heard professors in Bible colleges speak of their disbelief in the spiritual realm. One guest speaker in a college chapel service spoke of the belief in a spiritual realm as being nothing more than superstition. He actually stated that anyone who believes in an invisible spiritual realm is an uneducated fool.

I guess Paul would fit into that category as it is obvious that he believed in the realith of the spiritual realm. Read his words carefully:

> Finally, my brethren, be strong in the Lord and in
> the power of His might. Put on the whole armor
> of God, that you may be able to stand against the
> wiles of the devil. For we do not wrestle against
> flesh and blood, but against principalities, against
> powers, against the rulers of the darkness of this
> age, against spiritual hosts of wickedness in the
> heavenly places. Therefore take up the whole
> armor of God, that you may be able to withstand
> in the evil day, and having done all, to stand.
>
> (Ephesians 6:10–13)

It is obvious that we have a powerful enemy who uses tactics that blind the spiritual eyes. The devil, along with his evil cohorts, are doing all they can to keep us from seeing and discerning spiritual truth, especially in the arena of spiritual protection. There is an invisible battle raging around us at all times in which we are being assaulted by our enemy. He is doing everything within his power to deceive us, making us think lies about God. He did this in the garden of Eden, and it continues to be one of his most powerful weapons against us.

There is an example of the reality of this spiritual warfare in Second Kings. Elisha had been giving the king of Israel information pertaining to the movements of the army of Syria. The king of Syria is told that Elisha is the one giving this information to the king of Israel, and therefore assisting him in making strategic decisions in light of the information provided by Elisha. The king of Syria makes an all-out search for Elisha, and when he discovers that Elisha is in Dothan, he makes an attempt to arrest him.

The amazing story found in Second Kings:

> And when the servant of the man of God arose
> early and went out, there was an army, surrounding
> the city with horses and chariots. And his servant
> said to him, "Alas, my master! What shall we do?"

> So he [Elisha] answered, "Do not fear, for those who are with us are more than those who are with him." And Elisha prayed, and said, "Lord, I pray, open his eyes that he may see." Then the Lord opened the eyes of the young man, and he saw. And behold, the mountain was full of horses and chariots of fire all around Elisha.
>
> (2 Kings 6:15–17)

What a truly astounding sight Elisha's servant saw! What he had seen, and what he then saw, were two vastly different sights. First, he saw a powerful army surrounding them, providing no way of escape. Horses and chariots accompanied the soldiers, making it impossible for them to even contemplate a daring escape.

But then, Elisha prayed and asked God to open the eyes of the servant so that he might see the real battle. Then, when he looked again, the mountain was full of horses and chariots of fire all around them. They were protected by God's supplying grace, as He supplied a spiritual army which provided safety for Elisha and his servant.

This spiritual reality is still the same today. The battle rages all around. The prince of the power of the air is always busy about his disruptive work. His influence is deceitful and destructive. The tools he uses have so many blinded by his deceiving messages that are presented in a variety of forms.

The philosophies of man are works of our enemy. Any philosophical school of thought that begins with the premise that there is no God is a lie of Satan. Philosophy attempts to offer explanations for the existence of the universe without having God in the formula. Arguments are detailed and complex, as the existence of all things are explained from a god-less set of presuppositions.

Satan also uses the religions of the world to deceive masses of humankind. Man is religious at the root of his being. Satan appeals to this need for religious belief by presenting false religions that teach ways to heaven without the saving work of

Jesus Christ. His influence in false religions of the world blinds the spiritual eyes of multitudes, causing them to believe the lie.

Different theological schools of thought present attempts to explain the universe in terms of God's activity, but they still do not embrace the God of the Bible. They devise ways of believing in God without adhering to the Bible's clear teachings that He is actually Father, Son, and Holy Spirit – the Trinity. They come up with creative ways of talking in their own "God language" which may sound good and even theologically correct, but when close examination is made their theology is found to be heretical.

This spiritual battle is a constant reality, and it is happening all around us all the time. God supplies grace that is commensurate with the need of the moment, just as He did with Elijah's servant.

And the believer can take heart in the fact that the god of this world is still under the sovereign control of the God of the universe! Satan is powerful, but God is more powerful. And the Bible tells us that the One who is in us is greater than the one who is in the world.

These examples, along with so many others we could cite from the Biblical record, show clearly the reality of the grace of God at work in the world at large, as well as in the lives of individuals. Were it not for the grace of God operating in our daily lives we could not survive. In the lives of non-believers God works through the grace that is common to all. In the lives of believers His grace works in very specific ways, as the examples above illustrate.

God, by way of His supplying grace, supplies us with an abundant supply of everything we could ever need. But we must remember one vital truth: He promises to supply us with what we need, and not what we want. He knows that if we got everything we wanted it would not prove to be for our benefit, but rather for our harm. Out of His omniscience He knows what is best for each of us and works in our lives accordingly.

We need to guard ourselves against becoming bitter when we don't receive everything we pray for and thank God that in His wisdom He always knows what is best.

POINTS TO PONDER

1. How do we experience God's supply in our lives? List specific ways this is a reality.

2. What are we to understand from Paul's words that God will supply all our needs?

3. How would you describe the difference between a need and a want?

4. The author mentioned specifically the following types of supplying grace: physical nourishment, physical protection, physical healing and spiritual sight. Have you or someone in your family experienced one or more of these supplies of God? If so, tell the story behind them to someone who needs to be encouraged by your experiences.

5. Take time right now to spend some time thanking God for His abundant supply of grace in your life.

CHAPTER 8

Strengthening Grace

Do not be carried about with various and strange doctrines. For it is good that the heart be established by grace, not with foods which have not profited those who have been occupied with them.

Hebrews 13:9

A Mighty Fortress is Our God
A mighty fortress is our God,
a bulwark never failing;
our helper he amid the flood
of mortal ills prevailing.
For still our ancient foe
doth seek to work us woe;
his craft and power are great,
and armed with cruel hate,
on earth is not his equal.

Did we in our own strength confide,
our striving would be losing,
were not the right man on our side,
the man of God's own choosing.
Dost ask who that may be?
Christ Jesus, it is he;
Lord Sabaoth, his name,
from age to age the same,
and he must win the battle.
Martin Luther

Tiredness. Extreme tiredness. Overtiredness. Exhaustion. Fatigue. Weariness. Lack of energy. Debilitation. Faintness. Feebleness. Drained. Empty. Burnout.

These are all terms we have become much too familiar with in recent years. Let's admit it: we live in a rat-race, dog-eat-dog, frenzy-paced world. It is super easy to get so caught up in the fast pace of life that we find ourselves burning the candle at both ends, working long hours in the day, and too many days in a row. We go into our children's bedroom and kiss them goodbye in the morning as they sleep, and sneak into their rooms and kiss them goodnight in the evening, as they sleep. We are so dead set on being successful on our jobs that we become utter failures in our homes.

I read a column by Erma Bombeck years ago that illustrated this blight that is ravaging our land. She spoke of family albums filled with pictures in which the husband and father of the house is conspicuously missing. She made the observation that often the husband/father is so busy with his job and making enough money to give his wife and children all they could ever possibly need, that he was never present with them for the big events of life.

He was well on his way to total exhaustion, with nothing left to give his family.

Sadly, this is also true in the spiritual realm. Far too many get so caught up in being at every function the church offers, and doing everything the church does, and being at every meeting the church has, that we have little time left to care for ourselves, much less having time to care for our families. I have seen far too many pastors get so exhausted in the work of ministry that they walk away, not able to handle all the pressures of the work of the church.

I've been there. My wife and I were given a pastor's appreciation trip to the beautiful mountains of Colorado a few years ago. Reservations were made for us at a retreat center near Colorado Springs. The center was located at an altitude of a little more than ten thousand feet on majestic Pike's Peak. We were totally mesmerized by the beauty of our surroundings. But, we had no idea what awaited us upon our arrival.

As we pulled our car into the parking area we were met by a husband/wife counseling team. They very graciously welcomed us, walked us into the registration area, and gave us instructions for the evening. After checking in to our beautiful accommodations, we attended a short get-acquainted session with the other couples who were there. Teresa and I were under the impression that this would be a relaxing time of sight-seeing, rest, and physical as well as spiritual renewal. It proved to be anything but what we expected.

The name of the center included the word 'recreation,' so we anticipated it to be just that: fun, maybe some games, and a whole lot of recreational activities. However, upon looking more closely at the word, it was obvious that it contained a hyphen: re-creation. We learned quickly that it would be eight days of intense psychoanalysis by the host couple who were trained and licensed Christian counselors. Some of our sessions were spent one-on-one with the host couple, while at other times we were in group sessions with the other three ministry couples who were there for the same eight-day course of re-creation.

Teresa and I learned quite a bit about ourselves. It would be more accurate to say I learned quite a bit about myself, because as it turned out, Teresa already knew what the host couple revealed to me. On the last day of our stay, we had a concluding session with the hosts at which time they gave us their findings based on their time with us. They took into consideration the private conversations we had with them, and the things we shared in group sessions, along with the results of the questionnaires and self-assessments we had taken during the week.

The conversation began with the counselor saying, "Well, Steve, we guess you know that you are a perfectionistic workaholic." I literally laughed out loud, thinking that he was joking. But when I looked at his face it was quite obvious that this was no joke. So, I then said, "You are joking, right?" At this point he looked at Teresa and asked for her thoughts. She looked straight into my eyes, and with tears running down her cheeks, she said, "They are one hundred percent correct!"

I was crushed! What made this so much more serious was the fact that I had done the same thing years before. At that time, I had a dear friend who told me that I was losing my family. I did the same thing then: I laughed. But he suggested that I talk to Teresa about it and ask her opinion. So that night I asked her if she felt we were drifting apart. She burst into tears on that occasion just like the other. She then began telling me that I had time for everyone except her and our children. I was neglecting my family while taking care of the church family.

So, back to the concluding session at the re-creation center. I was told that I desperately needed to make some changes. I was encouraged to start taking a day off every week. I was also encouraged to take an annual vacation – a real vacation. I was told to make sure the leadership of the church knew that I needed time to tend to my family's needs, as well as taking care of myself.

I honestly had no idea what I had allowed to happen in my own life. All those words at the beginning of this chapter were true of me. I was told that if I didn't make some serious changes I would not make it much further in pastoral ministry. I was on the verge of total burnout. Teresa knew it. The counselors knew it. It seemed everyone knew it, except me.

When Teresa and I returned to our church family, I took the advice given me by the counselors and called a meeting of our church leadership. I shared with them what I had been told about myself, and that in their estimation I was on the verge of burnout. I then shared with them the counselor's suggestions to begin taking a day off each week and a true, annual vacation. I was totally shocked at the response of those men gathered around the conference table. They stood to their feet and gave me a standing ovation. The chairman then reminded me that they had been encouraging me to do those very things for quite some time

I discovered that I was in desperate need of grace: strengthening grace. And God gave me what I needed.

Have you ever been there? Are you there? Are you in need of the strengthening grace of God? Then please, read on.

Please understand that we are not talking here about physical strength, even though being exhausted spiritually will have a bearing on our physical well-being. Here, we are speaking specifically of spiritual exhaustion, and how to overcome it and its devastating power in our lives. The verse at the beginning of this chapter states clearly that we should strengthen our hearts with grace, not with food. Paul is speaking here of spiritual strength. He knew full well that we need physical nourishment to maintain health and wholeness, but here he is speaking of strengthening our hearts, not our bodies.

There are many today who place a tremendous amount of time and effort taking care of their physical bodies. They maintain a strict schedule of exercise. They go to the recreation center almost every day of the week with a detailed schedule of what muscle groups will be targeted on each day. They also have a healthy eating plan, not putting anything unhealthy in their bodies. These are to be commended for their rigorous commitment to their physical well-being. But, all-the-while they may be neglecting the more important task of taking care of their spiritual well-being.

It would be good for each of us to periodically take a self-assessment of how much time we spend taking care of ourselves physically compared to the time spent taking care of ourselves spiritually. Perhaps some of us would be shocked to realize that they are giving far too little time to caring for their spiritual needs.

So, let's remember that here the author of Hebrews is speaking of spiritual health and vitality. The only source that will help with this type of well-being is the grace of God. And thankfully, strengthening grace is always in good supply!

Strengthening grace is what we need to face the trials and difficulties in life. We pray that God would extend His grace to those in need – whether it be a physical need, a family need, a financial need, a spiritual need, or any one of so many others that could be named. But we need to constantly remind ourselves of our own personal need of this same strengthening grace.

It is also in those times of Satanic temptation that we ask for God's grace to strengthen us so that we might not succumb to the attacks of our enemy. Added to that, we are oftentimes drawn away by our own sinful desires, and again we desperately need God's strengthening grace to enable us to stand true to God.

How are we to be victorious in those times and situations that could so easily deplete us of our spiritual and physical strength? There are several observations that can be made which will help us better understand the need for, and the availability of, strengthening grace.

STRENGTHENING GRACE ENABLES US TO STAND

Since we have been justified by our faith in the Lord Jesus Christ, we now have access to the grace of God by which we are enabled to stand firm. Paul elaborates on this subject in more detail in his letter to the Ephesians. We have given consideration to this passage in an earlier chapter, but here we will look at a very specific word of instruction Paul gives in relation to the ability to engage in spiritual warfare.

> Therefore, having been justified by faith, we have peace with God through our Lord Jesus Christ, through whom we have access by faith into this grace in which we stand, and rejoice in hope of the glory of God.
>
> (Romans 5:1–2)

We all need encouragement at times to be strong in the fight against the onslaught and attacks of the devil. He has so many weapons in his arsenal that he uses to attack, and he seems to always know exactly where the point of attack should be. Of course, we need to be mindful of the fact that Satan does not have omniscience as does God. He does not have full knowledge of everything, past, present, and future. He only knows what we let him know about us personally. For example, he can't know that something is an area of weakness in my life until I reveal it. But once we have revealed an area of weakness, he uses that against us with his attacks on us personally.

We also know that he does not have the attribute of omnipresence. He can be in only one place at a time. But he is the prince of the power of the air and has a huge army of fallen angels who work in conjunction with him to tempt us individually and personally. These words of the apostle Paul should give insight into how we are to fend off satanic attacks.

> Finally, my brethren, *be strong* in the Lord and in the power of His might. Put on the whole armor of God, that you may be able to *stand* against the wiles of the devil.
> Therefore take up the whole armor of God, that you may be able to **withstand** in the evil day, and having done all, to **stand.**
> **Stand** therefore…
> (Ephesians 6:10–11; 13; 14a; emphasis added)

We don't have to have a conversation with the devil, letting him in on our strengths and weaknesses, for him to find out intimate details of our lives. All he must do is put a temptation before us. If we fall to the temptation and commit sin, then he knows from that point on that we have a spiritual weakness in that area. If we don't fall to it, then he knows that it would be a waste of time to tempt us with that particular temptation again. But if we do fall to the temptation and commit sin, then he knows that is a weak point in our lives, and he will then put that temptation before us when he finds us at a time in which we are spiritually and physically weak.

And rest assured, once he knows, he will use that against us every time he senses a weak moment in which we are vulnerable to the temptation. Your weaknesses will be different from mine, and mine from yours. We all need desperately to heed the words of Paul quoted above encouraging us to stand firm.

If we don't stand firm, then we open ourselves up to be deceived by the devil. For example, in our sexually permissive culture we often hear of individuals who have given in to the temptation to commit adultery. Many times, this will result in the destruction of a family as one leaves his or her spouse to enter into a relationship with the one with whom they have committed their sexual sin.

And to make matters worse, those who fall into these sinful sexual relationships will sometimes try to find Biblical justification for their decision. Families are destroyed in the aftermath of such foolhardy choices. If children are involved, then they are left in the wake of the destructive path set by their wayward parent. The destructive results of sinful actions are not confined to the one who has committed the sin. It begins a ripple effect that grows in intensity, doing damage to everyone caught in the wake of those continuing waves of adversity. Children are often left wondering if it was somehow their fault that their parents have now divorced. They carry deep scars for years to come as they struggle to make sense out of such senseless actions.

It is truly a heartbreaking thing to see when a once committed Christian turns his back on the principles of God's Word simply because they have decided to engage in actions clearly forbidden in the Bible. We might find a verse which seems to validate our sinfulness, but if it doesn't align with the overall teachings of the word of God then that should cause us to pause before taking that step of disobedience. Once that first step has been taken it is extremely difficult to go back. Sinful decisions bring about painful results that sometimes carry consequences for decades into the future.

Another example from our contemporary cultural climate is that of young couples engaging in premarital sexual relations. Many possible explanations, or excuses, for this behavior are often heard. Some might suggest that it is not adversely affecting anyone, and they are consenting adults, so why not go ahead and enjoy each other? God did create us as sexual beings, after all. Surely, He would not create us with these desires and then forbid us to enjoy the pleasure it brings.

Others might justify their actions by stating that they have decided to get married in the near future, so what's wrong with enjoying each other sexually now? After all, since they are committed to each other and are going to be legally married in just a short time God wouldn't mind if they go ahead and consummate their relationship now.

So many let their spiritual guard down and thus become weakened spiritually. They then become open prey for the onslaught of satanic persuasion. If we allow ourselves to become exhausted spiritually and physically, then we become susceptible to the attacks of Satan as well as the desires of the flesh. Paul gives us a list of some of the works of the flesh in his letter to Galatia. Read these sobering words slowly and allow them to serve as a warning against engaging in such behaviors.

> Now the works of the flesh are evident, which are: adultery, fornication, uncleanness, lewdness, idolatry, sorcery, hatred, contentions, jealousies, outbursts or wrath, selfish ambitions, dissensions, heresies, envy, murders, drunkenness, revelries, and the like; of which I tell you beforehand, just as I also told you in time past, that those who practice such things will not inherit the kingdom of God.
> (Galatians 5:19–21)

The examples could go on and on, but the point is clear. If we identify as believers in Jesus Christ, then we are to heed the Biblical admonitions to live lives of purity, holiness and righteousness. We are to put off the old habits of life and replace them with new Bible-centered habits and practices.

We all need to guard our hearts and minds carefully and prayerfully, putting on the whole armor of God that we might be able to stand firm against the tactics of our enemy.

STRENGTHENING GRACE ENABLES US TO SUFFER

I have never met a single individual who enjoyed suffering. There are probably some masochistic individuals who enjoy either inflicting self-pain or experiencing self-pain. But the vast majority of us would rather not suffer. We would rather live a life of health and happiness. The reality is, however, that we do sometimes suffer. It may be a physical illness, a mental ailment, a chronic disease, or some other type of personal suffering. When it invades our arena of personal experience, we need grace to deal with it properly.

The apostle Paul has some enlightening and instructive words taken directly from his own personal suffering:

> For we do not want you to be ignorant, brethren, of our trouble which came to us in Asia: that we were burdened beyond measure, above strength, so that we despaired even of life. Yes, we had the sentence of death in ourselves, that we should not trust in ourselves but in God who raises the dead, who delivered us from so great a death, and does deliver us; in whom we trust that He will still deliver *us*...
> (2 Corinthians 1:8–10)

Paul testifies that he was at a point of total despair. He described this experience as having the sentence of death on him. What got him through? God! This passage does not use the word "grace", but rest assured that is exactly what is operative in Paul's life. He is delivered by the grace of God. His suffering is relieved by grace.

There were many times in Paul's life during which he would not have survived had it not been for the grace of God. Read the following testimony of the apostle as he recites a list of his personal times of suffering:

> ...in labors more abundant, in stripes above measure, in prisons more frequently, in deaths often. From the Jews five times I received forty *stripes* minus one. Three times I was beaten with rods; once I was stoned; three times I was shipwrecked; a night and a day I have been in the deep; in journeys often, *in* perils of waters, *in* perils of robbers, *in* perils of *my own* countrymen, *in* perils of the Gentiles, *in* perils in the city, *in* perils in the wilderness, *in* perils in the sea, *in* perils among false brethren; in weariness and toil, in sleeplessness often, in hunger and thirst, in fastings often, in cold and nakedness...
>
> (2 Corinthians 11:23b–27)

Paul was a man acquainted with suffering. Suffering added to suffering. Suffering multiplied by suffering. Why did he not quit? Why did he not just turn and walk away? Why did he keep going knowing that to do so would just mean more of the same?

And, more than why, how? How did he manage to keep going in the face of all this suffering? To turn once again to his words in Romans, he says, "we have access by faith into this grace in which we stand." By faith, through grace, we stand.

There are two very important observations that should be made about how Paul handled adversity and suffering. First, Paul was a man of faith in God. It is obvious that he trusted God implicitly, and undoubtedly accepted the fact that everything he experienced in life was part of God's grand scheme of things. This enabled him to keep going even in the face of such extreme tribulation and personal trauma.

Second, Paul was a man of faithfulness to God. He testifies to the depth of his faithfulness in the following account taken from the book of Acts:

> And as we stayed many days, a certain prophet named Agabus came down from Judea. When he had come to us, he took Paul's belt, bound his own hands and feet, and said, "Thus says the Holy Spirit, So shall the Jews at Jerusalem bind the man who owns this belt, and deliver him into the hands of the Gentiles." Now when we heard these things, both we and those from that place pleaded with him not to go up to Jerusalem. Then Paul answered, "What do you mean by weeping and breaking my heart: For I am ready not only to be bound, but also to die at Jerusalem for the name of the Lord."
>
> (Acts 21:10–13)

Paul's faithfulness to God gave him the strength to face the horror that Agabus prophesied. Many, upon hearing such words as these, would take this as a warning from the Holy Spirit to stay away from Jerusalem. But Paul, who obviously felt strongly that the Holy Spirit was leading him to go to Jerusalem, makes that assertion that he is committed to go regardless of what it might cost him personally: Even to the point of costing his life. It is obviously through the strengthening grace of God that he managed to maintain this life of faith in God and faithfulness to God.

Another Person who suffered greatly and serves as an example of how to face suffering is the Lord Jesus Christ. As He faced the darkest hour of His earthly life, and knew the suffering He was about to experience, we get a glimpse of how He faced it in His prayer in the Garden of Gethsemane.

> And He was withdrawn from them about a stone's throw, and He knelt down and prayed, saying, "Father, if it is Your will, take this cup away from Me; nevertheless not My will, but Yours, be done." Then an angel appeared to Him from heaven, strengthening Him. [44] And being in agony, He prayed more earnestly. Then His sweat became like great drops of blood falling down to the ground.

This is a most graphic description of the intense struggle Jesus experienced as He faced the horror of the cross. The word "grace" does not appear in these verses, but it is clear that Jesus, in His humanity, was dependent on the grace of the Father. His prayers show that He was engaged in spiritual warfare as He peers into the "cup" that was before Him. Luke tells his readers that the personal struggle was so extreme that it caused His sweat to mingle with His blood, and the drops of perspiration appeared to be drops of blood falling to the ground.

This text also reveals that an angel ministered to Jesus during this time of intense struggle. And note carefully that we are told in the text that the angel strengthened Him. Strengthening grace was extended to Jesus in His humanity that enabled Him to face the horror of the cross.

The struggle was real. The suffering was real. The cries for the Father to allow the cup to pass were real. But through it all His dependence on the Father provided what Jesus needed to face the ordeal that lay ahead.

Suffering is real. We don't have to live very long to realize just how real it is. As we go through seasons of suffering, we can take heart in knowing God promises us the grace we need to face those dark periods through which we journey.

STRENGTHENING GRACE ENABLES
US TO GROW SPIRITUALLY

Sanctifying grace has been discussed in a previous chapter. However, we need to revisit that topic briefly in order to remember that we need strengthening grace to enable us to be consistent in the sanctification process. We have already learned that the sanctification process is a partnership with God. Think again about these words from the apostle Paul:

> Therefore, my beloved, as you have always obeyed, not as in my presence only, but now much more in my absence, work out your own salvation with fear and trembling; for it is God who works in you both to will and to do for *His* good pleasure.
>
> (Philippians 2:12–13)

We begin the process of sanctification the moment we are saved, and that process continues the remainder of our physical lives. We are called to work it out, but it is God who works within. So it is by His grace that we become more like Jesus as sanctification has its complete work in us.

There are three very real enemies that will fight against us as we strive to be consistent in the work of sanctification. These three enemies are the world, self, and the devil.

ARCH-ENEMY NUMBER ONE: THE WORLD

First, think about how the world fights against our sanctification. When we speak of the world fighting against us, we are speaking specifically about the world's system which is under the influence of the devil. Remember, the devil is described as the god of this world and the prince of the powers of the air. His influence is seen in political systems, philosophical systems, religious systems, and educational systems. The apostle John has a word of instruction and warning concerning how the world will hinder us from becoming fully what God desires us to be.

> Do not love the world or the things in the world. If anyone loves the world, the love of the Father is not in him. For all that *is* in the world—the lust of the flesh, the lust of the eyes, and the pride of life—is not of the Father but is of the world. And the world is passing away, and the lust of it; but he who does the will of God abides forever.
>
> (1 John 2:15–17)

We are not to love the world because it is an arch enemy of God. John says in this same letter that many anti-Christs were already at work in his day, so how much more prevalent is that work today. Liberal educational systems teach our children anti-God, anti-Bible theories as facts. By the time they reach college, liberal philosophy has been so ingrained in their minds that they have come to embrace and believe the lies of the devil.

Anti-God political systems hold their constituencies in check as they force upon them atheistic concepts, policies and promotions. Entire nations have been duped into believing there is no God. The world, under the intoxicating influence of the devil, fights against us, and it is only by the grace of God that we are able to grow in our sanctification in the face of the world's attacks on Biblical truth.

Our present cultural climate is one that has been influenced and deceived by the world. The dismantling of family values is one of the most glaring of those influences. God instituted the family and ordained its structure. He instructed that marriage should be between a man and a woman who would enter into a covenantal relationship that should only end with the death of one of the marriage partners. This biblical teaching has now been discarded and replaced with the practice of everyone doing what seems right in their own eyes.

As a result of this disregard, the divorce rate continues to soar. Alternate lifestyles are embraced and practiced by many who reject God's instruction on marriage. In our present state of confusion we are now witnessing a movement in which we no longer know what sex we are. Biologically there can be no confusion – we are either male or female. But now we can identify as either, regardless of our physical anatomy. Sadly, many parents are now allowing young children to decide for themselves what sex they choose to be with total disregard for their biological sex assigned at conception.

So many other examples could be cited to give more evidence of the influence of the world, but these should suffice to illustrate the point. But we have still two more arch-enemies that should be considered.

ARCH-ENEMY NUMBER TWO: SELF

Second, we must understand the seriousness of our own selfish desires standing against us becoming more like Christ. Our selfishness is obvious from the earliest age. Children are selfish by nature. This spirit of selfishness is seen in the nursery, when one child takes a toy from another. They both start screaming, claiming the toy is theirs. The nursery worker will try to intervene by explaining to the children that they should take turns playing with the toy being argued over, but there is little success in this endeavor. Why? Because they are selfish, demanding to have their way. And sadly, things don't improve much as we grow older. Our selfish behavior may look a little more civilized than it did when we were children, but it is there none-the-less. Listen to Jesus as He encourages us to fight against those selfish desires that are our common lot in life.

When He had called the people to *Himself,* with His disciples also, He said to them, "Whoever desires to come after Me, let him deny himself, and take up his cross, and follow Me."

(Mark 8:34)

Three things Jesus says we must do to be His disciples. First, we must deny self. Self cannot be on the throne of our lives. All through life prior to coming to faith in Jesus Christ we were self-centered, self-serving individuals. We were still able to do things for others, but for the most part we were focused on self-fulfillment. It was alright if others benefited in some way from our actions, as long as we attained what we were striving for. But Jesus says that we must deny ourselves. He doesn't say we must deny self of something, but to deny self. Place Christ on the throne of our lives and serve Him.

This matter of denying self is exemplified in Jesus' model prayer. He taught His disciples to pray for God's kingdom to come on earth as it is in heaven. Think for a moment about how this should affect the individual. If I sincerely pray that His kingdom come in my life, then it would entail first and foremost that my kingdom must go. I would have to denounce and even deny my selfish goals and ambitions, and seek after His.

The second thing Jesus says about being His disciple is that we must take up our cross. When Jesus spoke those words, the crowds listening to Him would have understood exactly what He meant: Death! Today, you see people wearing necklaces and bracelets with crosses on them. We see church steeples topped with ornate crosses. It's almost as if we look at it as a fine piece of jewelry.

It would have never been worn or displayed that way in Jesus' lifetime. It was a horrific portrayal of the most gruesome type of death penalty ever devised. It represented suffering beyond measure. It meant death! And that is exactly what Jesus meant when He spoke these words. If anyone would be His disciple, it required death to self. The apostle Paul understood this to be the case. He stated in his letter to the Galatians that he had been crucified with Christ. When he entered into a faith relationship with Jesus, he understood that this called for him to acknowledge the fact that he died to his old self and was now alive in Christ. So Jesus calls for us to deny self and then to die to self.

And third, Jesus says if we are to be His disciple, we must follow Him. To follow Him is to always keep Him in sight, as our focal point. Paul said that he pressed toward the mark of the calling of God in Christ Jesus. That is what we are to do. Press forward toward Jesus.

The combination of these three words of instruction from the Lord should help us to understand more fully what is entailed in dealing with our selfish ambitions and goals. To be a disciple is to deny self, die to self, and follow our Lord in word and deed.

ARCH-ENEMY NUMBER THREE: THE DEVIL

Discussion has already been made of the devil's fighting believers as they strive to live lives of righteousness, but we can never be reminded enough or warned sufficiently of his attacks. He is always working through his emissaries, the fallen angels, to catch believers off-guard with temptations to sin. It is only through the strengthening grace of God that we are enabled to withstand his attacks.

To make all of this a reality, we need God's strengthening grace. This is a grueling task. It is a lifelong journey. It demands nothing short of total self-denial, self-death, and having our sights set on Jesus. Only grace will enable us and equip us for the task.

POINTS TO PONDER

1. Have you ever been overwhelmed with the demands of life to the point that you were completely exhausted? If so, explain what caused this state, and how you overcame it.
2. The author spoke of strengthening grace giving us the ability to:
   a. Stand
   b. Suffer
   c. Grow spiritually
   d. Think of a time in your life when you experienced strengthening grace in these ways. Write down your thoughts and share them with friends or family members who would be encouraged by your experiences.

CHAPTER 9

Satisfying Grace

Now to Him who is able to do exceedingly
abundantly above all that we ask or think, according
to the power that works in us, to Him be glory
in the church by Christ Jesus to all generations,
forever and ever. Amen.

(Ephesians 3:20–21)

When I Survey the Wondrous Cross
When I survey the wondrous cross
on which the Prince of Glory died;
my richest gain I count but loss,
and pour contempt on all my pride.

Forbid it, Lord, that I should boast,
save in the death of Christ, my God;
all the vain things that charm me most,
I sacrifice them to his blood.

See, from his head, his hands, his feet,
sorrow and love flow mingled down.
Did e'er such love and sorrow meet,
or thorns compose so rich a crown.

Were the whole realm of nature mine,
that were an offering far too small;
love so amazing, so divine,
demands my soul, my life, my all.
Isaac Watts

H ave you ever been dissatisfied? Perhaps you started a new job with the hope that it would be fulfilling and satisfying for years to come. Maybe during the interview process you were really impressed with the potential of this new position, and you began your tenure there with great hope and anticipation of what the future might offer. However, it's not long before you discover that it was not at all that you had expected. The promises you had received from your new employer did not materialize. You felt betrayed and deceived. You became disillusioned and dissatisfied and began sending out the resumes in search of something different.

Or maybe you began your college experience thinking that you knew exactly what you wanted to focus your studies on, and what career you would prepare for. However, two years into your studies you became aware that this field of study was leaving much to be desired, and you were dissatisfied with where it was leading. So you found yourself frantically searching for a new major after spending those two years in frustration. You then felt as if you had wasted those two years and would now have to start over again.

Maybe you invested several years developing a relationship with the person you felt you would one day marry and then spend the rest of your life with. Much time and effort were put in to growing deep in the relationship. Everyone thought that the two of you were made for each other and were shocked to find out you had become dissatisfied with where the relationship was heading. Plans for the upcoming wedding were put on hold, and eventually cancelled altogether as you continued to drift farther and farther apart.

We all desire to live satisfying and fulfilling lives. And we invest much time, energy, and resources striving to make that a reality. However, it is not unusual for persons to become dissatisfied with their lot in life. This is evidenced in so many ways. People will move from job to job, looking for just the right one to bring a state of satisfaction. Others will go from one relationship to another, looking for the perfect mate with whom they feel they could spend the rest of their lives.

Then, there is another area of life that should never be a matter of dissatisfaction, but sadly, it oftentimes is. Our relationship with God should be consistently fulfilling and satisfying, but this is not always the case. Just as with any other relationship in our lives, if time, energy, and attention are not given this relationship then it can become unfulfilling and dissatisfying.

There are several possible reasons for this. We have already touched on some of these in previous chapters, but they need to be reinforced and given more emphasis so that we might guard ourselves against falling victim to any of them.

SELFISHNESS

It has been said that we all have the same worst enemy: self. Every morning when I gaze into the mirror, I see the reflection of the one person in all the world who causes me the most problems. I am my own worst enemy.

Oftentimes my desires take precedence over what I know to be God's desires for my life. Too many times I want to do what I want to do, regardless of what I know I ought to do. There are things I put on my to-do list that do not fit into what I know I should be investing my time and energy on.

Before committing my life to the Lord Jesus, I lived for me, selfishly. I invested time, resources, and energy in running after my personal, selfish goals. My all-consuming desire was to become a world-renowned drummer in a rock band. This desire consumed my every waking hour. No matter where I was, or what I was doing, or whom I was with, it was always the same: playing the drums was always on my mind.

Even after I was married, I still selfishly followed this desire. I was so consumed with playing the drums that it almost caused my marriage to end in divorce. I was not a good husband because I wanted to be a great drummer. I was not a good father because

I wanted to be a great drummer. I was not a good employee because I wanted to be a great drummer.

It was only because of the gracious intervention of God in my life that my marriage was saved. It was then that my whole perspective on life changed. My desires took a completely different direction. I became a follower of Jesus Christ, and I set my goal on being the best disciple I could possibly be.

I would love to say that this ended my struggles with selfishness, but sadly it did not. There have still been times when I have given myself over to my selfish desires.

And the reality is that when this happens it always causes me to lose my satisfaction with Jesus Christ. I cannot go my way and God's way at the same time. It calls for relinquishing one and running after the other. Jesus had much to say about this matter. These are extremely important words for anyone who desires to be a sincere follower of the Lord. It would be wise to read the following words slowly, carefully, and especially prayerfully:

> Our Father in heaven, hallowed by Your name, Your kingdom come, Your will be done, on earth as it is in heaven.
>
> (Matthew 6:9–10)

> No one can serve two masters; for either he will hate the one and love the other, or else he will be loyal to the one and despise the other. You cannot serve God and mammon.
>
> (Matthew 6:24)

> Teacher, which is the great commandment in the law? Jesus said to him, "You shall love the Lord your God with all your heart, with all your soul, and with all your mind. This is the first and great commandment."
>
> (Matthew 22:36–38)

There are some observations that need to be made from these words of our Lord. First, Jesus teaches us to pray that the kingdom of heaven would come. There is a universal aspect of this prayer as we are taught to pray that God's rule, His kingdom, would have full expression of perfection on earth as it is in heaven. But let's think about this in a more personal way. Could Jesus be teaching me, personally, to pray for God's rule to be done in my life? If so, then I need to understand that in order for His kingdom to come in my life, then my kingdom, my rule, has to go. I cannot possibly live according to my own selfish desires, ruling over my own kingdom, while at the same time allowing His kingdom to rule over me.

The second observation adds even more emphasis to this. Jesus asserts that we must make a choice because we cannot serve two masters. And when I try to serve both I will find myself in a state of total and utter frustration, completely dissatisfied with both because I am not completely committed to either.

This is a common mistake so many make. They attend church on Sunday. They make sure the family has that day set aside for God. They gather with other believers for a time of fellowship, discipleship, Bible study, and worship. There is never a question about what they will be doing on any given Sunday.

But if you see them Monday through Saturday, there is no difference between them and the world. They use the language of the world. They engage in activities that go along with the spirit of the world rather than the Spirit of God. Their Bible takes its usual place on the shelf, where it will stay until it is picked up the next Sunday to once again make its appearance. Ungodly business practices, ungodly relationships, ungodly vulgarity, ungodly desires are all the rule of the day. All outward appearances would identify them with the world and the spirit of worldliness.

Selfishness is the marker of their lives. But they are completely dissatisfied with both God and their ungodly ways. You cannot have both, but you must choose.

The third observation is from the response Jesus gave to the question about the greatest commandment. He encompassed the first four of the ten commandments into one and said that it was the greatest of them all. Love God with your entire being. This is the formula for overcoming selfishness. If we love the Lord with our hearts, souls, and minds then we will not strive to go after and serve other masters. We will always be seeking ways to follow Him even more closely, to obey Him even more consistently, and to live for Him even more carefully.

SINFULNESS

A second cause of dissatisfaction in our walk with the Lord is sinfulness. Selfishness, of course, is sin. And selfishness shows itself in so many ways. But in a more general sense, a spirit of sinfulness is a sure way to become dissatisfied with our relationship with the Lord.

We have talked about the difference between being called and being chosen in a previous chapter. I bring that distinction into the discussion here because the Biblical example we will consider of dissatisfaction because of sinfulness is Judas Iscariot. He was one of the twelve Jesus called to be His disciples. Judas, along with the other eleven, spent over three years with Jesus. He was privileged to hear the same teachings, to see the same miraculous works, to observe the sinless life, as did the others. And yet, he gave himself over to his own sinfulness which led to his self-destruction.

There are so many deep theological matters that could be discussed as we investigate the life of this man, but that is not the focus of this book, nor of this chapter. What we will focus on is the apparent dissatisfaction Judas experienced as he, along with the others, waited for Jesus to establish His kingdom.

There are several clear indications in the Bible that Judas Iscariot was not what others thought him to be. It does seem that he had the confidence of the other apostles as they appointed him treasurer of the group. However, he proved to be dishonest as the Bible reveals that he stole from the money bag:

> Jesus answered them, "Did I not choose you, the twelve, and one of you is a devil?" He spoke of Judas Iscariot, *the son* of Simon, for it was he who would betray Him, being one of the twelve.
>
> (John 6:70–71)

> This he said, not that he cared for the poor, but because he was a thief, and had the money box; and he used to take what was put in it.
>
> (John 12:6)

Jesus was fully aware that Judas was the one who would betray Him, and yet he called him to be one of the twelve. This was to fulfill Scripture, that Jesus would be betrayed for thirty pieces of silver.

That Judas would turn Jesus over for this amount of money not only fulfilled the prophecy, but it also showed again that he was more interested in money than he was in being a sincere follower of the Lord.

What could have possibly motivated Judas to betray Jesus? It is clear that he was interested in getting paid for his act of betrayal, but is that all there was to it? There is the very real likelihood that he had other motives in mind when he betrayed the Lord.

The leaders and teachers of the law had long taught the people of Israel that the Messiah would come as a powerful military leader who would liberate the nation from national bondage and reestablish Israel as a world power. After all, the prophets of old had prophesied about the coming of one in the likeness of David, the greatest military leader the nation had ever known. Could it be that Judas saw things slipping away when Jesus began to be threatened by the civil and religious leaders? Could it be that

Judas thought he was moving things ahead by forcing Jesus into the center of attention?

Maybe he thought that by doing what he did Jesus would reveal to everyone His amazing power. He had spoken of the kingdom of heaven being at hand, so why not hurry things along? This is certainly not to suggest that Judas had pure motives in doing what he did. But maybe, in his twisted way of thinking, he thought this would work for everyone's good. What he didn't realize is that he was playing right into the hands of the devil.

> Then I said to them, "If it is agreeable to you, give
> *me* my wages; and if not, refrain." So they weighed
> out for my wages thirty *pieces* of silver.
> (Zechariah 11:12)

Judas' actions were self-centered and sinful at the core. And, unlike Peter who came to sincere repentance after denying the Lord three times, Judas did not repent. Rather, he went out and hanged himself. Even after being with Jesus for over three years, he totally missed the point and gave himself over to his own sinful desires.

His dissatisfaction with the way Jesus was doing things led him to completely reject the direction Jesus was going. His decision led to his own destruction. If we allow ourselves to backslide on the Lord, going our own way into sinful behavior and practice, we will eventually become dissatisfied with Him and walk away from the best life we could ever experience.

DISCONTENTMENT

Still another way that we can become dissatisfied with the Lord is by being discontented with what He has provided. The apostle Paul spoke of this matter in his letter to the Philippians.

...for I have learned in whatever state I am, to be content: I know how to be abased, and I know how to abound. Everywhere and in all things I have learned both to be full and to be hungry, both to abound and to suffer need.

(Philippians 4:11b–12)

It is not very rare to see persons who are completely discontent with what they have. It is a common thing to compare ourselves with those who have more than we do. They have a bigger house, drive a more expensive car, have their children enrolled in the most prestigious schools, wear the latest styles, go on the best vacations – in short, they have the best of everything. But I don't. At least not comparatively speaking. I have a house, but mine is not as big as theirs. I drive a car, but theirs is a newer model with more bells and whistles. My children go to school, but it's not the best in the city in which we live. We go on vacations, but ours are no comparison to theirs.

God promises us that He will always provide us with our needs, but as we have already learned, sometimes those needs leave a lot to be desired. God might provide me with bologna, but I want a steak. I may have plenty of clothes in the closet, but they may not have the most popular labels.

If we don't guard our hearts, we can easily become dissatisfied with what we have. Paul says that he had learned how to be full and to be hungry. Carefully note the emphasis on the learning process. Satisfaction with God's supply is something we must learn in the classroom of life. There will be times in life in which we have an abundance, while at other times we struggle to get by. But in and through it all we can learn to be content with what we have, as we believe God always provides what is best for us in every season of life.

And again, we need to notice Paul's assessment about being content. He says he had learned contentment. Being content does not usually come naturally. We see someone else with something better than what we have, and we become discontented with ours. It could be anything from the most insignificant thing to the most extravagant. If we are no careful we can become envious of what they have and lose our contentment with what we have. Once again we can turn to Paul for wisdom and instruction on this important matter. If we fail to be content with what we have we open ourselves up for all manner of difficulty and heartache. But if we learn the principles found in the following passage of scripture it will prove to be a tremendous safeguard against developing a spirit of discontment.

> Now godliness with contentment is great gain. For we brought nothing into this world, and it is certain we can carry nothing out. And having food and clothing, with these we shall be content. But those who desire to be rich fall into temptation and a snare, and into may foolish and harmful lusts which drown me in destruction and perdition. For the love of money is a root of all kinds of evil, for which some have strayed from the faith in their greediness, and pierced themselves through with many sorrows.
>
> (1 Timothy 6:6–10)

Failure to abide in contentment with God's supply will result, as Paul says, in all manner of evil. This causes some to stray from their faith as they are dissatisfied with God's supply. We need to abide in the fact that God's satisfying grace always provides us with everything we need. We must learn to be satisfied with His supply.

DISTRACTION

There are so many other causes of dissatisfaction that could be discussed, but we will consider just one more: distraction. This is a subtle tool of Satan used to simply get our minds off our progress toward spiritual maturity. And there are countless distractions at his disposal. Some distractions will appeal to certain individuals while at the same time they have no appeal at all to others. There are things that I am personally drawn to that may have no attraction for you and may even prove to be repulsive to someone else. We are all different, with varying likes and dislikes.

> But each one is tempted when he is drawn away
> by his own desires and enticed. Then, when desire
> has conceived, it gives birth to sin; and sin, when
> it is full-grown, brings forth death.
>
> (James 1:14–15)

James gives a vivid description of how easily it is to be distracted. The distraction itself is not a work of the devil, even though he uses it against the individual. We are actually drawn into distraction by our own desires. As stated earlier, there are things that appeal to me that have no appeal at all to others. The desire is mine, and when I am placed in a situation in which the thing that appeals to me is all of a sudden before me, then I can be easily and quickly become distracted by it, drawn to it, deceived by it, and committed to it. This is a path of self-destruction which, according to James, will ultimately bring forth death.

For a non-believer this is of utmost importance, as it presents the picture of being so enthralled with and committed to those things that draw us away that they keep us from ever coming to realize our need of salvation. Therefore, the end result is death: physical, spiritual, and eternal. There is nothing more urgent in all of life than this.

But how does this verse relate to the believer? Is it possible for a genuine believer in Jesus Christ to be enticed and drawn away by those things that distract them? And, if it is possible, does it result in a loss of their salvation? James does say that it brings forth death!

It is possible to be drawn away, and it is possible for this to give birth to sin. This, in turn, can lead to losing our spiritual fellowship with God. It can't, however, cause us to lose our eternal life. The individual who has been called and chosen and birthed into the family of God can never lose their relationship with God (this will be discussed at length in the chapter on securing grace).

It is, though, a very serious thing for the believer to be distracted by those things that draw them away. It will result in becoming dissatisfied with the Lord. Those things that entice us tend to capture our hearts, and we are not satisfied until we have them, even though they are drawing us away from the intimacy of our fellowship with God.

These four – selfishness, sinfulness, discontentment, and distractions – are enough to show beyond doubt that it is possible to become dissatisfied with what God has provided. So the question that remains is how do we safeguard ourselves against becoming dissatisfied? For the remainder of this chapter we will try to answer that question.

HOW TO LIVE A SATISFIED LIFE

Paul has some much-needed instruction on this matter of living a satisfied life. Read these words slowly, taking time to meditate on the important message he gives.

> If then you were raised with Christ, seek those
> things which are above, where Christ is, sitting at
> the right hand of God. Set your mind on things

above, not on things on the earth. For you died,
and your life is hidden with Christ in God.

(Colossians 3:1–3)

The foundational thing that we must do in order to live a satisfied life is to set our minds on things above. It is obvious that in order to be distracted by the things of the world we must first take our minds off the things of God. This is so extremely easy to do. We live in the world. We are engaged in worldly activities. We work on secular jobs. Our businesses deal with worldly wisdom. We are taught worldly principles with which we conduct ourselves in our private lives, our public lives, our careers, and our classrooms. Our minds are focused on the world most of the time.

So this makes it so difficult to maintain an other-worldly mindset. It takes discipline to make this a reality. We do not automatically become heavenly minded when we are born into the family of God. Just as in the matter of sanctification, it takes effort on our part. There are several Christian disciplines that it would be wise for each of us to endeavor to put into habitual practice in our lives. Even though there are many more that could be added to the following, to put these few into practice would give us a good start on experiencing and enjoying the satisfying grace of God.

READING THE BIBLE

A regular time set aside every day to read the Bible is a wonderful Christian discipline. There are so many reading plans that will assist us in reading through the Bible. My personal practice has been to read through the Bible every year. I have been doing this for more than forty years, and it has always proven to be such an enriching practice. Reading through different translations will give more insight and understanding to some of the more difficult passages in the Bible – and there are plenty of those!

The psalmist gave a bit of helpful advice about the discipline of reading the Bible.

> Your word is a lamp to my feet and a light to my
> path.
>
> (Psalm 119:105)

If we are going to set our minds on things above, then we must allow the Bible, God's inspired word, to shed light on the path of life. The Bible will give guidance to those who need direction. It will give comfort to those who are hurting. It will bring healing to a sorrowful heart. It will give principles for living to the glory of God. It will give instruction for those seeking to know God's will.

Far too often we turn to other sources for help, guidance, and comfort. The Bible should be the believer's first source to turn to when in need.

It doesn't matter what plan you choose to follow – just do it. Choose the time that best fits your schedule. Strive to make sure it is a time of the day when you will have the least chance of being disturbed. Turn the cell phone off. Turn the TV off. Get into your secret place, wherever that happens to be, and read God's word. Ask that He would speak to you through the passage you will read that day. Listen for His voice to speak through the words of the passage.

God will speak, sometimes in a shout, and at other times in a whisper. But He will speak. He desires to speak. Let's allow Him to do so through the discipline of reading the Bible.

STUDYING THE BIBLE

A discipline that should then be added to reading the Bible is having time allocated for studying the Bible. There are certainly parallels and commonalities that are observable between these two disciplines but studying goes much farther than reading. Paul shares some insightful words on why we should not only read the Bible, but study it as well.

> All Scripture *is* given by inspiration of God, and *is* profitable for doctrine, for reproof, for correction, for instruction in righteousness, that the man of God may be complete, thoroughly equipped for every good work.
>
> (2 Timothy 3:16–17)

> Be diligent to present yourself approved to God, a worker who does not need to be ashamed, rightly dividing the word of truth.
>
> (2 Timothy 2:15)

The Bible is the word of God. From the very first word in Genesis to the last word in Revelation, it is God's word. Notice that Paul says all Scripture is given by inspiration of God. The phrase literally means that the Scriptures are God-breathed. This would carry the idea that the Bible originated with God, not with man. The human authors received the inspired word and recorded it as God revealed it. There are many things to be learned from this, one being that since the Bible is inspired by God then it carries the weight of His authority.

Paul further states that, since it is inspired by God, then it is profitable to the reader and student of the Bible. He gives four things that should motivate us to study Scripture. First, it is **profitable for doctrine**. This cannot possibly be over-emphasized in our secular society. Too many people, churches, and even entire denominations seem to be moving away from Biblical doctrine in the present day. Doctrinal disagreements cause division among believers. Instead of engaging in spiritual warfare against our common enemy – the devil – we are far too often seen fighting among ourselves. And, also far too often, our doctrinal disagreements are caused by trying to embrace and implement false doctrine. We argue over societal issues, and instead of turning to Scripture we turn to worldly theories and ideas. We argue over philosophical issues, and again we turn to the philosophies of man rather than the teachings of Scripture. We argue over theological concerns, and squabble and fight over matters that are of no eternal consequence.

Paul says we need to turn to Scripture for a clear and correct understanding of doctrine. Second, he says that Scripture is **profitable for reproof**. The Bible is the authoritative source to which we can turn to receive rebuke, or reproof, for wrong actions, attitudes, and activities. If we allow ourselves to become involved in some sinful activity, whether it be a one-time offense or an on-going behavioral pattern, the Bible will confront us over that sin. James speaks clearly and powerfully concerning this matter in his epistle.

> For if anyone is a hearer of the word and not a doer, he is like a man observing his natural face in a mirror; for he observes himself, goes away, and immediately forgets what kind of man he was. But he who looks into the perfect law of liberty and continues *in it,* and is not a forgetful hearer but a doer of the work, this one will be blessed in what he does.
>
> (James 1:23–25)

The sincere believer who truly desires to be a disciple of the Lord Jesus Christ will look into the word of God with an open heart and mind, seeking doctrinal instruction and Biblical reproof for his actions, and then do as the Bible says. The Bible, when studied sincerely, will provide reproof that is intended to guide us in our ongoing sanctification process. It is imperative that we gaze intently into the mirror of the word of God, seeking the Holy Spirit's assistance in understanding it correctly and applying it properly. We need desperately to seek God's truth, and then be a doer of the truth He reveals.

There is a third benefit of studying the Bible pointed out in the passage from Second Timothy: Scripture is **profitable for correction**. Reproof and correction can be thought of as two sides of the same coin. They should go together in the development toward spiritual maturity of the truth-seeking believer. God reproves us through a study of His word. That is the negative side of the coin. Reproof is looking into that mirror, and seeing the blemishes, the scars, the scratches, the imperfections. Correction is looking into that same mirror and being able to see clearly how to make things right. Let's be reminded of something we learned from the writings of Paul in a previous chapter. He spoke of putting off and putting on. One example he gave was if anyone stole, let him steal no more but work honestly with his own hands. So, if a thief were reading this message from Paul, then the word would rebuke him by pointing out his sinful behavior, and then correct him by showing him what he must do to turn away from the sin and walk in righteousness.

This is actually the fourth profit Paul mentions that will come about by being a sincere student of the word of God: **instruction in righteousness**. The process begins with true doctrine, which will lead to reproof, which is followed by correction, and finally by instruction. But let us not look into that mirror, see the imperfections, try to mask them with some sort of spiritual make-up to hide them from others, and go our way, forgetting what we have seen. Study with the intent that we become fully mature, and fully equipped as a worker who does not need to be ashamed.

MEMORIZING THE BIBLE

There is another discipline that has to do with scripture: memorizing the Bible. This is a much-needed discipline as it puts into our minds verses that God can and will bring to our remembrance when the message in a passage is pertinent to a life situation we find ourselves in.

> Your word I have hidden in my heart, that I might not sin against You. Blessed are You, O Lord! Teach my Your statutes.
>
> (Psalm 119:11–12)

Memorizing Scripture has many benefits, one of which is mentioned here by the psalmist. When we find ourselves in a situation in which we are faced with the choice to engage in a questionable behavior, passages of Scripture committed to memory will come to mind, pointing in the direction God would have us go. It will guard us against engaging in activities that may seem appropriate, but when placed beside the clear teachings of the Bible we see that it would be sin.

Memorizing Bible verses will also prove to be helpful when we are given the opportunity to share a witness with an unbeliever. Verses committed to memory will come to mind, enabling us to address specific questions raised by the person with whom we are speaking.

There are many other benefits to scripture memorization. It is truly a beneficial discipline for the devoted follower of Jesus Christ.

PRAYER

Prayer is still another discipline desperately needed in the Christian life. Prayer can be thought of as a lifeline between the believer and God. All through the Bible we see examples of individuals engaging in prayerful communication with God. Prayer is a vital part of the Christian disciplines.

Jesus taught His disciples to pray. He led in this by example as well as instruction. The disciples saw how important prayer was to Jesus as they observed Him investing time in communication with the Father in prayer.

There are so many different components of prayer. As we talk with the Father we go to Him with adoration, confession, thanksgiving, petition, and supplication. We are encouraged to come boldly before the throne of grace, and to cast all of our cares upon the Lord realizing He cares so compassionately for us.

We need to be careful not to misuse prayer. It is possible to go to God in prayer for wrong reasons and with wrong motives. We need to submit ourselves to God as we go into a time of prayer, asking Him to reveal His desires to us so that we can in turn pray those desires back to Him. To pray correctly we need to have our minds and motives surrendered to Him so that He might have access to both, and so that He can have no obstacles to overcome in speaking to us.

If we aren't careful in this matter, we can turn a time of prayer into a selfish "give me what I want" session, speaking to God as if He were a magic genie at our beck and call. Prayer is a Christian discipline, and it takes discipline on our part to learn to pray, and to pray properly.

Admittedly, it is sometimes difficult to pray. I remember quite vividly a season of my spiritual pilgrimage in which I was finding it nearly impossible to pray. It seemed that every time I tried to engage in prayer my mind would go off into a thousand different directions. So many things would crowd into my mind, causing me to lose focus.

I became so bothered by this that I went to my pastor for counsel. I shared with him my dilemma, feeling ashamed because I had convinced myself that no other Christian had ever gone through such an intense struggle with their prayer life. My pastor gave me words of encouragement, assuring me that I was definitely not the first to experience this kind of spiritual battle. Then, he made a remark that was so simple and yet so profoundly powerful. He said that when we are going through a season of prayerlessness, pray. When we don't feel like praying, pray. When we feel that our prayers are bouncing off the ceiling, pray. Pray, and keep praying, until you feel like praying.

That certainly wasn't earth-shattering theology, but it was life-changing practicality. Prayer is an absolutely essential discipline we are to practice in our walk with the Lord. It is one of those component parts of the Christian life that will prove to be a tremendous safeguard against becoming dissatisfied in our Christian walk.

FELLOWSHIP

Fellowship with other believers is another much needed Christian discipline. We need each other, and it is through fellowship with other believers that this need can be met, at least partially. There are several reasons that should be mentioned here to show how important this aspect of the Christian life is.

> Two are better than one, because they have a good reward for their labor. For if they fall, one will lift up his companion. But woe to him who is alone when he falls, for he has no one to help him up. Again, if two lie down together, they will keep warm; but how can one be warm alone? Though one may be overpowered by another, two can withstand him. And a threefold cord is not quickly broken.
>
> (Ecclesiastes 4:9–12)

We need fellowship for mutual encouragement. It is difficult to stay the course of true discipleship without receiving and giving encouragement. We don't have to stand alone in the spiritual battle we all face in life. Alone we are vulnerable to the onslaught of the enemy. We have no one to watch our back. In times of discouragement, we can become distraught if we try to face that discouragement alone. But we draw strength in numbers.

Oftentimes being alone seems so overwhelming we feel as if we will never be able to cope with the harsh realities of life. Being alone means we have no one to come to our aid, to stand by our side, to pick us up when we fall. But being in fellowship with others means that we have those who will hold us up and, if the need arises, pick us up.

It is also through fellowship around the word of God that gives us opportunity to share our questions and concerns about issues of importance. These may be theological issues, or theoretical issues, or societal issues, or cultural issues. In times of fellowship, we can ask for assistance in understanding the Bible's teachings on matters of concern to us.

We are also able to seek spiritual guidance in times of fellowship. A situation may arise to which you have no idea as to how to respond. You have no idea what the Bible might say about the matter at hand, so you ask others for insight and advice. It is through these times of fellowship that we find strength in numbers. As we learn what God's word teaches, we become more satisfied with His ways and are enabled to discard the world's ways.

One of the practices of the early church was spending time together. An insightful testimony to this is found in the book of Acts.

> Then those who gladly received his word were
> baptized; and that day about three thousand souls
> were added to him. And they continued steadfastly
> in the apostles' doctrine and fellowship, in the
> breaking of bread, and in prayers.
>
> (Acts 2:41–42)

Note the emphasis on fellowship and prayer. They drew strength from one another as they spent time together, leaning on one another and encouraging each other.

SILENCE

A much-neglected Christian discipline is silence – being still, quiet, and attentive to the still, small voice of God. We are too often so busy that we don't feel that we have time to be silent before the Lord. Deadlines approach, appointments await, project deadlines draw close, family events need to be attended, children's activities have to be watched – something is crammed into every moment of every day. How in the world can we be expected to find time to be quiet, to sit in silence, listening for God to speak? If He is going to speak to me, He had better make it quick so I can make it to the next thing on my schedule.

> God is our refuge and strength, a very present help
> in trouble.
> Be still and know that I am God; I will be exalted
> among the nations, I will be exalted in the earth!
> The Lord of hosts is with us; the God of Jacob is
> our refuge.
> (Psalm 46:1, 10, 11)

That may be one of the biggest hindrances to being satisfied with God: busyness. Too busy for God. Too busy to spend any time waiting for Him to communicate with me. Too much activity crammed into too little time.

Psalm 46 begins and ends with the same assertion: God is our refuge. He is our place of shelter, safety, and security. The circumstances surrounding the writing of this psalm are not known, but it seems to be a time of national upheaval when the pagan nations are opposing and oppressing the people of Israel. In the midst of the uncertainties of life, the psalmist says that we should be still and focus on God. He is in control, and He is a present Help in times of trouble.

Regardless of the circumstances of life we face at any given time, God is still God, and He is established on the throne. So be still and remember who is truly in in control. It will help us be satisfied with His grace. There are situations and circumstances in which we feel that there is no way of escape. We feel as if we must busy ourselves with striving to come up with a plan that will enable us to get through. We are so busy that we have no time to seek God's guidance, much less to sit in silence while we wait. We find ourselves living out the old adage, "Don't just sit there, do something!" But what God would like for us to understand is that in those times we actually need to say, "Don't just do something, stand there!" Stand, sit, kneel, but by all means be quiet before the Lord. Listen for that voice of God speaking in the midst of the difficulty. Be silent before Him, and allow Him time to address you in the midst of the storm.

CELEBRATION

Consideration will be given to one more of the Christian disciplines: celebration. We would all be amazed if we realized how much this discipline could benefit our personal level of satisfaction with God's grace. We celebrate a lot of things: birthdays, anniversaries, graduations, promotions, gender reveal parties, engagements, retirement, and more. We love to celebrate those big, important moments in life. So why do we neglect to celebrate spiritual milestones? There is so much to be celebrated, and in doing so we would grow in our level of satisfaction.

> And do not be drunk with wine, in which is dissipation; but be filled with the Spirit, speaking to one another in psalms and hymns and spiritual songs, singing and making melody in your heart to the Lord, giving thanks always for all things to God the Father in the name of our Lord Jesus Christ, submitting to one another in the fear of God.
>
> (Ephesians 5:18–21)

The admonition against being drunk with wine is compared to being filled with the Spirit. To understand Paul's comparison let's consider first being drunk with wine. One under the intoxicating influence of alcohol is actually controlled by the alcohol in his system. His speech is impaired, his ability to maneuver is adversely affected, his sight is blurred, his mental faculties are compromised. Every aspect of his life is affected by the influence of alcohol.

Compare that to the person who is filled with the Spirit. His speech is also affected, but not in the same way. Whereas the one under the influence of alcohol has his tongue loosened and he speaks perversely and with vulgarity, the one under the influence of the Spirit has his tongue affected by the control of the Spirit. Vulgarity, profanity, perversity are all replaced by speaking with psalms, hymns and spiritual songs.

The one under the influence of alcohol is affected in his ability to maneuver physically. He is no longer able to walk without staggering and stumbling, perhaps running into things, or tripping over things. Sometimes the level of intoxication may render one totally incapable of walking at all.

The person controlled by the Spirit is now no longer walking by the dictates of the world and under the influence of the world, but walks in the Spirit and is therefore able withstand the temptations of the flesh and the influence of the world.

This is where the Christian discipline of celebration becomes so important. When we engage in singing and making melody in our heart to the Lord, it has an amazing positive affect on us. As we celebrate the person and work of Jesus Christ, we grow in our appreciation for His satisfying grace, and we begin to lose the desire for anything other than what He supplies. When we begin to sing to the Lord from the depths of our innermost being, we experience refreshing seasons of closeness and intimacy with Him. Our level of satisfaction in the Lord grows exponentially as our minds are focused on things above and not on things of the earth.

Celebration, along with the other disciplines mentioned in this chapter, enhance our understanding of the amazing grace of our Lord. So, by putting into practice these disciplines we begin to understand more fully just how amazing the grace of God really is. As the hymn says, the things of earth will grow strangely dim as we gaze into His wonderful face.

Maybe it's time we start gazing!

POINTS TO PONDER

1. Have you ever been dissatisfied with something or someone in your life?
2. If you answered yes, write down the experiences: why you were dissatisfied, with whom you were dissatisfied, how you were able to bounce back from the state of dissatisfaction.
3. The author wrote of some specific causes of dissatisfaction. Think about these and write down any experiences you have had with them:
    a. Selfishness
    b. Sinfulness
    c. Discontentment
    d. Distraction
4. Add to this list other causes of dissatisfaction that come to mind.
5. The author wrote of several things we can do to assist us in living a satisfied life. Think about them and strive to put these Christian disciplines into practice:
    a. Reading the Bible
    b. Studying the Bible
    c. Memorizing the Bible
    d. Prayer
    e. Fellowship
    f. Silence
    g. Celebration

CHAPTER 10

Securing Grace

My sheep hear My voice, and I know them, and
they follow Me. And I give them eternal life, and
they shall never perish; neither shall anyone snatch
them out of My hand. My Father, who has given
them to Me, is greater than all; and no one is able
to snatch *them* out of My Father's hand. I and *My*
Father are one.

(John 10:27–30)

Crown Him with Many Crowns
Crown him with many crowns,
The Lamb upon his throne;
Hark! how the heavenly anthem drowns
All music but its own:
Awake, my soul, and sing
Of him who died for thee,
And hail him as thy matchless king
Through all eternity.
Crown him the Lord of heaven!
One with the Father known,--
And the blest Spirit, through him given
From yonder triune throne!
All hail! Redeemer,--Hail!
For Thou hast died for me;
Thy praise shall never, never fail
Throughout eternity!
Matthew Bridges

F eeling insecure is a common plight in life. One might feel insecure on his job, in his relationships, in the community – almost anywhere. On the job he could possibly feel insecure because of mistakes he has made, and warnings he has received. The supervisor may have issued a verbal statement that the next time he makes a major blunder he will be terminated. So, he feels completely insecure, always looking over his shoulder for the axe to fall.

Or one might feel insecure on the job simply because he feels inadequate to perform the required tasks the job demands. Perhaps he feels he never received sufficient training which would enable him to do the job efficiently, so he is always looking over his shoulder, anticipating that one day he will be reprimanded for doing something wrong.

In his relationship with his wife, perhaps he has begun to see warning signs that things aren't the way they once were, the way things should be. Maybe he has noticed that they have been drifting apart – he is going his own way, doing his own thing, while at the same time his wife is doing the same. Perhaps their interests have taken a sharp turn in opposite directions. He no longer enjoys being with her friends, and she doesn't like his. He begins to feel very insecure in the relationship that he thought would last a lifetime.

The neighbors, who used to speak, and even drop by unannounced, now keep a significant distance between them. It used to be that if they met up in the grocery store, or the department store, or on the street, they would stop and have a lengthy conversation. Now, if the neighbors see them on one aisle in the store, they quickly make their way to a different aisle just to keep from coming into contact.

Friends have a dream of going into business with each other. They have worked long and hard at putting all the pieces together, saving the needed funds, securing sponsorships for their new business venture, and stockpiling an ample amount of supplies to get the business started. Opening day finally arrives and they excitedly throw the doors open to a large number of people who have responded to the opening day hype.

However, a few years into the joint venture, the partners begin to sense that a new direction should be implemented. But they begin to have a difference of opinion as to what that new direction should look like. One wanted to be overly aggressive in a rebranding of their business, while the other wanted to take a more cautious approach. The aggressive approach would require taking seventy percent of their accrued profits to launch the rebranding. If it failed, then they would probably end up filing bankruptcy.

The more cautious partner in the venture refused to take such a huge risk due to a feeling of insecurity. The disagreement led to a total dismantling of the business, and an end to a long-term friendship.

There are so many other examples we could cite, but these will suffice to show that insecurity can invade any area of life. When it comes, it can cause us to feel like we can't be sure of anything. Our minds can begin playing tricks on us, making us feel that we are in this – whatever 'this' is – all alone, with nowhere to turn and no one to whom we can turn.

In more than forty years of pastoral ministry I have met quite a number of individuals who were having a difficult time feeling secure in one or another of these areas of insecurity, or one of many others. But the one that was, in my estimation, the worst of all was when someone would come to me feeling totally insecure in their relationship with God. They had no assurance of their security in Christ Jesus.

What could cause a person who has been born into the family of God to begin doubting that relationship? How could one who has come into an intimate relationship with the God of the universe through His Son, Jesus Christ, ever have feelings of insecurity in that relationship? There are many different potential causes of this type of insecurity. So, before we consider passages of Scripture which would verify the promise of eternal security, we will consider some of the possible causes of insecurity.

NOT PRACTICING THE CHRISTIAN DISCIPLINES

In the previous chapter consideration was given to several of the Christian disciplines. We learned that by practicing these disciplines we grow in our state of satisfaction in our relationship with God. His satisfying grace makes us more aware of His tremendous love for us, which in turn causes us to love Him more. Then, as we become more aware of His love for us, we grow in our love for Him, and we feel more secure in the relationship.

But the reverse of that is just as true. If we don't practice those disciplines that help us grow in our relationship with Him, and further assist us in our spiritual development through sanctification, then we lose our intimacy with Him. This will result in a loss of the security we should have in our relationship with the Lord.

The disciplines discussed in the previous chapter – reading, studying, and memorizing Scripture, silence before God, fellowship with other believers, etc. – are all essential in helping us enjoy the most intimate closeness with God that is possible. But when those are neglected, we begin to sense a wedge of separation being driven between us.

It is like the illustrations given at the beginning of this chapter. Personal relationships – husband/wife, parent/child, employee/employer – can suffer when time and energy are not expended in keeping them strong. When we fail to do the things that are necessary to strengthen those relationships, we begin to feel insecure.

My wife and I have been conducting marriage retreats for more than twenty-five years. One of the most important topics of discussion we address is the importance of investing time and energy in each other. If we don't do this, then there will come the day in which we look at each other over the dinner table and wonder who this person is sitting across from me. Married couples can easily become strangers living under the same roof, even sleeping in the same bed, if effort isn't expended in maintaining the intimacy of the relationship.

And so it is with our relationship/fellowship with God. When we fail to do the things that are necessary to continually build it up, it will immediately begin to deteriorate. The closeness will begin to erode. The desire to spend time with Him will lose its appeal. We will begin cutting our time short with Him through the disciplines noted above and will begin spending that time doing other things. Practicing the Christian disciplines is vitally important if we desire to be secure in our relationship with God.

NOT WALKING IN THE SPIRIT

A second possible cause of feeling insecure in our relationship with God is that we are not walking in the Spirit. Not walking in - conducting ourselves, behaving in a manner of – the Holy Spirit will definitely cause us to feel insecure in our relationship with God.

The matter of walking in the Spirit will be discussed later in this chapter, but for now let it suffice to say that walking in step with the Holy Spirit of God is one of the most powerful ways a believer can be secure in his relationship. Paul warns us that if we do not walk in the Spirit we will be walking according to the desires and dictates of the flesh. And, if we are walking in the flesh then we will be living according to the fleshly desires. This, in turn, will cause us to be very insecure in our relationship with God.

John speaks clearly about this matter in his first epistle. He says that if we choose to be friends with the world, then we become enemies of God. What exactly does this mean for the child of God? It means that if a true believer becomes involved in an act of sin, or an on-going behavioral pattern of sin, then he sets himself in opposition to God. God will allow this to continue for an indefinite period of time, but He will not let it go on forever.

But there is one thing He will do: He will bring the believer under severe conviction. God promises that He will discipline His children if they return to a life of sin. This will not result in the loss of salvation, but, as we learned earlier from the example of King David, it will result in the loss of joy, which will also lead to a sense of insecurity in the believer's relationship with God. Remember, David's prayer was for God to restore to him the joy of His salvation, but not salvation itself. The joy of the relationship was gone because the intimacy of the relationship had eroded and subsided.

NOT ABIDING IN CHRIST

Another cause of insecurity that is closely related to not walking in the Spirit is not abiding in Christ. The apostle John, recording words spoken by the Lord Himself, shows clearly how important this matter is.

> Abide in My, and I in you. As the branch cannot bear fruit of itself, unless it abides in the vine, neither can you, unless you abide in Me. I am the vine, you are the branches. He who abides in Me, and I in him, bears much fruit; for without Me you can do nothing.
>
> (John 15:4–5)

Jesus is here speaking of the relationship between a believer and Himself. If the branch does not abide in the vine, he cannot bear fruit. The life of the branch is drawn from being connected to the vine. If the branch is removed from the vine, then it withers and dies.

Some would suggest that this portrays losing one's salvation. However, we will see clearly a little later that this cannot possibly be the case. Once an individual is saved by the grace of God he cannot be unsaved. Once one is born into the family of God he cannot be unborn. Rather, it is teaching that the branch cannot possibly bear fruit without abiding in the vine, and if severed from the vine the branch loses the vine's life sustaining, fruit-bearing flow.

This is such an important matter in the life of the believer. It is speaking of how crucial it is for the believer to remain consistently in Christ. We are told in Galatians that we are to bear the fruit of the Spirit, which is love, joy, peace, longsuffering, kindness, goodness, faithfulness, gentleness, self-control (see Galatians 5:22-23). Jesus says that in order to bear fruit the branch must remain in the vine. So, if a believer does not remain steadfastly in the vine, receiving the vine's life-sustaining flow, then the branch will not be able to bear the fruit of the Spirit.

A believer in Jesus Christ can become unloving, unkind, with no joy, no peace, no goodness, no faithfulness, and no self-control if he does not abide in Christ. The fruit of the Spirit becomes conspicuously missing, and the works of the flesh become the prominent feature of his life. This doesn't necessarily mean that all of the works of the flesh are manifested in his life at once, but they begin to show the very moment the branch is severed from the vine. This will result in a state of increasing insecurity in his relationship with God.

We need to understand how negatively these things affect our intimacy with God. When we are not walking in the Spirit, not abiding in Christ, and not practicing the Christian disciplines, our fellowship with God is interrupted, and we lose our sense of security in our relationship with Him.

So what can we do to safeguard ourselves against this happening to us?

How to Feel Secure in our Relationship with God

The remainder of this chapter will focus on how to feel secure in our relationship with God. It is safe to say that we desire security in our relationships. Husbands and wives want to have confidence that their spouses are committed to the marriage, and they have a sense of security in the relationship. How awful it would be to have an ongoing sense of insecurity in the marriage relationship. It could cause one to have no trust in their spouse. If something has happened in the past that has eroded the trust that spouses should have in one another, then it is very difficult to have that trust reestablished and the feeling of security restored. I have counseled with couples in the past concerning difficulties they were experiencing in their marriages. One of the major reasons they sought counseling was because one or the other had done something to cause a sense of distrust and insecurity. Sometimes they were able, by the grace of God, to work things out and move ahead. Other times the distrust was too great to overcome, and the marriage ended.

The same can be true of parent/child relations, and business partner relations. Once the trust factor has been compromised it is difficult, sometimes impossible, to regain. This is one of the main reasons I have always suggested to parents to strive to never make a promise that they do not keep. Children need to feel secure in their relationship with their parents, and if promises are made and then broken, the trust factor erodes. This causes the child to feel very insecure. There are times when things happen unexpectedly and we cannot keep a promise we have made to our children. This should happen as infrequently as possible, and when it does we need to explain to our children why we could not do as promised. The same is true in all other relationships as well. Broken promises will result in broken trust, which will ultimately result in insecurity.

But there is one thing that we can rest assured of: God is completely trustworthy. What He has said He will do: He WILL do. One thing He has promised is that He will give eternal life to those who believe. As we learned in chapter three, those who are called and chosen will believe unto salvation, and it is these who will abide in Christ.

There are two ways to view this matter of abiding in Christ in the life of the believer. First, when one is born into the family of God, he is positionally "in Christ" from that moment on. It is the same as with our sanctification. At the moment of salvation, the person who has become a new creation in Christ is positionally sanctified, set apart for God and to God. So it is with the matter of abiding in Christ. At the exact moment of the new birth, the believer is positionally abiding in Christ. This position can never be altered or changed.

> For God so loved the world that He gave His only begotten Son, that whoever believes in Him should not perish, but have everlasting life.
>
> (John 3:16)

> My sheep hear My voice, and I know them, and they follow Me. And I give them eternal life, and they shall never perish; neither shall anyone snatch them out of My hand. My Father, who has given them to Me, is greater that all; and no one is able to snatch them out of My Father's hand. I and My Father are one.
>
> (John 10:27–30)

However, in the practical sense of abiding in Christ, we are to put forth the effort to remain in Him – that is, in fellowship with Him, in submission to Him, and in service for Him. This is a great challenge for the believer because the temptations of the flesh, the world, and the devil are sometimes seemingly insurmountable. When we fall prey to any of them, we, for some period of time, are not practically abiding in Christ.

In order to feel totally secure in our relationship with God, we need to constantly remind ourselves of our position in Christ. And what exactly is that position? We are God's children! We have been born into His family of faith.

Those who believe have everlasting life. And who are those who believe? According to Jesus in the passage quoted above, it is His sheep who listen, follow, and then receive eternal life. Jesus adds to that a word of great encouragement and comfort: they shall **never** perish! And then, as if He knew that some would still have difficulty believing such a wonderful word of promise, He further strengthens His statement by adding a two-fold assertion: 1) no one can snatch them out of Jesus' hand, and; 2) no one can snatch them out of the Father's hand. The believer is doubly secured in his relationship with God being in the hand of Jesus, who is in the hand of the Father.

Another passage that is quite helpful in gaining greater clarity on this matter is also found in the third chapter of John's Gospel. It is another very familiar passage, recording a conversation between Jesus and a religious leader by the name of Nicodemus. This conversation actually concludes with Jesus' words quoted above (John 3:16).

> There was a man of the Pharisees named Nicodemus, a ruler of the Jews. This man came to Jesus by night and said to Him, "Rabbi, we know that You are a teacher come from God; for no one can do these signs that You do unless God is with him." Jesus answered and said to him, "Most assuredly, I say to you, unless one is born again, he cannot see the kingdom of God."
>
> (John 3:1–3)

It is very important to take note of the terminology Jesus used. He spoke of being born again. Nicodemus goes on to question Jesus as to how this could possibly take place. He completely misunderstood the true meaning of Jesus' words. Nicodemus was thinking in physical terms, as is seen in his response to Jesus.

> Nicodemus said to Him, "How can a man be born
> when he is old? Can he enter a second time into his
> mother's womb and be born?"
>
> John 3:4

To Nicodemus, hearing Jesus speak of being born again was the epitome of absurdity. How can a fully grown, adult man be born again? That is a biological impossibility! And indeed, it is. But Jesus was not speaking in physical terms. Rather, He was speaking about a spiritual birth. As one has been born physically into an earthly family, so the one born again is born into a spiritual family.

How many individuals have you known to be born a second time physically? Take a moment to think about it – it's a very important question (said with extreme sarcasm!). Of course, the answer is NONE! No one has ever been born a second time physically.

But many have experienced a second birth – spiritually. Jesus, still wanting Nicodemus to understand, continues explaining the details of this second birth. He does not want this religious leader of Israel to leave in a state of spiritual confusion. Jesus further elaborates on this matter of the second birth by stating plainly the following clarification:

> Jesus answered, "Most assuredly, I say to you,
> unless one is born of water and the Spirit, he
> cannot enter the kingdom of God. That which is
> born of the flesh is flesh, and that which is born of
> the Spirit, is spirit."
>
> (John 3:5–6)

We have physical life because we have had a physical birth. My parents were W.C. and Evelyn Stewart. I was the third child born to them. My sister, Ada, is the oldest of the three, with my brother, Wayne, being the second born. We have been siblings all these years. And we have been children of the same parents, all these years.

Did I ever do anything that was a source of heartache to my parents? More times than I would want to recount. Have I done or said things to or about my parents that I now regret? Have I caused them pain through some of my actions, attitudes, friend selection, behavior choices? Yes!

But, through it all, I am still their son (even though both have entered into the presence of our Lord years ago). They never disowned me, and I never disowned them. I continue to bear the name of my father.

My siblings and I were totally different from our very earliest ages. My sister and I never really had anything in common, and, since there is a five-year difference in our ages, there was very little we ever wanted to do together. (This is no longer the case, as we both enjoy spending time together) My brother and I, only separated by two years in age, never had anything in common either. Our choices in music, movies, friends, hangouts, hobbies, were all very distinct from each other. We never did anything together, except for those things we did as a family.

But through all these years, we are still siblings. We are brothers and sister because we were born to the same parents. Nothing can ever change the fact that we are siblings. That relationship will never end.

Those who have been born again have spiritual life because they have experienced a spiritual birth. And, just as those who are born physically to a set of parents will be their children forever, so will those who are born of God. Once an individual is born into the family of God, the relationship is forever. You cannot be unborn spiritually, just as you can't be unborn physically. Remember, Jesus said that He gives us eternal life.

This means, for the child of God, we are now living physically, spiritually, and eternally. When we are born again, we have been taken out of spiritual death and placed into spiritual life. We belong to a spiritual family. We have brothers and sisters all around the world. But we have one Father, who has adopted us into His family. We are now sons and daughters of God.

But even having these reassuring promises from the Lord, there are still times when some will doubt that relationship. They will begin thinking one of two things: either I was never really born again, or, I was born again but have now fallen from grace. Let's examine those two claims.

First, there are those who may have lost the assurance of their salvation and have begun doubting that they were ever really saved. We have noted earlier in this chapter some possible causes of losing one's sense of security in their relationship with God, and also noted that it is a very real possibility that we lose that sense of security. How is one to regain his sense of security, and once again be assured of his eternal relationship with God?

One thing that is absolutely crucial to remember: salvation is all of God, and not of us. To quote the apostle Paul again:

> For by grace you have been saved through faith, and that not of yourselves; *it is* the gift of God, not of works, lest anyone should boast. For we are His workmanship, created in Christ Jesus for good works, which God prepared beforehand that we should walk in them.
>
> (Ephesians 3:8–10)

The entire process of salvation is from God. We play no part in it whatsoever. If we played any part in the salvation process, we would be able to boast about the role we fulfilled. We could brag to others that we did this, or we gave that, or we served them. But God did it all. He preordained the plan. He sent His Son. His Son gave His life. The Holy Spirit brings us to the realization of our desperate need. He quickens us – brings us out of death into life. And once we are spiritually alive, we accept His amazing gift of eternal life.

So, since we had nothing to do with it, we can take heart in knowing that God has done all that is necessary to secure our eternal salvation. What this means for the individual who is doubting his salvation and his eternal security is that he has been placed in the hand of Jesus Christ; Jesus' hand is then placed in the hand of the Father, and we are safe and secure in their firm grasp.

Paul has more helpful words of enlightenment on this matter earlier in his letter to the Ephesians.

> Blessed *be* the God and Father of our Lord Jesus Christ, who has blessed us with every spiritual blessing in the heavenly *places* in Christ, just as He chose us in Him before the foundation of the world, that we should be holy and without blame before Him in love, having predestined us to adoption as sons by Jesus Christ to Himself, according to the good pleasure of His will, [6] to the praise of the glory of His grace, by which He made us accepted in the Beloved.
>
> (Ephesians 1:3–6)

There are some key words and phrases in this passage that should be noted: chose, predestined, adoption, and the good pleasure of His will. Brief attention was given to this passage in chapter three as we considered saving grace. Here we are focused on securing grace. It only stands to reason that if God, from before the foundation of the world, chose, predestined and adopted us into His family, that we could have had nothing to do with it. He did not choose us because we were worthy, or because He looked down through the ages of human history and saw something good in us. No, He saw a world filled with sinners who deserved his pronounced judgment on sin.

But God, according to the pleasure of His will, chose us and adopted us. Since this passage testifies to this amazing truth, then we should never doubt the fact of our salvation. We should believe that we are saved by grace, and once saved we are secure in the powerful hands of God.

Then there are others who fear the possibility of losing their salvation. What if we revert to our lives of sin after trusting the saving power of Jesus? What if we backslide completely on God? Will that not cause us to lose our salvation? If we have been born into the family, we may not be able to be unborn; but can a saved person be lost again?

First of all, let's understand that if it is possible to lose God's gift of salvation, it would indicate His inability to hold onto us. As has already been mentioned, we are in Jesus' mighty hand, and His hand is in the powerful grasp of the Father. No one can snatch us out of their hand.

But someone might object to that by asserting that even if it is true that no one else can snatch me, is it not still possible for me to jump out of His hand? Is it possible for me get out of His hand on my own, by my own choice? Or if I revert to a life of sin, can't I fall out of His hand?

These are questions that have been debated through the ages of the church. Is it possible to lose one's salvation? The doctrine of the eternal security of the believer would say no, but is the doctrine correct? Doctrine is, after all, man's interpretation of scripture. Could man not make a mistake? Also, there are some who believe that losing one's salvation is a very real possibility, while others say it isn't. So, how do we know who is correct? Both can't be right, right?

Since it is correct that two contradictory statements cannot both be true, then how are we to determine which is the correct doctrine? The only course of action we have is to turn to scripture and strive to find the solution there.

One of the most controversial passages on this subject is found in the letter to the Hebrews. In the sixth chapter of this letter, the writer is speaking of the miraculous work of salvation. He presents a situation which has been interpreted in two ways: one views the text as dealing with believers while the other views it as dealing with non-believers. However, no matter which view is taken, the passage gives a weighty argument for the eternal security of the believer.

> For *it is* impossible for those who were once enlightened, and have tasted the heavenly gift, and have become partakers of the Holy Spirit, and have tasted the good word of God and the powers of the age to come, if they fall away, to renew them again to repentance, since they crucify again for themselves the Son of God, and put *Him* to an open shame.
>
> (Hebrews 6:4–6)

First, think of the passage as referring to non-believers. If this view is taken the terminology could be a bit confusing. The terms "enlightened", "tasted", and "partakers" all sound as if the passage is speaking about a genuine believer. However, if the passage is speaking of non-believers then we must understand these words in a little different way. "Enlightened" would be a reference to those who have their minds exposed to some level of biblical truth, but not that they have accepted what they have heard. "Tasted" could be understood in the sense of a momentary experience, and not a life-changing conversion. And finally, "partakers" could be that they have received the witness of the Holy Spirit but have not embraced the life-changing message.

Second, if we think of the passage as referring to believers, then it could be thought of as a hypothetical statement made by the author to show the absurdity of a genuine believer losing his salvation. Several translations of the Bible begin this passage with the word "if": "If they fall away." The argument is that if it is possible for a believer to fall away from the faith and lose their salvation, then it is impossible for them to be saved again. This would require Jesus dying a second time on the cross, which is the height of absurdity.

In Jesus' parable of the seed sown on four different types of soil we see this same principle. The seed that fell on rocky places sprang up quickly, showing signs of life, but just as quickly withered and died because it had no depth of earth to take root. They appeared to be the real thing but were proven to be false.

It is possible for non-believers to show signs of genuine life to the point that even other believers are fooled. The apostle John shares some thought-provoking insight on this matter that could help.

> They went out from us, but they were not of us; for if they had been of us, they would have continued with us; but *they went out* that they might be made manifest, that none of them were of us.
>
> (1 John 2:19)

John is describing some who had undoubtedly lived a life of deceit. They had been so convincing in their behavior that it is obvious many true believers had been deceived by them. They appeared to be sincere believers. But now John says they had left the church, and it proved that they were never genuine believers in Jesus Christ. Their actions validated the fact that they had been living a lie.

I would like to close this chapter by addressing a question that has been posed to me on several occasions: How about the hypothetical case of an individual who has been in church for a long period of time? They made a profession of faith, were baptized, and became members of a local body of believers. For several years they were actively involved in the churches many ministries.

But suddenly, with no forewarning at all, they quit attending. Before long it was discovered that they had reverted to their old lifestyle of partying, drinking, smoking pot, and using drugs.

A few of the leaders from the church go to visit them and try to find out what has caused this drastic change of behavior. They casually reply that church just wasn't for them. They tried it, but it did not have any appeal. They were now living in open sinful lifestyles and showing no sign of being convicted by the Holy Spirit over their behavior.

Were they saved, and then lost again? Or were they never saved? Or were they saved and backslidden? From our previous remarks we can rule out the first as a possibility, because once an individual is saved, he is saved eternally.

Both the second and third questions are real possibilities. First, it is possible, even probable, that he was never saved. The Bible makes the assertion that God will discipline His children when they fall into sin. It goes so far as to say that if a professing believer falls into sin and does not experience the conviction of the Holy Spirit, then he is an illegitimate child because God is not his Father. This is one of the true litmus tests of genuine Christianity: a true believer cannot live in habitual sin without experiencing the Holy Spirit's power of conviction.

The third question – "were they saved and backslidden?" – is also a possibility. However, they will not be able to enjoy their sinful behavior because of being convicted by the Spirit.

Eternal life is the gift of God to those who sincerely recognize their sin, turn to Jesus for forgiveness, and are born into the family of God. It is our possession now through Jesus Christ. God wants us to live in the full awareness of being eternally secure in His hands. When doubts arise, then be reminded that Paul says if we confess with our mouth the Lord Jesus and believe in our heart that God has raised Him from the dead, we will be saved. Believe it. Trust it. By faith embrace it.

POINTS TO PONDER

1. Have you ever experienced a feeling of insecurity? Was it in a relationship, or on your job, or in the classroom, or some other area of your life? If so, what caused the insecurity, and what did you do about it?
2. The author discussed some possible causes of insecurity. Do you identify with any of these?
    a. Not practicing the Christian disciplines.
    b. Not walking in the Spirit.
    c. Not abiding in Christ.
3. If you have been guilty of any of these, what did you do, if anything, to rectify the problem?
4. What are some specific actions you can take to help ensure that you will not fall to the feelings of insecurity in the future? Write down any ideas that come to mind.
5. Have you ever felt insecure in your relationship with God? If so, what did you do to rectify the problem?
6. Take time to review the passages the author used in this chapter to give you assurance of your relationship with God.

CHAPTER 11

Sufficient Grace

"And lest I should be exalted above measure by the abundance of the revelations, a thorn in the flesh was given to me, a messenger of Satan to buffet me, lest I be exalted above measure. Concerning this thing I pleaded with the Lord three times that it might depart from me. And He said to me, "My grace is sufficient for you, for My strength is made perfect in weakness." Therefore most gladly I will rather boast in my infirmities, that the power of Christ may rest upon me."

(2 Corinthians 12:7–9)

His Grace is Sufficient for Me
Many times I'm tried and tested
As I travel day by day
Oft I meet with pain and sorrow
And there's trouble in the way
But I have a sweet assurance
That my soul the Lord will lead
And in Him there is strength for every need.
Oh, His grace is sufficient for me
And His love is abundant and free
And what joy fills my soul
Just to know, just to know
That His grace is sufficient for me.
Anna B. Russell

S ufficiency is an important concept in so many different areas of life. It is the idea of having adequate amounts of the essential needs in life. Parents want to provide sufficiently for their children. We want them to have proper, weather-compatible clothing. We would not send them out barefooted, in shorts and a T-shirt when it is fifteen degrees outside with seven inches of snow on the ground. Nor would we send them to school on a ninety-five-degree day wearing a pair of winter boots, insulated pants, three layers of shirts, a down-filled coat and a toboggan. How utterly ridiculous to even think such things!

We also want them to be fed properly, with healthy, nourishing meals that will help them grow and develop mentally, physically, and emotionally. We would not feed them a constant supply of candy, popcorn, sugary soft drinks, and other food items with little to no nutritional value. A good, healthy, balanced eating plan will prove to be sufficient in helping them grow into strong, healthy adults.

We would all love to have jobs that would provide sufficiently for the needs of our families. It is certainly not necessary to be extremely wealthy, but we would like to have incomes that would allow us to live comfortably, without undue concern about the food in the pantry, gas in the automobile, resources to meet our financial obligations, and, hopefully, some left over to store away for another day.

It is not necessary to have the newest, the biggest, the brightest, and the best, in order to have a sufficient supply. We just simply need to have an adequate supply to meet our needs.

When we think of sufficient grace, we are speaking of an adequate amount of grace to meet all our spiritual needs. And thankfully, we have ample testimony in scripture that would validate the claim that God's grace is, indeed, an all-sufficient grace.

Thinking about the Bible's teachings on this subject, it is easy to see that sufficient grace is presented in at least four distinct ways. These four will give us confidence in the sufficiency of God's grace.

First, we have the sufficiency of the Bible. This aspect of sufficiency will be our first consideration as we look at this subject. Second, the Bible then presents us with the sufficiency of God the Father. Third, the Bible also presents us with the sufficiency of Christ. Then, fourth and finally, the sufficiency of the work of the Holy Spirit is clearly evidenced in the Bible.

THE SUFFICIENCY OF THE BIBLE

Consideration will first be given to the sufficiency of the Bible. This means that the Bible is everything we need to live a life of victory, being equipped for the service of God, and guiding us into a fullness of faith. The progressive revelation of God that is developed throughout the pages of scripture leads the reader into a deeper understanding and appreciation of all God has done to bring about the redemption of fallen man, and then how the redeemed individual can experience a life of sufficient grace in all areas of life.

From the very beginning of the first book in the Bible, to the very end of the last book, Revelation, we see the consistent unveiling of the purposes and plans of God. It begins with the majestic plan of God to create the universe. Just by speaking the word, everything that exists was brought into existence. This creative work of God culminated with the creation of man. And this begins the saga of how the story of man, the history of man, developed.

The creation of man was followed by the fall of man, after which man, now bearing the marks of the fall, and the scars of sin, is banned from the garden. However, this did not take God by surprise, forcing Him to come up with a new plan. Rather, He knew what man would do and had already preordained the plan by which sinful man could be redeemed.

The unfolding plan culminated with the birth of Jesus Christ, the preordained sacrifice who would give His life to pay the penalty for the sin of man. And now, through the forgiving grace of God in Jesus, redemption is offered.

The Bible is sufficient in its ability to make this message known. It is sufficient in bringing the message of salvation, as well as the means of salvation, to lost mankind.

But it is sufficient in so much more. The foregoing is a brief summation of the sufficiency of the Bible in presenting us with the development of the history of the human family. But what we will focus on now is the sufficiency of the Bible in the life of individuals. It is sufficient in presenting the big picture, but it is also sufficient in bringing us smaller pictures – pictures of how man is brought into the family of God, and how he then grows and develops in his new life in Christ.

Many believers are obviously malnourished when it comes to spiritual things. Even years after trusting in the saving work of God offered through the sacrifice of Jesus Christ they remain in spiritual infancy. They have not grown and developed into spiritually mature believers but are still needing to be nurtured and fed as babies in Christ. The following passages speak of the reality of stunted spiritual growth in the life of some believers.

> And I, brethren, could not speak to you as to spiritual *people* but as to carnal, as to babes in Christ. I fed you with milk and not with solid food; for until now you were not able *to receive it,* and even now you are still not able; for you are still carnal.
>
> (1 Corinthians 3:1–3a)

> For though by this time you ought to be teachers, you need *someone* to teach you again the first principles of the oracles of God; and you have come to need milk and not solid food.
>
> (Hebrews 5:12)

This is a very sad state for believers to find themselves in. It can also be added that it is a fairly common thing in the lives of many believers. If we fail to maintain close fellowship with God then we open ourselves up for the possibility of ceasing to grow toward spiritual maturity. But this does not have to happen, nor does it mean that one can't get out of this spiritual state once he has allowed himself to fall into it. It would be wise to take a moment and review a passage we gave attention to in a previous chapter.

> All Scripture *is* given by inspiration of God, and *is* profitable for doctrine, for reproof, for correction, for instruction in righteousness, that the man of God may be complete, thoroughly equipped for every good work.
>
> (2 Timothy 3:16–17)

As a quick review, let's remind ourselves that the Bible is the inspired word of God. In this book we have instructions, teachings, stories, history, poetry, law, letters, and Gospels. We may read them and wish God had inspired more authors to write more books which would give us more insight and instruction. But we acknowledge that God has given us everything we need to enter into a relationship with Him, to grow to maturity in Christ, and to live lives which glorify Him.

Perhaps one of the best passages that speaks of the sufficiency of the Bible is found in the book of Psalms. This is a powerful testimony to the important role the Bible should play in the life of all who believe in the Lord.

> The law of the Lord is perfect, converting the soul; the testimony of the Lord is sure, making wise the simple; the statutes of the Lord are right, rejoicing the heart; the commandment of the Lord is pure, enlightening the eyes; the fear of the Lord

is clean, enduring forever; the judgments of the
Lord are true and righteous altogether. More to
be desired are they than gold, yea, than much fine
gold; sweeter also than honey and the honeycomb.
Moreover by them Your servant is warned, and in
keeping them there is great reward.

(Psalm 19:7-11)

The Bible converts the soul, makes the simple wise, causes the
heart to rejoice, enlightens the eyes, and should be desired more
than gold! What an amazing book, indeed!

So, in review, the Bible is sufficient in showing us why we
need to be saved; how we can be saved; how to grow in faith and
in the knowledge of the Lord; how to live a life of righteousness;
how to discern personal spiritual giftedness and then how to
use those gifts for His glory. This is reason enough to commit
ourselves to read, study, apply, and live according to God's Word.

THE SUFFICIENCY OF GOD THE FATHER

Attention will now be turned to the sufficiency of God the Father.
What is meant by God the Father being sufficient? The Bible
reveals the work of the Father in creation, in preordaining His Son
to be the One who would give His life as the sacrifice for sin, in
electing those who would be saved, in drawing sinful individuals
to the Son, and now holding those redeemed individuals safely
in His hand. This is all an amazing testimony to the sufficient
grace of the Father.

I have often wondered why God didn't just give up on us.
Why would He invest so much in His human creation? Even
more than that, why would He even create humans knowing
that we would rebel against His commands, and knowing that it
would cost the life of His Son to make redemption possible?

Surely it was not because man met a need that was lacking

in God. Think back to that timeless span that was before time. It doesn't matter if the creation took place ten thousand years ago, or ten million, or ten billion, or ten trillion: At some point prior to the creation there was nothing, except God. Was there anything lacking in God then? Did He need something that man would provide? Of course not! God was not lacking in anything. In that timelessness before time God was perfectly fulfilled within Himself. He had no need of anything, and still has no need for anything.

So why did He create the universe? And as the crown of that creation why did He create man in His own image? The Bible tells us that He did it all for His own good pleasure. God is sufficient in and of Himself, with no need for anything outside of Himself to make Him more complete.

In His state of total self-sufficiency, He proves to be more than sufficient to create, control and guide His created order to His preordained end. God is on the throne of the universe and, as the psalmist declares, He cannot be moved. Even though the nations should rage against Him, He is neither threatened nor afraid. The psalmist states this truth powerfully in this passage.

> Why do the nations rage,
> And the people plot a vain thing?
> The kings of the earth set themselves,
> And the rulers take counsel together,
> Against the Lord and against His Anointed, *saying,*
> "Let us break Their bonds in pieces
> And cast away Their cords from us."
> He who sits in the heavens shall laugh;
> The Lord shall hold them in derision.
> Then He shall speak to them in His wrath,
> And distress them in His deep displeasure:
> "Yet I have set My King
> On My holy hill of Zion."
>
> (Psalm 2:1–6)

As I write this chapter the armies of Russia are encircling the Ukraine, ready to invade at any moment. There are so many dynamics at work in this act of aggression, and it is not within the scope of this work to delve into those dynamics. However, the point I would make concerning this is that Russia has long been a nation that has been strongly atheistic. This certainly doesn't mean that all Russians are atheists, but they are led by a political machine that is propagating atheism to its citizens.

Russia has always been a threat to the West, and right now we are witnessing a battle of words between President Biden of the United States and President Putin of Russia. But as I think of the words of the psalmist quoted above, my mind is drawn to the throne of the God of the universe, and to Him seated on that throne. He is not in the least bit threatened by what He sees happening. The tensions between these nations, and how it might affect other nations around the world, causes Him no stress at all. As a matter of fact, He laughs, and holds those in derision who would take it upon themselves to fight against His authority.

God's sufficiency can be viewed in so many ways. We have spoken in earlier chapters about His omnipotence and omniscience. We can add to that His omnipresence. He knows all things; He can do all things; and He is always everywhere. Dr. Kenneth Ridings, my homiletics professor at Fruitland Baptist Bible Institute (now College) used to say, "No matter how far man is able to travel in space, when he reaches his destination, God will already be there. You can't go anywhere that God isn't." His power, knowledge and presence assure us of His sufficiency in all things.

THE SUFFICIENCY OF JESUS CHRIST

The Bible also reveals to us the sufficiency of Jesus Christ. There are several areas of Jesus' life and ministry that show clearly that He was sufficient in everything the Father had sent Him to accomplish. There is an interesting episode in Jesus' life that will illustrate this point.

> The Pharisees heard the crowd murmuring these things concerning Him, and the Pharisees and the chief priests sent officers to take Him.
>
> Then the officers came to the chief priests and Pharisees, who said to them, "Why have you not brought Him?" The officers answered, "No man ever spoke like this Man!"
>
> (John 7:32; 45–46)

This event in the life of Jesus intrigues me every time I read it. Jesus had become increasingly popular with the crowds. As His popularity grew with the common people, his unpopularity continued to grow with the religious leaders, and it caused them to try to find ways to entrap Jesus. They even go so far on this occasion to send a delegation to arrest Jesus. But they return without bringing Him, and when questioned as to why their response is simply one of amazement at the way Jesus spoke.

As we think about their amazement, several areas of Jesus' life and ministry should amaze us. Think with me about a few of these.

SUFFICIENT IN HIS TEACHING

It is obvious as one reads through the Gospels that Jesus was more than sufficient in His teaching. His teachings cover a wide array of topics, such as the Kingdom of God, repentance, the distinction between the letter of the law and the spirit of the law, righteousness, heaven, hell, the necessity of the new birth, and so many others.

It is clear from what we have recorded in scripture that Jesus was a master teacher. He was always teaching, whether it be in private with His disciples, or in public as crowds would gather to hear Him speak. He was always investing Himself in sharing the truth with those who would take time to listen.

Jesus taught often publicly before the masses. On several occasions He taught crowds that numbered in the thousands. As His popularity grew, the crowds grew in number. Several passages speak of large crowds gathered to hear Him teach.

One thing that attracted these large crowds was the way Jesus taught. After Jesus gave the sermon on the mount (see Matthew 5–7) the reaction of the people speaks volumes about Jesus' teaching.

> And so it was, when Jesus had ended these sayings,
> that the people were astonished at His teaching, for
> He taught them as one having authority, and not
> as the scribes.
>
> (Matthew 7:28–29)

It is interesting to note the reason for the people in the crowd being astonished at His teaching. He spoke with authority, which set Him apart from the scribes, who could only quote other sources to validate their teachings. Jesus, however, had no need to quote anyone: He was His own source of authority. His authority was based on His identity with the Father. He had all authority in heaven and earth, as He was and is the sovereign Ruler of the universe.

Jesus also taught privately to the twelve He had chosen to be His apostles. Jesus often spoke in parables, which are extended stories used to teach spiritual truths. Some of these parables could be understood in different ways, and even the apostles did not fully understand what He was teaching. So, when they were alone with Jesus, they would ask Him to explain further the meaning of the parable. On one of those occasions, Jesus said something that sounds rather strange. The apostles asked Him privately why He spoke in parables, and He answered by saying:

Because it has been given to you to know the
mysteries of the kingdom of heaven, but to them it
has not been given. For whoever has, to him more
will be given, and he will have abundance; but
whoever does not have, even what he has will be
taken away from him. Therefore I speak to them
in parables, because seeing they do not see, and
hearing they do not hear, nor do they understand.
And in them the prophecy of Isaiah is fulfilled,
which says:
"Hearing you will hear and shall not understand,
And seeing you will see and not perceive;
For the hearts of this people have grown dull.
Their ears are hard of hearing,
And their eyes they have closed,
Lest they should see with *their* eyes and hear with
their ears,
Lest they should understand with *their* hearts and
turn,
So that I should heal them."

(Matthew 13:11–15)

There were, obviously, some things that were not clearly
explained to the large crowds gathered to hear Jesus teach. Jesus
did explain to the apostles, however, that His reason for this was
based on a prophecy from Isaiah. The people to whom Isaiah
wrote, and the people to whom Jesus spoke, were undoubtedly
there to hear Jesus teach out of curiosity, not a sincere desire to
know the truth. Their eyes and ears were open, yet they were
not there to gain an understanding of the true meaning of Jesus'
teaching. So, Jesus taught in parables on some occasions for that
reason.

Jesus spent much time with the twelve men whom He had
called to be apostles. He taught them so much more than He
taught the crowds, preparing them for the ministry they would

perform after Jesus' death, burial and resurrection. But Jesus also knew that He could not possibly teach them everything they would need while He was with them so He promised that when the Holy Spirit had come that He would guide them into all truth. The Holy Spirit would take up where Jesus left off, so they could be assured of continued teaching and training after Jesus' ascension back to the Father.

Regardless of whether He was speaking publicly to multitudes, or privately to the twelve, Jesus was always teaching in order to share the truth. And more often than not, the truth Jesus taught ran contrary to the traditional teachings of the Jewish leaders. This, along with so many other things, led to His arrest, trial, and execution.

SUFFICIENT IN HIS WORKS

Another area of Jesus' life and ministry that shows His sufficiency can be seen in the works He performed. John makes a most remarkable statement about Jesus' works in his Gospel.

> And there are also many other things that Jesus did, which if they were written one by one, I suppose that even the world itself could not contain the books that would be written. Amen.
> (John 21:25)

What we have recorded in the Gospels is only the tip of the iceberg as it relates to the reader the many things Jesus said and did. He was constantly going about doing good. His works displayed His desire to show men the truth.

Jesus stood in the face of opposition and hatred, speaking the truth and doing good works to show the failures of the Jewish leaders to guide the people in the ways of God. Jesus' works were always performed intentionally and purposefully. The intent was to reveal the truth about the kingdom of God. The Jewish leaders had taught error-laden messages about the kingdom, placing emphasis on a Messiah who would come and reestablish Israel as a powerful kingdom as it was under the rule of King David. They were teaching the people that the kingdom of God would be an earthly kingdom.

The purpose of His works was just as clear: He came to teach by His words, and reveal by His actions, that the kingdom was not an earthly kingdom, but a spiritual kingdom, of which He was King. Thus, the teachings and the works of Jesus go hand-in-hand in pulling back the veil so that we could understand the truth of and about the kingdom of God.

His words and His works were sufficient to show that He was truly God, and yet the religious leaders hated Him because of those very things. They were certainly threatened by His popularity with the masses, and they were fearful that His followers would continue to grow in number and strength. These are some of the reasons they plotted and planned ways to entrap Him, sometimes in His words and sometimes in His works. Their hatred for Jesus had no bounds.

SUFFICIENT IN HIS MIRACLES

Jesus' miracles are part of His works but are not to be identified as one and the same. His miracles are works, but there are many works that are not miracles. Jesus performed physical healings: He restored sight to the blind, hearing to the deaf, healed diseases, made the lame to walk, and even raised the dead. He also performed miracles over the natural realm: He multiplied food to feed thousands, calmed raging storms, and walked on the water. And He performed miracles over the spiritual realm by casting demons out of individuals who had been possessed by one or more evil spirits.

It is not the purpose of this work to consider in detail each individual miracle Jesus performed. It is the purpose to show Jesus' sufficiency in all things, and His miracles are powerful displays of His absolute sufficiency over the physical, natural, and spiritual realms. For those who had eyes to see and ears to hear, these were all powerful attestations to His true identity, but to those who were spiritually blind and deaf they were nothing but the words and works of a charlatan who must be destroyed at any cost.

SUFFICIENT IN HIS LIFE

Jesus' life shows His sufficiency in perfectly obeying and fulfilling the will of His Father. The purpose for which Jesus came into this world was to provide the means by which sinful man could be reconciled to God. To do that Jesus would have to live a perfectly sinless life. If He failed to accomplish that, His death would have only paid for His own sin, meaning He could not provide salvation for fallen man.

But He did accomplish this amazing feat. A huge theological debate that has raged from the very earliest stages of church development centers around Jesus' sinlessness. The debate and discussions focus on the question as to whether Jesus was able not to sin, or not able to sin. The following verses will show why this debate continues to the present day.

> For we do not have a High Priest who cannot sympathize with our weaknesses, but was in all *points* tempted as *we are, yet* without sin.
>
> (Hebrews 4:15)

> And being found in appearance as a man, He humbled Himself and became obedient to *the point of* death, even the death of the cross.
>
> (Philippians 2:8)

227

Look carefully at two phrases in these passages: "In all points tempted as we are," and "became obedient to the point of death." Was the temptation real? And, since the text says He became obedient, does that mean He could have chosen to disobey? Many attempts have been made at giving a reasonable explanation in response to those questions. No satisfactory answer has been given that has consensus among scholars. It does seem clear that the writer's intent is that the reader would understand that Jesus, in His humanity, faced real temptation to which He could have fallen, and He truly had to "become" obedient, choosing to obey rather than disobey the will of the Father.

If that is indeed the proper interpretation of these verses, then we see even more clearly how sufficient Jesus was in His life. He was foreordained to be the Lamb slain for the sin of man, but it was His choice to accept or reject that plan. His struggle is clearly seen in the garden of Gethsemane as He prayed that the Father would remove the cup from Him. Luke even records that His sweat because as drops of blood falling to the ground. But He ultimately decided to obey the Father's will by stating that He wanted God's will to be done. He was sufficient in His life to the very end.

SUFFICIENT IN HIS DEATH

This leads directly to another sufficiency of Jesus: He was sufficient in His death. His death on the cross was sufficient to bring about the salvation of sinful man. There are some vitally important issues relative to this particular aspect of Jesus' sufficiency.

First, consideration will be given to the word, "atonement." Oftentimes we will hear someone refer to the atoning death of Jesus, or the fact that Jesus is the atonement for sin. However, the word "atonement" is never found in the New Testament. There is one exception to this in the King James Version of the Bible, where in Romans we do find the word "atonement".

When compared to other translations, however, we find that a different word is used to translate the Greek word into English. The following quote is the verse from Romans that contains the word "atonement". This will be followed showing how other translations interpret the same word under consideration.

> And not only so, but we also joy in God through
> our Lord Jesus Christ, by whom we have now
> received the atonement.
>
> (Romans 5:11, KJV)

The word translated "atonement" in the KJV is translated by the word "reconciliation" in these Bible versions: New King James, New International Version, New American Standard, Holman Christian Study Bible, Young's Literal Translation, The Lexham English Bible, American Standard Version, as well as many others.

Is there any reason not to use the word "atonement" in this verse? First of all, it must be understood that in every other place this Greek word is used, it is always translated as "reconciliation", never atonement. This would be an extremely important argument in favor of the word "reconciliation" being used here.

But second, and even more importantly, is the meaning of the word "atonement". It actually means a temporal covering over of sin. In the Old Testament, the High Priest would enter the Holy of Holies on the Day of Atonement with a blood sacrifice which would atone for the sins of the people, but only temporarily. This day of sacrifice took place every year, depicting that these sacrifices could not provide permanent forgiveness. They were all pointing to an ultimate sacrifice by which sin would be, not atoned for, but propitiated. The covering over of sin did not appease the just wrath of God. It was only through the sacrificial, propitiatory death of Jesus Christ that the penalty of sin was met, thereby making it possible for sinful man to be reconciled to God. Hence, the use of the word "reconciliation",

Jesus' death was sufficient in fulfilling the just demand of the law, and the just penalty for sin. It is through this act of grace that we are able to be justified, reconciled, by Jesus Christ who appeased the wrath of the Father as our substitutionary, propitiatory sacrifice.

Jesus gave His life as the sacrifice for the sin of humankind. His life of sinless perfection made it possible for Him to complete this amazing work of grace. His death was indeed sufficient for this purpose.

SUFFICIENT IN HIS RESURRECTION

When speaking of the death of Jesus we often hear that He was killed by the Jews, or by the Romans, or, more specifically, by Pilate, or Herod, or some other individual or group. However, according to Jesus, none of these killed Him. It is true that they all played a role in the drama of Jesus' passion, but Jesus states plainly that they did not take His life. He gave His life. He had the authority to lay it down, and to take it up again.

Jesus spoke these remarkable words about His death:

> I am the good shepherd. The good shepherd gives His life for the sheep.
>
> I am the good shepherd; and I know My *sheep,* and am known by My own. As the Father knows Me, even so I know the Father; and I lay down My life for the sheep.
>
> Therefore My Father loves Me, because I lay down My life that I may take it again. No one takes it from Me, but I lay it down of Myself. I have power to lay it down, and I have power to take it again. This command I have received from My Father.
>
> (John 10:11; 14–15; 17–18)

Jesus' resurrection from the grave is the validation of His identity as the Son of God. He had announced to His disciples that He would be betrayed into the hands of wicked men who would crucify Him. But, He also told them that after three days He would arise from the grave. It is obvious that none of them actually understood what He was telling them. It is also clearly stated that after the crucifixion none of them seemed to even remember Jesus revealing His impending death to them. They were all so stupefied by the events of the betrayal, arrest, trials, savage beatings, and finally crucifixion that they were paralyzed with fear and anxiety until they had personally experienced the risen Lord.

But once they realized the resurrection was a reality, and they experienced the power of the resurrection in their own lives, they literally turned the world upside down as they boldly proclaimed this amazing truth.

But why is the resurrection so important for us? What exactly is the significance of the resurrection of Jesus Christ from the grave? Listen to the words of Jesus as He speaks concerning the power of the resurrection.

> Jesus said to her, "I am the resurrection and the life. He who believes in Me, though he may die, he shall live. And whoever lives and believes in Me shall never die. Do you believe this?"
>
> (John 11:25–26)

> Jesus said to him, "I am the way, the truth, and the life. No one comes to the Father except through Me."
>
> (John 14:6)

The resurrection is important for us because without the resurrection we would all be hopelessly lost in our sin with nothing awaiting us after this life but eternal torment in hell. Jesus states assertively that no one can come to the Father through any means other than Himself. And the only way He could make that possible was through His death, burial, and resurrection.

The Apostle Paul presents a substantial case for the necessity of the resurrection in his correspondence with the Corinthians.

> But if there is no resurrection of the dead, then Christ is not risen. And if Christ is not risen, then our preaching *is* empty and your faith *is* also empty. Yes, and we are found false witnesses of God, because we have testified of God that He raised up Christ, whom He did not raise up—if in fact the dead do not rise.
>
> (1 Corinthians 15:13–15)

> But now Christ is risen from the dead, and has become the firstfruits of those who have fallen asleep. For since by man came death, by Man also came the resurrection of the dead.
>
> (1 Corinthians 15:20–21)

The argument is simple: if Christ has not been raised from the dead, then we have no hope in this life or the life to come. But, since Christ is risen from the dead, we have the assurance of being resurrected by the power of His resurrection. His resurrection is sufficient to provide resurrection and eternal life for those who believe.

SUFFICIENT IN HIS ASCENSION

An aspect of the life, ministry, death and resurrection of Jesus Christ that is often overlooked is that of His ascension. After His resurrection, Jesus made appearances to His disciples over a period of forty days. There are eleven of His post-resurrection appearances recorded in the Gospels. These appearances were made to individuals, small groups, and on at least one occasion Jesus appeared to more than five hundred people at once.

After making all these post-resurrection appearances He ascended back into heaven. It was a most wonderful and remarkable day in the life of the apostles as they were given the opportunity to be eyewitnesses of this amazing event. The wonder of the ascension is recorded in these words:

> Now when He had spoken these things, while they watched, He was taken up, and a cloud received Him out of their sight. And while they looked steadfastly toward heaven as He went up, behold, two men stood by them in white apparel, who also said, "Men of Galilee, why do you stand gazing up into heaven? This *same* Jesus, who was taken up from you into heaven, will so come in like manner as you saw Him go into heaven."
>
> (Acts 1:9–11)

Yes, it was wonderful and amazing to witness this event, but it must have also been a most challenging and anxious day for them as well. Why? Because Jesus would no longer be with them physically. Of course, as far as we know, Jesus had only made eleven appearances over that forty-day period of time. So, it had not been like it was before Jesus' death, burial and resurrection. But still, He had been there, and surely we are to understand that His physical presence was a source of strength and encouragement for them. But now they would no longer be able to see Him, to speak with Him face-to-face, to ask questions and receive instructions.

But the ascension was necessary to complete the cycle of salvation. Jesus had to come; He had to live; He had to die; He had to be resurrected; and He had to ascend back to the Father to complete the work. His ascension was the last thing necessary to complete the work the Father had preordained from before the foundation of the world. Jesus completed that assignment as He obeyed the Father's will to lay down His life and then take it up again. His ascension completed the work in full, thus making it possible for man to be saved.

SUFFICIENT IN HIS INTERCESSION

And now, Jesus is in constant intercession for us! For us! Think about that; meditate on that wonderful truth. Jesus is praying for us.

> Therefore He is also able to save to the uttermost those who come to God through Him, since He always lives to make intercession for them.
>
> (Hebrews 7:25)

> My little children, these things I write to you, so that you may not sin. And if anyone sins, we have an Advocate with the Father, Jesus Christ the righteous.
>
> (1 John 2:1)

While Jesus was on earth, during His ministry, He spent time in personal communication and communion with the Father. He also let His disciples know that He was praying for them, personally. But in these verses we are told that now He is in a ministry of intercession, always making intercession for us.

He had already let the disciples know of His ministry of intercession in His prayer recorded in John 17. The prayer is divided into three sections: in the first, He prays for Himself; in the second, He prays for His disciples; and in the third, He prays for all who will believe. Even then, Jesus was praying for us!

How wonderful to think that He has prayed for us and continues to make intercession for us now in His constant ministry of intercession. His intercession is sufficient for us.

THE SUFFICIENCY OF THE HOLY SPIRIT

Jesus wanted to alleviate any undue stress and anxiety the apostles and disciples might have after His ascension back into heaven, so He assured them that they would never be alone. He assured them that after His departure the Holy Spirit would come and would continue the work He had begun. Of course, in some ways His work was not only begun, but it was also finished. Jesus completed His assigned task. Then He promised the disciples that a Comforter would come upon His departure, but He could not come until Jesus had ascended back to the Father.

The Holy Spirit comes on the Day of Pentecost. Many signs and wonders validated His arrival. He came in order that He might carry on the work of the Lord Jesus. It is His ministry to bring about conviction of sin, and to warn of the impending judgment of God that is yet to come on the earth. It is His ministry to guide believers into the truth of God as opposed to the pseudo-truth of the world. It is His ministry to empower believers to carry on their personal ministries in their service to God.

The Holy Spirit's work and ministry in the world at large, as well as in the life of individuals, is absolutely sufficient for the task. The following passages will clearly show the sufficiency of His work as He empowers believers.

> But you shall receive power when the Holy Spirit
> has come upon you; and you shall be witnesses to
> Me in Jerusalem, and in all Judea and Samaria,
> and to the end of the earth.
>
> (Acts 1:8)

However, when He, the Spirit of truth, has come, He will guide you into all truth; for He will not speak on His own *authority,* but whatever He hears He will speak; and He will tell you things to come.

(John 16:13)

And when He has come, He will convict the world of sin, and of righteousness, and of judgment: of sin, because they do not believe in Me; of righteousness, because I go to My Father and you see Me no more; of judgment, because the ruler of this world is judged.

(John 16:8–11)

This brief overview has reminded us of the fact that God in His fullness – Father, Son, and Holy Spirit – is at work in the world. We are never left alone to carry out His work on our own but are always in the presence of the living God. Be encouraged by the sufficient grace of God that is manifested in our lives here and now and will be manifested in our glorified lives in the very presence of the living God.

POINTS TO PONDER

1. Explain in your own words the concept of the sufficiency of the Bible.
2. Explain in your own words the sufficiency of God the Father?
3. Explain in your own words the sufficiency of God the Son?
4. Explain in your own words the sufficiency of God the Holy Spirit?
5. What does the sufficiency of the three persons of the Trinity mean to you personally? Write down several talking points relative to each of the three, and then share your ideas with a friend or family member.

CHAPTER 12

Sustaining Grace

And lest I should be exalted above measure by the abundance of the revelations, a thorn in the flesh was given to me, a messenger of Satan to buffet me, lest I be exalted above measure. Concerning this thing I pleaded with the Lord three times that it might depart from me. And He said to me, "My grace is sufficient for you, for My strength is made perfect in weakness." Therefore most gladly I will rather boast in my infirmities, that the power of Christ may rest upon me. Therefore I take pleasure in infirmities, in reproaches, in needs, in persecutions, in distresses, for Christ's sake. For when I am weak, then I am strong.

(2 Corinthians 12:7–10)

It is Well with My Soul
When peace, like a river, attendeth my way,
When sorrows like sea billows roll;
Whatever my lot, Thou hast taught me to say,
It is well, it is well, with my soul.

It is well, with my soul,
It is well, it is well, with my soul.

Though Satan should buffet, though trials should come,
Let this blest assurance control,
That Christ has regarded my helpless estate,
And hath shed His own blood for my soul.
Horatio Gates Spafford

There are so many dangers, toils and snares that confront us as we go through life. These come in a wide variety of types: personal, family, business, financial, natural disaster, man-made disaster, illness, and so many others. We face them in every season of life. Sometimes we are able to see them coming from a distance, but most of the time they come suddenly, without any prior notice, and we find ourselves frantically trying to make it through.

The world has been in the throes of one of these major dangers for over two years. On December 31, 2019, it was announced by the World Health Organization that a mysterious form of pneumonia was sickening dozens of individuals in China. Since then, the disease has become a world-wide pandemic. The toll in the United States (as of April 19, 2022) stands at 82,397,033 confirmed cases and 1,016,037 deaths.

Alongside this ravaging disease are so many other diseases – short-term, chronic, terminal, infectious, non-infectious – that are always attacking the human family. And disease is only one type of the dangers, toils and snares we face through life.

Up through the age of fifty, I had enjoyed excellent health. But when I reached that milestone in age things began to quickly deteriorate. For the twenty years I have now lived beyond my fiftieth birthday, I have experienced health issues of different kinds. I began having constant sinus infections, which resulted in two sinus surgeries. I also was diagnosed as a type two diabetic, resulting in being prescribed oral medication and insulin injections. My rotator cuff in my right shoulder had to be surgically repaired, and I also had surgery on my lower back for a herniated disc.

These particular health issues are nothing compared to what I have seen others go through, but they do give testimony to the fact that we as individuals face certain dangers, toils and snares as we go through life. And some of these are so overwhelming we find ourselves wondering if we will be able to survive. We are so consumed with those things going on in our life – the pain we suffer, the surgeries we face, the physical deterioration we experience – that they oftentimes become the focus of our life. If we are not careful we can become embittered toward God and belligerent toward our loved ones because we can see nothing good in our dilemma.

We have probably all witnessed family members and friends go through a dark season of life. Perhaps we have been by the bedside of a spouse, parent, sibling or child as they suffered the ravages of a terminal illness. We have tried to encourage them, comfort them, and in some way make their present plight a little less painful. But still, day after day we have watched as they have grown weaker, with no hope for recovery.

My parents were godly individuals who lived exemplary lives. I never heard either one ever speak a single word of profanity. They never argued, at least not in my presence, and I never once heard either of them raise their voice at me or my siblings. They were examples of godly living.

My father, at the age of fifty, suffered a massive heart attack that disabled him, and only two years later, at the age of fifty-two, he suffered a second attack that took his life. My mother was one of the godliest people I have ever known. She was one of the most kind, gentle persons you could ever meet. In her last couple of years of life she began showing signs of Alzheimer's disease. It was almost imperceivable at first, but gradually grew noticeably worse. For her safety, and to assure she received the care she needed, my siblings and I made the difficult decision to find a health facility where her needs could be met.

When you watch someone suffer the ravages of this awful disease you know that certain things are coming. For me, I knew the day would come when I would walk into her room, and she would not recognize me. I tried to mentally prepare myself for that day, but when it finally happened I found myself totally unprepared. When I walked in the door and looked into her eyes, even before speaking a word, I knew she had no idea who I was.

I walked over and sat down in the chair next to her bed. She had an inquisitive look on her face as she tried to remember who I was. I finally began asking her a series of questions, making a feeble attempt to perhaps jog her memory. Do you know what day it is? Do you know where you are? Do you have any children? Grandchildren? To each question the answer was always the same: No. This awful disease had robbed her of her memory, at least for the moment. Thankfully there were other days in which she would recognize me and we would carry on a decent conversation, but still, to this day, I am haunted by that day – that first day when I experienced the emptiness in her eyes, and the hollowness in her voice.

Yes, dangers, toils, and snares are a very real and very painful part of life. The question is: how do I make it through when they become part of MY life? What will sustain me in the midst of the dark seasons? Again, as stated in an earlier chapter, it would be wonderful if there was a manual which provided a point-by-point process through which we could progress that would help get us through those difficult seasons. However, we all know all too well that there is no such thing. But there is help and hope. The hope that we have as believers rests in God's grace. More specifically, God's sustaining grace. That is the subject of this chapter: sustaining grace.

BIBLICAL REASONS FOR DANGERS, TOILS, AND SNARES

One of the major reasons cited by non-believers for their not believing is because of the manifold troubles and evils in the world. The age-old question centers on the goodness of God: If God is good, then why is there evil in the world? Why do we see such bad things happening to good people? Even more, why do bad things happen at all, regardless of whether it is experienced by a good person or a bad person? If God is indeed all-powerful, with the ability to eradicate all forms of evil, and if He really is good, then why doesn't He do something? Why does evil, suffering, sickness, murders, rapes, assaults, wars, earthquakes, tornados, hurricanes, floods, etc. exist?

The Bible supplies the answer to those probing questions: God has done something. Once again we need to revisit the garden of Eden. God had pronounced to Adam and Eve the prohibition against eating fruit from one particular tree in the garden. All they had to do was simply stay away from that tree. One of the best ways to guard ourselves against falling prey to temptation is simply to refrain from placing ourselves in a place that we know will entice us to sin. I feel sure the garden was plenty big to allow ample room for the first couple to stay away from that one forbidden tree.

But they disobeyed, and as we have seen in a previous chapter, they then passed down their sin nature to the entire human family. Man was then given the freedom to make decisions based on his will and pleasure. This meant that man was able to choose to murder, rape, rob, assault, engage in war, and any other evil practice he chose.

The goodness of God is evidenced in the fact that He gave man the liberty to choose. Of course, we are not truly free to choose, because in our fallen state we are prone to sinful behavior. Just as a reminder, we have learned that we sin because we are sinners – born with a sin nature and born with a propensity to sin. Every vestige of evil is a result of that fallen nature.

God cannot be blamed for what man has brought upon himself, and yet multitudes continue to blame Him and refuse to accept the message of His grace because they are given over to their own sinful tendencies. They fail to see that God in His amazing love and grace has provided all that is necessary to save man from sin and also provide an eternal home in that wonderful place Jesus has gone to prepare for us. But, in this world there will continue to be all manner of evil because of the curse of God on sin.

To summarize, we could say that every sickness of every kind, every murder, every rape, every theft, every war, every act of hatred and bitterness – every evil thing, every bad thing, everything that causes suffering of any kind – is a direct result of sin.

But?

Let's get a little more specific with our investigation into this matter. It is true that all manner of suffering and evil is a direct result of sin, but is it a direct result of *personal* sin? Was my mother's Alzheimer's a direct result of her personal sin? Is my diabetes a direct result of my personal sin? Is every person's suffering, difficulties, troubles, tribulations, all a result of personal sin?

Absolutely not! Good, godly, sincerely righteous individuals suffer just as much as the bad, ungodly, horrifically unrighteous individuals. Suffering is a result of sin – original sin. The sin committed by Adam and Eve resulted in their sin nature being passed down to us.

To get a better grasp on the complexities of human suffering, and how God sustains us through those dark seasons of life, let's look to scripture to find specific answers to why there is so much suffering and evil in the world.

Premise #1 - God is the "First Cause"

To begin our discussion, attention will be given to a most difficult topic relative to God. Since He is the first cause of all that exists, then we much strive to understand how this applies to the presence of evil in the world. God is the sovereign ruler of the entire created order, and therefore nothing can happen outside of His control. This being true, then we must understand that the presence of suffering in all its varied forms has to fit somehow into His creative activity.

This raises the question as to whether God is the author of sin and suffering. It is true, as we have previously seen, that God created Adam and Eve with the ability to obey or to disobey. They had perfect free will to choose from no predisposed position. They chose to disobey, and thus sin entered the world. Then, through the first human couple the sin nature passed to all succeeding generations.

This shows clearly that God allowed the sinful actions of man. This is a matter of grave importance as we strive to understand the presence of suffering and evil. If this means that man did something that God was not previously cognizant of, then it shows that man subverted the authority of God, and thus proved to be sovereign over Him. It would mean further that in some inexplicable way man was able to circumvent the control of God over the universe He had created.

This problem presents no difficulty at all for those who believe that God does not, even cannot, know the future because the future is unknowable. No one, not even God Himself, can know something that is yet to take place. Process theology teaches that God is actually in process of "becoming". They believe that God can make extremely accurate guesses about the future based on His perfect knowledge of the past and the present, but He cannot guarantee any future event simply because it cannot be known.

However, for the student of the Bible who believes the testimony of scripture that God knows everything, this is an absurdity of the highest order. God did not relinquish His sovereign rule, nor did man somehow exert his authority over that of God. God is the sovereign ruler of the created order – the universe that He created for His purposes and His pleasure. It must be understood that His authority extends to all that happens within the confines of His creation.

This is a topic that could not possibly be discussed at length in a work such as this. And delving into these deep theological debates is not the purpose of this book. But it must be noted in any discussion of the presence of suffering in the world that God, being the First Cause of everything, had to have a purpose for the introduction of sin and suffering in the world. To understand it in any other way would, again, put man in a position of authority over God, and that is a completely untenable position to accept. Therefore, God being the first cause of everything means that the presence of suffering has to be understood in terms of His divine plan.

PREMISE #2 – GOD IS GOOD, ALL THE TIME

With that being said, it would be wise for us to remind ourselves of an important theological truth: God is good, all the time. Nothing can change that. No matter what happens in the world at large, or in the life of an individual, He is good.

> For the Lord is good; His mercy is everlasting, and
> His truth endures to all generations.
>
> (Psalm 100:5)

One thing that makes this assertion difficult to understand is that sometimes the goodness of God is equated with the good things He does. It is interesting to hear people make the remark that God is good after they have experienced some amazing work of God in their lives. Perhaps they have prayed for God to heal a loved one, and healing takes place. They are then quick to give God praise for being so good. The praise is certainly warranted, but the question I would pose is would not God have been just as good if the healing did not take place? What if God had chosen to allow the person to remain ill, to continue to struggle with the chronic illness, or even to die. Would that lessen the goodness of God?

Of course not. God is good, all the time. His goodness should never be equated with good things. He is good even when bad things happen. Many Bible characters experienced bad things in their lives, but none of these negated the goodness of God. Job suffered horribly as he lost all his possessions and all ten children in just a matter of hours. But the goodness of God never failed.

David suffered at the hands of King Saul, who had decided that he would kill David. Jeremiah suffered greatly at the hands of his enemies, simply because He was faithful in proclaiming the message of God to the people. Paul suffered at the hands of those who opposed his preaching of the Gospel. Church tradition teaches that all the apostles, with the exception of the apostle John, were martyred for their faith.

Suffering is real, but it never negates the goodness of God. Our problem is that we have a distorted understanding of what the goodness of God truly entails. God is good and can be nothing but good. The presence of suffering should never be allowed to cause us to question that fact.

And we could go a step further. If we are ever tempted to question the goodness of God all we should have to do is look at the cross. God's goodness is seen in the most awful event to ever occur. When Jesus died on the cross to pay the penalty for sin God's goodness was displayed as never before. On that horrible day in the life of Jesus God's goodness was made manifest to sinful man, so that man's suffering could be swallowed up in the enormity of God's act of love and goodness. By focusing on the cross our doubts concerning the goodness of God should be destroyed forever.

PREMISE #3 – GOD CAUSES SUFFERING AS A JUDGMENT AGAINST THE WICKED

Still another Biblical premise is that God sometimes causes suffering as a judgment against the wicked. This is clearly seen in the pages of the Old Testament where God oftentimes brings judgment against the pagan nations because of their harsh treatment of the Israelites. At other times God brings judgment against the Israelites because they have rebelled against Him by disobeying His commands. Either way, God is actually the author of suffering when it is warranted to bring about His judgment against those who are going against His will.

An example of His judgment against a pagan nation because of their treatment of Israel can be found in the book of Exodus. The Israelites had been in Egypt over 400 years, in servitude to the commands of Pharaoh. God sends a series of ten plagues against the Egyptians in order to convince Pharaoh to let the Israelites go free.

One of the interesting matters that must not be overlooked in this record of the plagues is that Pharaoh's heart was hardened so that he would not let the Israelites go. Three times the Bible tells us that God announced that he would harden Pharaoh's heart (Exodus 4:21, 7:4, and 14:4), and six time He actually did the hardening (9:12, 10:1, 10:20, 10:27, 11:10, 14:8). Through this process of hardening Pharaoh's heart, God performed ten plagues against the nation of Egypt through which the people of the nation suffered tremendously. The last of the ten plagues was the death of all the firstborn of the entire nation, after which Pharaoh released the Israelites so that they might leave the nation. These plagues were not natural phenomena, but rather super-natural occurrences orchestrated by God Himself. God orchestrated these ten plagues to reveal His power to His people which bringing judgment against the Egyptians for their mistreatment of Israel.

On other occasions God's judgment was against the people of the nation of Israel due to their rebellion against His guidance and law. This occurred many times during the years of the monarchy, especially during the reigns of kings who led the nation to worship the gods of other pagan nations. So, the Bible makes it clear that there are times in which God actually orchestrated and initiated suffering to fulfill His purposes.

PREMISE #4 – GOD USES SUFFERING TO HELP HIS CHILDREN GROW IN FAITH

Another Biblical premise to consider is that God sometimes used suffering to teach His children and to facilitate their spiritual growth. We see this principle clearly in both Testaments. Abraham was chosen by God to be the father of the nation of Israel as well as the father of the faith family of New Testament believers. But it was not an easy path for Abraham to follow. One of the biggest tests of Abraham's faith was when God commanded that he offer his son, Isaac, as a sacrifice to God. It is difficult to imagine how horrific this must have been for Abraham.

I have three children and six grandchildren. It is extremely difficult for me to fathom such a command as this. To contemplate such an awful command would send me into a tailspin like none I have ever faced. I feel sure that I would at least present an argument to God on behalf of my child/grandchild. I feel that I would try to negotiate with God, trying to come up with a alternate plan. This would prove to be a test of faith that would have the potential to break me.

Yes, I would love to say that I am sure I would do the right thing and obey God regardless of how it might turn out. Yes, I would love to be able to say that I feel my faith is strong enough to stand the test and come out victorious. And even if I could muster the faith to follow through, it would be with a broken heart and a crushed spirit.

So how did Abraham do when faced with this task? He passed the test with flying colors. He took Isaac to the place God commanded, prepared the altar, placed his son on the altar, and drew back the dagger to slay his son. Just before the blade was plunged into Isaac's flesh, God stayed Abraham's hand. God then provided the ram for the sacrifice. But Abraham had to come to the very moment of taking his son's life before his hand was stayed. This entire episode was commanded by God, and even though He stopped Abraham before he took Isaac's life, the awful reality is that he followed through on this direct command of God.

In the New Testament we see several different individuals whose faith was tested to the exteme. Mary and Martha, the sisters of Lazarus, were tested severely when their brother became sick. They sent a message to Jesus informing Him of Lazarus' sickness with the hopes that Jesus would arrive quickly and heal their brother. Jesus, however, purposefully stays away long enough for Lazarus to die and his body to be in the tomb four days. The sisters must have been overwhelmed with questions as to why Jesus stayed away, as they knew He could have cured Lazarus. When Jesus did arrive, He was met with the same message from both sisters:

> Now Martha, as soon as she heard that Jesus was coming, went and met Him, but Mary was sitting in the house. Now Martha said to Jesus, "Lord, if You had been here, my brother would not have died. But even now I know that whatever You ask of God, God will give You."
>
> (John 11:20–22)

Martha and Mary had their faith tested to the max, and even after their brother had died and was buried Martha still shares a statement of faith when Jesus arrives. She boldly proclaims her belief that whatever Jesus asked of the Father, the Father would do. Even in the midst of extreme grief and sorrow she professes faith in Jesus. Their faith grew exponentially as a result of this time of extreme suffering.

As we face the difficulties of life, we should pray that God would help our faith to grow as we go through them. It is in the dark seasons of life that our faith usually grows the most.

PREMISE #5 – GOD ALLOWS SUFFERING THROUGH SPIRITUAL WARFARE

A final Biblical premise about suffering is that God sometimes allows suffering in our struggle with spiritual warfare. We are engaged in a battle that cannot be seen with the eyes. It is a spiritual struggle in which we are at war with the devil and his evil emissaries. They are out to deceive and defeat us so that we lose our testimony of glory to the Lord. Peter says that our enemy is like a lion who is roaming the earth seeking someone to devour. We know that he cannot cause us to lose our salvation, but he can certainly be of such an influence that we lose our personal witness for the Lord Jesus.

Suffering is a reality in this world. We experience it in so many ways, and at so many different levels of intensity. As noted above there are a variety of reasons God allows suffering to come our way. His ultimate desire is that it would serve the purpose of helping us grow in our faith as we go through those periods.

Now we will turn our attention to the matter of facing those periods of suffering victoriously. Once again, the answer is grace – more specifically, sustaining grace. It is through the sustaining grace of God that we are able to make it through and come out stronger on the other side. The passage quoted at the beginning of this chapter will prove to be very helpful as we consider the subject of God's sustaining grace.

> And lest I should be exalted above measure by the abundance of the revelations, a thorn in the flesh was given to me, a messenger of Satan to buffet me, lest I be exalted above measure. Concerning this thing I pleaded with the Lord three times that it might depart from me. And He said to me, "My grace is sufficient for you, for My strength is made perfect in weakness." Therefore most gladly I will rather boast in my infirmities, that the

power of Christ may rest upon me. Therefore I take
pleasure in infirmities, in reproaches, in needs, in
persecutions, in distresses, for Christ's sake. For
when I am weak, then I am strong.

(2 Corinthians 12:7–10)

Special attention needs to be given to a few statements Paul
made in these verses. First, Paul says that he was given a thorn
in the flesh. The idea of being given something sounds as if Paul
is saying that this thorn was a gift from God. To protect Paul
from becoming conceited and proud of the fact that he had been
caught up to the third heaven, God gave him this thorn for his
own benefit: to keep him humble.

But he also says that this gift of God was a messenger of Satan
given to buffet him. This is one of those rare occasions where we
see God working in conjunction with Satan to bring about His
will. It is the same thing that we see in the book of Job. It was God
who pointed Job out to Satan, and it was God who gave Satan
the opportunity to put Job's integrity and faith to the test. Satan
could only do what God allowed him to do, but his involvement
was clear in the lives of Job and Paul.

Second, Paul informs the reader that he prayed three times
that God would remove the thorn. This shows that it is proper
for the believer to ask for God to heal in times of sickness. Paul
was undoubtedly thinking that he would be able to do so much
more for the Lord if he was not encumbered with this thorn, so
he prayed for its removal.

When we are faced with difficulties of different kinds, we
should take those difficulties to the Lord in prayer. God is
pleased when we show our dependence upon Him as we take
our problems to Him. He is not bothered by our many petitions
and supplications but is rather honored that we come to Him as
the source of our every need.

A third insight we can draw from this passage is that Paul
willingly accepted God's answer to his prayers. And what was

God's answer? He spoke to Paul in some undisclosed manner and told him that He was not going to remove the thorn but would supply Paul with the grace to sustain him as he continued to suffer from the thorn. As stated above, it is proper for the child of God to take our requests for the removal of the difficulty, but it is incumbent upon the child of God to accept God's answer.

This leads us to a fourth important insight: Paul's response to God's answer. Read these words again very carefully, asking God to speak to your heart as you read.

> Therefore most gladly I will rather boast in my infirmities, that the power of Christ may rest upon me. Therefore I take pleasure in infirmities, in reproaches, in needs, in persecutions, in distresses, for Christ's sake. For when I am weak, then I am strong.

Take special note of the two times Paul uses the word "therefore". He says that based upon God's answer to his prayer he will most gladly boast about his infirmities, and that he will take pleasure in the infirmities, reproaches, needs, persecutions, and distresses. This is a powerful display of God's sustaining grace.

The fifth insight we need to draw from this statement is Paul's reasoning for making this statement of commitment. He says that he will accept God's answer "for Christ's sake". He has committed his life to service to Jesus Christ and his desire is to bring Him glory in every way possible. This means that he will accept anything and everything God brings into his life in such a way as to point people to Him.

There is another passage in which Paul gives even more helpful insight on this important matter.

> But we have this treasure in earthen vessels, that the excellence of the power may be of God and

not of us. *We are* hard-pressed on every side, yet not crushed; *we are* perplexed, but not in despair; persecuted, but not forsaken; struck down, but not destroyed—always carrying about in the body the dying of the Lord Jesus, that the life of Jesus also may be manifested in our body.

(2 Corinthians 4:7–10)

The Gospel, referred to here as "treasure", is entrusted to God's children, referred to as fragile earthen vessels. In our present human condition, we are fragile and weak, prone to suffering in its various forms. We do not have the power to carry on the work of God in our own strength. Paul describes our precarious state by using four contrasts.

First, he says that he was hard-pressed on every side, yet he was not crushed. The New Living Translation translates the phrase "hard-pressed on every side" as "pressed on every side by troubles". Paul's life was filled with adversity from the moment his ministry began, (see Second Corinthians 11:22ff) but, through all the adversity he was not crushed. The word "crushed" could be thought of in terms of total hopelessness. Paul testifies that even though the pressure was intense he was not brought to a point of hopelessness. Why? Because of the power of God's sustaining grace.

The second phrase Paul uses is "perplexed but not in despair". In the Christian life many things come our way that can cause a state of confusion and perplexity. Often, we find ourselves asking the "why" question. Why me? Why this? Why now? Situations arise that cause us to question why God is allowing something to happen to us, and we begin the barrage of questions that are generated in our state of confusion. However, we need to make special note of Paul's statement in its entirety: "perplexed but not in despair". Despair is debilitating and paralyzing. It can cause us to withdraw, to quit, to throw in the towel and walk away. But, by the power of God's sustaining grace we can keep going even in those situations that cause a state of confusion.

253

Paul then says that he was "persecuted but not forsaken". He was indeed persecuted. Persecuted by those who would reject his presentation of the Gospel. The book of Acts records many episodes of Paul being harassed, driven out of cities, arrested, beaten, deserted by friends and persecuted by foes. But he testifies that he was not forsaken. Paul was giving personal testimony to the comforting promise of God that He would never leave us nor forsake us. No matter what happens in this life, we are always in the presence of the living God who is our very present help in times of trouble.

And then the fourth and final contrast Paul gives is "struck down but not destroyed". Paul was struck down on many occasions, but by God's sustaining grace he was always able to get back up again. God's grace is the only means of getting through the intensity of the hardships of life. Whatever form the hardship takes, God's grace is always enough to sustain us in the midst of it.

Going a little farther in the passage quoted above, Paul gives a summary statement that all believers need to hear and heed.

> Therefore we do not lose heart. Even though our outward man is perishing, yet the inward *man* is being renewed day by day. For our light affliction, which is but for a moment, is working for us a far more exceeding *and* eternal weight of glory, while we do not look at the things which are seen, but at the things which are not seen. For the things which are seen *are* temporary, but the things which are not seen *are* eternal.
>
> (2 Corinthians 4:16–18)

As we live in this physical body – this fragile, earthen vessel – we experience hardships of different types and differing degrees of difficulty. During these we are "perishing". But notice how Paul identifies these hardships: Light afflictions which last only a moment. When we read his litany of troubles and trials (2 Corinthians 11) we wonder how he could ever refer to them as "light afflictions".

What we must see in this passage is that Paul is looking at a much bigger picture. He compares the temporal with the eternal. If we pause for a moment to think about this temporal, physical, earthly existence – this life in earthen vessels – in comparison with our eternal home in the glories of heaven, then we can begin to understand what Paul is saying. No matter how long those afflictions last in this temporary earthly life, it does not even begin to compare with all that awaits us in heaven. The troubles and trials of this life are like a blink of the eye in comparison.

We need to keep our eyes of faith focused on the prize that is before us. As we look by faith into the eternal future God has prepared for us, the "weight" of those afflictions is diminished by the "sight" of our eternal home.

Jesus, in wanting to prepare His followers for future afflictions, made the following statement:

> These things I have spoken to you, that in Me you may have peace. In the world you will have tribulation; but be of good cheer, I have overcome the world.
>
> (John 16:33)

Jesus does not want us to be caught off guard when afflictions come our way. He told us clearly that we would have tribulations in this life. But He also promised peace in the midst of the storm, and that He had already overcome the world so the victory is already ours through Him.

Sustaining grace: grace that keeps us going in the midst of the turbulent storms of life. We are able to stand firmly on the solid foundation of grace. When we are in the throes of the affliction, then through the eyes of faith we trust and believe the promise we have received: peace and grace.

This will enable us to praise Him in the storm. Praise Him that He has a plan that will work out in our lives for our good as well as His glory. We may not be able to see the good while we are in the throes of the affliction, but as we gaze through the lens of faith we embrace the victory.

I will close this chapter with a wonderful invitation extended to children of God. This invitation also contains a most beautiful promise from God to His child.

> Therefore humble yourselves under the mighty hand of God, that He may exalt you in due time, casting all your care upon Him, for He cares for you.
>
> (1 Peter 5:6–7)

My personal favorite translation of this verse is found in the J.B. Phillips translation of the New Testament.

> So, humble yourselves under God's strong hand, and in His own good time He will lift you up. You can throw the whole weight of your anxieties upon Him, for you are His personal concern.
>
> (1 Peter 5:6–7; J.B. Phillips New Testament)

The invitation: "throw the whole weight of your anxieties upon Him." The promise: "You are His personal concern." God's sustaining grace will get us through. He cares for us; He provides for us; He will be with us before the affliction, in the midst of the affliction, and on the other side of the affliction.

Take heart, child of God: His sustaining grace is sufficient for the task. Trust Him, and watch Him work!

POINTS TO PONDER

1. Write down the details of an occasion when you were sustained by the grace of God.
   a. A time of sickness.
   b. A time of family crisis.
   c. A time of financial crisis.
   d. A time of death.
2. Have you or a member of your family suffered from the Covid-19 pandemic? How did God's sustaining grace get you through the ordeal?
3. How do you understand the author's discussion of the following premises related to God's sustaining grace?
   a. God is the "First Cause".
   b. God is good, all the time.
   c. God causes suffering as a judgment against the wicked.
   d. God uses suffering to help His children grow in faith.
   e. God allows suffering through spiritual warfare.
4. In Second Corinthians 11, Paul lists several of his personal times of suffering and tribulation. What can we learn from his experiences that might help us better handle suffering in our own lives?
5. In Second Corinthians 1, Paul talks about an experience in which he despaired of life. What did he learn, and what could we learn from his experience?

---------- CHAPTER 13 ----------

Serving Grace

As each one has received a gift, minister it to one another, as good stewards of the manifold grace of God. If anyone speaks, *let him speak* as the oracles of God. If anyone ministers, *let him do it* as with the ability which God supplies, that in all things God may be glorified through Jesus Christ, to whom belong the glory and the dominion forever and ever. Amen.

(1 Peter 4:10–11)

I Surrender All
All to Jesus, I surrender,
All to Him I freely give;
I will ever love and truth Him,
In His presence daily live.

All to Jesus I surrender,
Humbly at His feet I bow;
Worldly pleasures all forsaken,
Take me, Jesus, take me now.

I surrender all,
I surrender all,
All to Thee, my blessed Savior,
I surrender all.
Judson W. Van De Venter

We live in a consumer driven society. We want to get the best service available to meet the need of the hour. When we go to a restaurant for a nice evening meal, we want to receive quality service. Our drink should never be less than half full. We want our server's undivided attention, regardless of the fact that they may be serving five other tables besides ours. We want our meal served promptly, just the way we ordered it. If I ordered my steak well-done then I don't want to see any pink when I cut into it. If I ordered it medium rare, I don't want it cooked until it is so dry and tough that I can't even cut it. When I bite into my food, I don't want what is supposed to be a hot meal to be lukewarm.

When I visit my favorite electronics store, I don't want to have to wait for a salesperson to seek me out. I want him to approach me, offering his assistance as soon as I walk in the door. And when he approaches me, I want him to be knowledgeable of the product I am shopping for. I want him to have all the answers to all my questions, about every brand and every model of that product. I don't want him to waste my time looking something up on the web page, as it is his job to be up to date on all the latest products.

When I'm in the market for a new car, as soon as I pull into the dealership, I want a sales representative to immediately approach me. I would like for him to reach me before I even exit my automobile, but if not that quickly then at least before I reach the door. When I tell him what make and model I am looking for I expect him to instantly tell me exactly what they have in stock, with all the details of each one.

After all, each of these are here to serve me, right? I am the one who is going to make a purchase that will provide them with a hefty commission. I am the one who is putting food on their tables, and clothes on their backs. I am the most important person in the world to them at the moment of our meeting. Their undivided attention should be focused on me and me alone. They are here to serve ME!

At least, that's the way we think it should be. We feel that we should be served, always. No questions asked.

But is that the way God would have us live? Would He be pleased with someone who looks at others as those who should grovel at our feet, bending over backwards to make sure our every need is met with the least amount of stress on our part? Would He commend us for being so demanding of others so as to get what we want, how we want it, and when we want it?

The Bible presents a far different picture than that. Jesus had much to say about this subject that would be extremely helpful to consider. We will look first at Jesus' instructions concerning our service, and then we will consider His example of service.

Biblical Instructions Concerning Our Service

Jesus taught so very much on this subject. He wanted His followers to understand the importance of the believer being involved in acts of service. The following passage of scripture will illustrate just how important this topic was to our Lord.

> And when He was in the house He asked them, "What was it you disputed among yourselves on the road?" But they kept silent, for on the road they had disputed among themselves who *would be the* greatest. And He sat down, called the twelve, and said to them, "If anyone desires to be first, he shall be last of all and servant of all."
>
> (Mark 9:33b–35)

Who wants to be a servant? Really – who wants to be a servant? Don't we all want to be served? Probably, if we were sincerely honest with ourselves, we would have to admit that we would rather be served than to serve.

The apostles were obviously having a pretty animated discussion as they walked along the road. They must have thought to themselves that Jesus was far enough out away that He would not know the topic of their debate. And what was that topic? They were debating who among them would be the greatest in Jesus' kingdom.

They were undoubtedly still thinking in terms of Jesus establishing an earthly kingdom. Jesus would, of course, be on the king's throne. There was absolutely no question about that. But who would be the greatest in the court of the king from among the twelve? They were all desirous of being at the top. They were all giving their best arguments as to why each one thought he would be the best choice.

Try for a moment to listen in on their conversation. Peter, Andrew, James and John could argue that they were the first four Jesus called, so they had seniority over the rest of the apostles. Then, out of those four, three of them – Peter, James and John – were the inner circle that Jesus often allowed to share in experiences from which the others were excluded. They may have thought that one of them should be Jesus' choice.

Matthew may have presented his case by stating that he could more easily and readily identify with the outcasts, since he was one himself, being a hated tax collector. Judas Iscariot could have argued that he was already in a position of authority since he was the treasurer of the group, so he should certainly hold a prominent position among them.

Methodically, one by one, they all are presenting their cases, thinking that they should have those positions of greatness. Jesus obviously allowed them to discuss and debate about this matter for a good while, as it seems they continued until they reached their destination. It was not until they were in the house that Jesus asked them about the topic of their discussion.

This must have been a most embarrassing moment for the apostles. No one responded to Jesus' question. They must have felt it was alright to discuss it among themselves, but when Jesus confronts them they realize how their petty dispute would appear to Him. So, they keep silent.

It must have been a most powerful moment as Jesus looked at them. Perhaps His gaze would move from one to another to another. Maybe He would stare into the eyes of each one for a few uncomfortable moments. They all begin to look down, not wanting to feel the piercing stare of Jesus as He seems to be looking not just at them, but into their very soul. They may have begun to shuffle their feet uncomfortably in a feeble attempt to distract Jesus from staring so deeply and painfully.

Jesus is about to teach them a powerful lesson. He does this by offering a word of instruction:

> "If anyone desires to be first, he shall be last of all,
> and servant of all."

Can you imagine the looks of bewilderment on the faces of the apostles as they hear these words? How in the world can anyone be first by being last? That simply doesn't make any sense whatsoever. Have you ever seen a race where the last one to cross the finish line was crowned the winner? Have you ever witnessed an Olympic event where the participant who finished last was given the gold medal at the awards presentation? Of course not! The winner is first, not last. So how can it be that the greatest is last?

And even more perplexing, how can the greatest be servant of all? The greatest is supposed to be served by all. His greatness has earned him the right to be served. So, what could Jesus possibly mean when He made this most ridiculous statement?

This is one of those occasions at which Jesus turned things on their heads. This was certainly not the traditional way of thinking then, and it is still not today. The first is supposed to be first, not last. The greatest among us are to be served, not serve. And yet, that is exactly what Jesus wanted them, and us, to understand. We achieve true greatness when we become servants of all.

But what does that service look like? Whom are we to serve? Paul shares an insight that will prove to be helpful.

> For we are God's fellow workers; you are God's field, you are God's building.
>
> (1 Corinthians 3:9)

What a phenomenal thought: we are fellow workers with God. We are in a joint venture with the Lord. The truly amazing thing about this is the fact that God doesn't need us in the sense that there is something that can't be done without us. He has all power to accomplish all His will without any assistance from anyone.

We need to realize that it is a God-given privilege to be fellow workers with Him. And it is important to notice how Paul explains this. In the preceding verses he has been talking about the joint ministry he has been sharing in with Apollos. He and Apollos had been serving together in ministry to the Corinthians, and he reminds the people of Corinth of the ministry they had performed among them.

> Who then is Paul, and who *is* Apollos, but ministers through whom you believed, as the Lord gave to each one? I planted, Apollos watered, but God gave the increase. So then neither he who plants is anything, nor he who waters, but God who gives the increase. Now he who plants and he who waters are one, and each one will receive his own reward according to his own labor.
> For we are God's fellow worker.
>
> (1 Corinthians 3:5–9a)

This helps us understand a little better the meaning of Christian service. Paul says that he and Apollos are ministers to the people of Corinth, and that they are the ones through whom the Corinthians believed. They have served the people of Corinth by ministering the Gospel to them. They have been faithful to God by serving the Corinthians.

But that isn't the only way they served the Corinthians. He mentions that the people in Corinth are God's field and God's building. These are two very powerful word pictures. First, Paul says that they are God's field, and he and Apollos are workers in that field. This is an illustration from the agricultural world. The workers in the field would till the land, pull the weeds, plant the seed, irrigate the soil, and finally harvest the crop. Much labor and toil are put into working the field.

Then, second, he says the Corinthians are God's building. This is an illustration from the world of construction. Again it is the portrait of much hard work. The work would consist of planning, securing materials for the project, making sure the foundation is solid, ensuring that all the corners are square, making sure the project is structurally sound in every phase of the project. It is tedious and painstaking work. Paul says that he and Apollos are fellow workers with God in His building.

Service to God and for God is not for the faint-hearted and weak-kneed. And Jesus says that if we would be great then we must become servant of all.

The biblical principle of service is an Old Testament principle as well as a New Testament principle. God gave it to Moses as He revealed His law:

> And now, Israel, what does the LORD your God require of you, but to fear the LORD your God, to walk in all His ways and to love Him, to serve the LORD your God with all your heart and with all your soul...
>
> (Deuteronomy 10:12)

According to this verse, it is the Lord's requirement that we serve Him with all our heart and soul. In other words, our entire being is to be given over to service to the Lord. Our commitment in life, first and foremost, is to the Lord, and out of that commitment we are to serve Him with the fullness of who we are.

There are many other verses we could consider that would help us further understand the believer's service is focused on the Lord. But might ask why? Why should we serve the Lord? What is the logical reasoning behind believers giving themselves to the Lord as His servants?

WHY SHOULD WE SERVE THE LORD?

The Bible offers several answers to that question. First, foremost, and foundational is the fact that Jesus taught that His followers should serve. When Jesus was led by the Spirit to the place at which He would be tempted by Satan, He was presented with three temptations which were designed to appeal to Jesus in different ways. The one that is pertinent to the subject of service is the second temptation. The following account from the Gospel of Luke is a powerful testimony to Jesus' teaching on this subject.

> Then the devil, taking Him up on a high mountain, showed Him all the kingdoms of the world in a moment of time. And the devil said to Him, "All this authority I will give You, and their glory; for *this* has been delivered to me, and I give it to whomever I wish. Therefore, if You will worship before me, all will be Yours."
>
> And Jesus answered and said to him, "Get behind Me, Satan! For it is written, '*You shall worship the Lord your God, and Him only you shall serve.*'"
>
> (Luke 4:5–8, emphasis added)

When faced with the temptation to have all the kingdoms of the world, Jesus quoted the passage from Deuteronomy.

Note carefully that the passage concludes with the command to serve only God. We won't get into the theological discussion of the temptations, as that is not the focus of this book. What we want to see is that Jesus taught the importance of the disciples' responsibility to serve God. This is the foundational answer to the question of why we should serve God.

A second answer to the question is that we should serve God out of the abundance of our love of God. When a rich young ruler quizzed Jesus about the greatest commandment, Jesus said the first and greatest commandment was to love God with our whole being. Then, He added that the second commandment was to love our neighbor just as we love ourselves. In that passage Jesus did not specifically mention service, but it is clearly insinuated in His response. If we truly love our neighbor, then we will have his best interest at heart. We will do him no harm, but we will do good for him when the opportunity and the need arise.

So, I am to serve God out of my sense of duty and obligation to Him, and out of the abundance of my love for Him. Still another reason to serve Him should be our desire to become more like Jesus. The apostle Paul spoke of this in Romans and Colossians.

> For whom He foreknew, He also predestined *to be* conformed to the image of His Son, that He might be the firstborn among many brethren.
>
> (Romans 8:29)

> ...till we all come to the unity of the faith and of the knowledge of the Son of God, to a perfect man, to the measure of the stature of the fullness of Christ.
>
> (Ephesians 4:13)

We are to strive to become more like Jesus. Our goal in the Christian life, our goal in our process of discipleship, our goal in the ongoing work of sanctification, should be to become more like our Savior.

So what does this have to do with serving the Lord? Simple: If we become more like Jesus, we will take upon ourselves His character traits. One of the outstanding traits Jesus constantly and consistently displayed was His servanthood. He made this clear in the following proclamation:

> Yet it shall not be so among you; but whoever desires to become great among you shall be your servant. And whoever of you desires to be first shall be slave of all. For even the Son of Man did not come to be served, but to serve, and to give His life a ransom for many.
>
> (Mark 10:43–45)

Jesus, the Son of God, the second person in the Trinity, the Lord over all creation, did not come to be served, but to serve. What an astounding thing to consider. Jesus is the ultimate portrait of servant leadership. He was a powerful leader, but He led out of servanthood.

Some may think that there is a clear line of delineation between leading and serving. They think that the two terms are diametrically opposite of one another. But Jesus taught that they should be one and the same. Of course, there is a distinction between the two in terms of position. And it is obvious that leaders attain the position of leadership by displaying qualities that are conducive to leadership.

But even though one attains the position of leadership, it doesn't necessitate him exerting his authority over those under him. Leadership, when done with a servant's heart and attitude, will encourage those who are following to strive to give their best. People are more apt to follow a leader whom they feel is truly one of them, and one who leads them by serving them.

Jesus gives the greatest example of sincere servant leadership on the night of His betrayal. He had gathered with the twelve for the observance of Passover. It was there, in the hours just before He would be betrayed by Judas Iscariot, that Jesus did something no one would have expected.

> Jesus, knowing that the Father had given all things into His hands, and that He had come from God and was going to God, rose from supper and laid aside His garments, took a towel and girded Himself. After that, He poured water into a basin and began to wash the disciples' feet, and to wipe *them* with the towel with which He was girded.
>
> (John 13:3–5)

It is difficult for us to even imagine Jesus doing this. It is Peter who speaks out of his incredulity. He can't believe what he is seeing. He's probably trying to figure out just exactly what in the world Jesus thinks He's doing? This is the job of a common household servant, not the job of the one who is going to be King. But he is probably just verbalizing what all of them were thinking. Read the following dialogue between Peter and Jesus, and let the power of Jesus' words sink in:

> Then He came to Simon Peter. And *Peter* said to Him, "Lord, are You washing my feet?"
>
> Jesus answered and said to him, "What I am doing you do not understand now, but you will know after this."
>
> Peter said to Him, "You shall never wash my feet!"
>
> Jesus answered him, "If I do not wash you, you have no part with Me."

It is obvious that Peter does not understand the actions of Jesus. And rightly so. It is difficult for us to understand what

Jesus was doing as well. This does not fit into our understanding of the mission and ministry of the Lord. He is, after all, the Son of God, the second Person of the Holy Trinity, and the Savior of man. This doesn't fit our picture of the Lord over all creation.

But this is exactly who He is, and this is exactly what He came to do. He came to be servant of all. To help us grasp the significance of His actions let's read on a little further into the text:

> Do you know what I have done to you? You call Me Teacher and Lord, and you say well, for *so* I am. If I then, *your* Lord and Teacher, have washed your feet, you also ought to wash one another's feet. For I have given you an example, that you should do as I have done to you.
>
> (John 13:12b–15)

Jesus has stated clearly that He did not come to be served, but to serve. Here, He gives a vivid, living display of His servant leadership. By His example He is teaching His disciples, then and now, that we are to lead by serving. One of the main things that should be understood from Jesus' action is that leadership is not to be thought in terms of position, but in terms of attitude. Jesus clearly teaches, by His words as well as His actions, the true meaning of servant leadership.

The remainder of this chapter will focus on Jesus washing the disciple's feet, as there are several points of emphasis that should be noted by anyone who is sincerely interested in following Jesus' example of servant leadership.

First, it should never be thought of as condescending to serve others. It is actually a testimony to our commitment to be like Jesus. We are not below others when we choose to serve them. Jesus took it upon Himself to do the menial task of washing feet, a task that was usually assigned to a household servant. However, there was no such servant where Jesus and the twelve assembled for the observance of Passover, and none of the disciples took it upon themselves to perform this task. So, Jesus took it upon Himself to wash the feet of the disciples.

It would have been a testimony of a lesson well learned if one of the twelve had taken it upon himself to perform this job upon their arrival. But they have now been gathered in that room for a good while, and no one had taken the task upon himself. It would probably be safe to assume that none of them even thought of doing such a thing. It may not have been thought of as being beneath their dignity to wash the feet of the others in the room, but it was simply that they thought this should be done by someone else.

So, when Jesus took a basin of water and a towel, and then began to go from one to another, washing their feet, it must have been a matter of great conviction to them. The text doesn't specifically speak of their reactions, but I can picture in my mind that they were sitting in stunned silence. It was not until Jesus came to Peter that anyone spoke, and it would have been far better if he had not!

It is interesting to note that Peter's statement was contradictory. Listen again to his two statements: "Lord, are You washing my feet?" "You shall never wash my feet!" The contradiction is seen in the fact that Peter calls Jesus "Lord", but then turns around and makes an assertion that clearly shows that, at least at that moment, he was not submitted to Jesus' lordship. If He is really Lord, we can't say "No" to anything He does or says.

The second observation we can make is that serving others is an expression of our love for them. It is hard to imagine a more loving act than Jesus' washing the feet of the twelve. Of course, His most unbelievable act of love was His sacrificial death on the cross. But here, just a matter of hours before His arrest, His attention is focused on a need that had been left unaddressed. Knowing what was just ahead, and all that He would go through, He still focused His attention and His energy on serving others.

Service to others is a powerful testimony of our love for them.

This brings to mind a gentleman I had the privilege of knowing several years ago. Soon after I met him he asked if I would like to visit his wife who lived in a nearby nursing facility. Upon arrival, we made our way to her room where I met her. He went over, took her by the hand, and began telling her how beautiful she was and how glad he was to be there with her. It was obvious from her non-response that she had no idea who he was.

He held her hand as we walked down the hallway toward the main sitting room. He talked to her about the weather, about their children and grandchildren, about things at the church – just small talk. She walked alongside her husband; her arm cradled in his. She stared straight ahead, never saying a word, never responding in any way to him as he talked with her.

He then sat with her in the dining room and fed her lunch. Then, we walked her back to her room where he helped her get comfortably settled in bed. We waited until she drifted off to sleep, and then we left. I sat quietly in the car for a few moments, thinking to myself that I had just witnessed one of the greatest displays of love and commitment that I had ever seen. When I finally spoke I asked him how long she had been living in the nursing facility and was shocked to hear that she had been there five years. She had not recognized him in all that time. But he had gone three times a day, every day, to walk with her, talk with her, feed her, and care for her. He served her out of his love for her.

This could have been done simply because of his love for his wife, with no further display of this type of servanthood. But this is the reason I wanted to share his story. He not only displayed this type of servant leadership with her, but he was the same in his service to the Lord through the church. He led others by serving them. This is the way we should all be – serving God by serving others.

This leads to a third observation: Jesus saw a need and took the initiative to address it. My wife and I have been working at amusement parks for almost a decade. On several occasions I have been approached by a guest in the park and asked how the park is kept so clean. Of course, the basic answer is that we have a department whose task it is to make sure the park is kept as clean as possible. But that is only part of the answer. It is not uncommon to see people in high positions, all the way up to park manager, walking around with a picker in hand, picking up pieces of litter as they make their rounds. Granted, this is a small task to perform, but it shows that good leadership doesn't only tell others to do the job, but they lead by example.

Jesus took the initiative to meet a need by performing what appeared to be a menial task. He then instructed the twelve that since He had done this for them that they should do it for one another. Serve the Lord by serving other.

A final observation from this episode in Jesus' life is that He was willing to put others' needs ahead of His own. He was not chained to His own agenda but was willing to make His agenda accommodate the needs of others. This is seen so many times in the Gospels as Jesus goes out of His way to minister to those in need. On several occasions, after He had been busy from a long day of serving and ministering, He would still welcome those who came seeking help. He was truly the perfect example of servant leadership.

Sometimes our personal agendas can be a huge detriment to serving others. We can get ourselves so chained to our plans for the day that we pass right by several opportunities to serve the Lord by serving others. Perhaps on your way into work you pass a vehicle beside the road with a flat tire. You notice that it is a young mother with two very small children. It is obvious that she is distressed about her present situation. In a split second you have to decide what is more important: your agenda, or your desire to serve the Lord by serving others.

Or maybe you are in the check-out line at the grocery store. The elderly lady in front of you has now had her items added up by the cashier and is two dollars short of the amount owed. You have the extra money, and it certainly wouldn't hurt your personal budget to help out with this small amount. We can choose to very quietly hand the cashier the balance she owes, or we can choose to become irritated because she is wasting our time. After all, our agenda is much more important than standing here waiting for this to be straightened out. We need to see this as a great opportunity to serve the Lord by serving others.

To bring this chapter to a close let's be reminded once again of the personal testimony of our Lord. He said that He had not come to be served, but to serve. He is our example, and He is our Lord. Since He is both, then we need to submit to His lordship, and follow His example.

Granted, we are not able, nor are we motivated, to do this on our own. That is the reason we need God's grace that enables us to serve Him and others. Once we appropriate His grace by faith, we are then able to serve, and we will also find ourselves motivated to serve. We will then find that there is a sense of satisfaction and fulfillment as we give ourselves in service to the Lord by serving others.

POINTS TO PONDER

1. Would you rather serve, or be served? Make an honest assessment of your true feelings.

2. What can we learn from Jesus' statement about His not coming to be served, but to serve?

3. When Jesus washed the disciples' feet, what do you think He was trying to teach His disciples?

4. Explain what you think Jesus meant when He said that if anyone desires to be first, he shall be last of all, and servant of all?

5. Explain what you think Paul meant when he said that he had planted, and Apollos had watered, but it was God who gave the increase.

6. What do you think Paul meant when he said that we are God's fellow workers?

7. Why should we serve the Lord?

CHAPTER 14

The Stewardship of Grace

Let a man so consider us, as servants of Christ and stewards of the mysteries of God. Moreover it is required in stewards that one be found faithful.

(1 Corinthians 4:1–2)

As each one has received a gift, minister it to one another, as good stewards of the manifold grace of God.

(1 Peter 4:10)

More About Jesus
More about Jesus I would know,
More of His grace to others show;
More of His saving fullness see,
More of His love who died for me.

More, more about Jesus,
More, more about Jesus;
More of His saving fullness see,
More of His love who died for me.

More about Jesus let me learn,
More of His holy will discern;
Spirit of God, my teacher be,
Showing the things of Christ to me.
E.E. Hewitt

I f you placed your financial future in the hands of a well-known, highly respected financial consultant, it would be wise to do some research to make sure his reputation was not a sham. You would want to make sure he had a proven track record, and that there were plenty of testimonials from past and present clients who would vouch for his integrity and honesty. You would do your research, using every source available to you to check his background, his track record with previous clients, his profit to loss ratio, and his satisfaction rating from every tracking agency possible. You would check the Better Business Bureau to see if there are any complaints, past as well as current, that would be a possible sign of serious problems you might encounter if you chose to use his services.

If there are any minor areas of concern you would most likely go back to the research table and look for more areas of concern that might mean he is not all that he is reported to be. If, with the further research, you discover even more warning signs, you would surely begin looking in other directions for a consultant who would serve you better. You would want a good steward to watch over your financial resources.

Employers look for employees who will prove to be good stewards on the job. They want employees who are people of integrity. They are looking for individuals who can be trusted to give an honest day's work for an honest day's pay. The employee should be a good steward of their attention to their responsibilities, good stewards of their time, and good stewards of the use of their skills and talents. Employers are looking for individuals whom they can trust to be good stewards over the tasks and assignments given them. They want employees who will also always take responsibility for their actions on the job. They want employees who will prove to be a good steward who would be willing to sacrifice for the sake of getting a job done on time, and to get it right the first time. A good steward in the workplace will bear certain character traits that will endear them to the employer.

Those traits are the very things an employer will look for as they interview potential employees.

Good stewardship is so important in every area of life. This is especially true in the life of a disciple of Jesus Christ. The two verses at the beginning of this chapter will prove to be a good starting point for our discussion of this important matter.

> Let a man so consider us, as servants of Christ
> and stewards of the mysteries of God. Moreover it
> is required in stewards that one be found faithful.
> (1 Corinthians 4:1–2)

Paul understood his role and responsibility was to be a servant of the Lord. He oftentimes identified himself in this way. He had enslaved himself to the work of sharing the message of salvation through Jesus, and his life bore the marks of that servanthood.

In the New Testament era, the word Paul uses is usually used in reference to one who was in a permanent position of servitude. The bondservant was considered the personal possession of his owner. He was property. He had no rights, and if he displeased his master he could be punished severely, and even executed if the owner so desired.

The servant would be responsible for the possessions of his master. This would include several aspects of the servant's life, and he would be accountable to his master for his management of those possessions. Servants would be responsible for the areas of the master's possessions that were put under his care. For example, if his area of responsibility was the grounds around the master's property, he would be held accountable for the care of those grounds. The servant was the possession of his master and was accountable to him in all areas.

Paul identifies himself as the servant of Jesus Christ. He had been bought with the precious blood of the Lamb of God and was thus His possession. He had given up all personal rights and privileges and was at the beck and call of his Master.

This is true of every believer in the Lord Jesus. We have been bought with the blood of Jesus just as Paul had been. Therefore, we are His possession. And now we are commissioned to be good stewards over that which has been assigned to us.

In order to understand this matter of servanthood a little more clearly we will focus our attention on three areas of the servants life in which we are accountable: time, personal abilities, and resources. First, we are all accountable to God for the use of our time. Time is one commodity that we all have an equal amount of, at least in terms of the time in a day. As we know, there are twenty-four hours in a day. This computes to 1440 minutes, which in turn computes to 86,400 seconds. This is the time each of us has each day.

The discrepancy comes in the number of days each individual has allotted to them. If a person lives exactly twenty-three years, then his time on earth is 725,328,000 seconds, whereas the person who lives exactly eighty-three years has a lifespan of 2,671,488,000 seconds.

Attention here is not focused on the length of life, but on the 86,400 seconds each of us has in one day. Thinking about our lives in increments of one day, we are to be good stewards of the use of that time allotment for that period. What does that look like? Does that mean that we are constantly praying, constantly reading the Bible, constantly ministering to others in Jesus' name? Just how are we to be good stewards of our time?

To bring it down to its most simple understanding, we are to do what Paul admonished us to do in his letters to the Colossians and Corinthians. He says:

> And whatever you do in word or deed, do all in the
> name of the Lord Jesus, giving thanks to God the
> Father through Him.
>
> (Colossians 3:17)

> Therefore, whether you eat or drink, or whatever
> you do, do all to the glory of God.
>
> (1 Corinthians 10:31)

We are to be good stewards over our time allotment by doing everything for His glory. I tell new students coming into my class for a new quarter of study that they should do their class assignments as if they were going to hand them to the Lord Jesus Himself. When I was a student, I tried to keep this uppermost in my mind. If I was preparing to take an exam, or writing a paper, or completing a written assignment, I tried to focus on the fact that I was doing those things for Jesus, not for my professor. This always motivated me to do my best.

If you are a housewife, taking care of the children while your husband works outside the home, then you should do your housework as if Jesus would personally inspect it. If you are the husband who goes to work every day to keep the family financially solvent, then you should do your job as if you were doing it for the Lord.

Whatever we do, in word or deed, should be done for the glory of God. To keep this uppermost in our minds day-by-day will facilitate us being good stewards of our time.

Second, we should be good stewards of our personal abilities. Every individual, whether a Christian or a non-Christian, has certain talents that enable them to do certain things. When I was a young boy I would daydream about playing football for the Dallas Cowboys. I would envision myself in a close game, with only seconds to play before time ran out, making the game-winning catch in the end-zone as time expired. Or kicking the last second field goal that gave the team the victory. But, alas, they were only dreams. I didn't even make the starting line-up on my middle-school football team.

But I did have some talents that those football players did not have. I was very interested in music and taught myself how to play the drums. I then played in a rock and roll band for twelve years, using my talent to the best of my ability and to the enjoyment of many who heard me play. Then, after I was saved by the grace of God I used that talent for His glory by playing in the praise band at church. Talents are to be used for the glory of our Lord.

We all have talents, some of which set us apart from others, while other talents might simply enable us to get a job and do it well. Whatever talents we have as believers in the Lord should be used for the glory of the Lord.

For the person who has been born into the family of God, there is another dimension of ability for which we are accountable. Every believer in the Lord Jesus has been entrusted with at least one spiritual gift, and, from my personal observations, most have more than one. Listen again to the words of the Apostle Paul in his correspondence with the Corinthians:

> There are diversities of gifts, but the same Spirit. There are differences of ministries, but the same Lord. And there are diversities of activities, but it is the same God who works all in all. But the manifestation of the Spirit is *given to each one for the profit of all*...
>
> But one and the same Spirit works all these things, distributing to each one individually as He wills.
>
> (1 Corinthians 12:4–7; 12:11; emphasis added)

We all have been assigned a spiritual gift which is to be used, as Paul says, for the profit of all. Paul gives a list of some of these spiritual gifts in his letter to the Romans. In the twelfth chapter of that letter he mentions the spiritual gifts of prophecy, ministry, teaching, exhortation, giving, leading, and mercy. This is not to be considered an exhaustive list, but a sampling of gifts assigned to individuals by God.

And we are to use our spiritual gift(s) for the profit of everyone in the body of Christ. I would even suggest that this should be taken to apply to our local assembly with which we meet regularly. It is the personal belief of this author that God makes sure that each individual local body of believers will have every spiritual gift manifested that is necessary for the effective and efficient fulfillment of that local body's assignment.

And every gift is necessary! Your gift is necessary for the efficient and effective fulfillment of the ministry of your local assembly. If you are not doing your part, then something is lacking in that body. Paul uses the analogy of the human body to illustrate this point. He says the eye cannot do the work of the ear, nor can the ear do the work of the eye. Both are necessary to perform their assigned function. And so it is with the body of the church: each member needs to perform their assigned function.

In being good stewards of our personal abilities, each of us is to use our talents and our spiritual giftedness in such a way as to profit the entire body, and ultimately bring glory to God.

Third, we are to be good stewards over our personal possessions – our resources. The underlying principle that must be understood to properly understand our responsibility over our resources is to grasp the fact that we really have no resources. There is absolutely nothing that we can claim possession of. Granted, we may have a title that states that we are owners of a certain automobile. Or we may have a deed that says we own a certain plot of land. We may have receipts that show we purchased a certain item, and thus claim ownership of it. But in reality, we are not owners – we are only stewards. God owns it all.

Remember, we are His possession. He purchased us (believers) with the precious blood of His Son. He owns us. Of course, even non-believers are His possession as well. He gave them life, and sustains their lives, and thus everything they own is on loan from God. They would never acknowledge that fact, but it is true none-the-less.

But for believers, we are to accept and acknowledge the fact that we, and everything we own, are the rightful belongings of the Lord. Therefore, we are responsible to Him for how we use our personal resources, and we will give an account to Him on a future day as to how we used, misused, or abused the resources.

It is the responsibility of each individual believer to be good stewards over our time, talents (both natural talents as well as spiritual gifts), and our personal resources. But Paul has more to say about being good stewards.

Second, he identifies himself as a steward of the mysteries of God. The mysteries of God would include the Gospel of the Lord Jesus. We learned in an earlier chapter that Paul said we have this treasure, the Gospel, in earthen vessels. We are weak, frail humans who have been entrusted with the most amazing treasure there is. We have actually been entrusted with the lifesaving, life-changing, life-improving message of the Gospel. What an awesome thing to consider!

So how are we to be good stewards of the mysteries of God – the Gospel of Jesus Christ? There are several ways we can prove to be good and faithful stewards of this treasure.

First, to be a good steward of the mysteries of God we should be involved in protecting them. In one very important sense we would have to acknowlege that God needs no help with the protection of this treasure. He is more than capable of protecting that which belongs to Him. It is not that He needs us to protect it, but He has entrusted it to us, and, in this physical realm, we are called to protect it.

But what exactly are we protecting if from? The Bible itself testifies to the fact that the word of God never returns to Him void, but always accomplishes it's intended purpose. So, if God is capable of protecting it, and if it has all power to accomplish its purpose, then why do we need to be involved?

History records the attempts of those who made attempts to destroy the Bible. Atheistic governments have attempted to keep the Bible out of the hands of the common man. Atheists have attempted to explain the intricacies of the universe without any reference to God. Philosophers have attempted to replace God with a man-centered concept of reality.

Evolutionists have propagated a theory as if it were fact. They teach us that everything that exist came into existence from a massive "big bang" billions of years ago. This big bang, which was an explosion of preexisting matter, hurled everything out from the center, and somehow these space objects locked into an orbital pattern around the center of the universe. They have no explanation as to where this preexisting matter originated, nor do they have an answer as to how this matter somehow locked into this orbital pattern. They present this fanciful theory as fact, and they embrace it by faith. They believe in their man-made explanation of the existence of the universe. This is an all-out assault on the Bible's teachings about the origin of all things. The mystery of the Gospel must be protected from this assault from unbelievers who have replaced God with their own theories.

Added to these philosophies of man are the many false religions that have kept God in the formula, but they propagate a Christ-less message. Or, if Christ is part of their religious teaching, He is not accepted as the Son of God, the third Person of the Trinity. He may play an important role in the message of these false teachers and preachers, but He is not the only begotten Son of God who gave Himself as the propitiating sacrifice for sin. So we need to be good stewards of the mysteries of God because they are under constant attack from a world that is becoming more and more antagonistic toward the Gospel.

Second, we can be good stewards of the mysteries of God through our profession. This may not sound like a very powerful protective activity, but in reality it is extremely powerful and seriously needed. I will personally meet people with whom you will never cross paths. These individuals need to hear the Gospel message, and I, or you, may be the only person from whom they will ever have the chance to hear. Our profession is vitally important in our personal circles of influence. Our friends and family members need to hear the message of the mysteries of God. Our fellow employees and our classmates need to hear. We need to be good stewards in professing our faith so that others might hear.

There will be times when being that good steward might call for us to get out of our comfort zones. Perhaps we find ourselves in a situation where we are given the privilege to share the Gospel with a stranger. It could very likely be that God has orchestrated our meeting for the express purpose of sharing the hope we have with a person in need. We don't know the need, but God does, and He has strategically placed us there, right where we need to be at just the right moment in time. We need to be good stewards in sharing our personal profession with others.

It would be beneficial if we thought of these encounters as divine appointments. There have been many such encounters throughout my Christian life. Some of them I took advantage of as I quickly realized that God had placed me in that place at just the right time. However, there have been other times in which I felt that divine nudging, and yet, instead of taking advantage of that opportunity to be a witness for the Lord I walked away. I can only pray now that God sent someone else to make up for my inaction.

I don't mean to suggest by this personal example that any of us are indispensable in the Lord's work. He can easily make up for my mistake, but His choice was at that moment in time to use me rather than someone else. I will give an account for those missed opportunities, but I trust God's grace in sending someone else to share His love.

Still another way we can be good stewards is by propagating the mysteries of God. How does this differ from sharing my profession? It goes so much farther than my profession could ever reach. Usually, our profession of the mysteries of God does not go very far. We may be able to share a testimony before a gathering of people, and it could possibly be a crowd of hundreds or even thousands. But it is still a limited number, and a one-time event.

But there are ways to propagate the mysteries of God that will reach so many more. We just simply need to learn to avail ourselves to these avenues. One way I have through the years propagated the mysteries of God is through the written word. I have written letters to the editors of newspapers in cities where I have resided. This is a relatively simple thing to do. When certain social issues have been prominently discussed in the public forum, I have written responses to these by addressing letters to the editor. These have sparked much discussion from readers who would respond – sometimes negatively and sometimes positively. However, regardless of the response, I was able to propagate the message.

Now, with the growing popularity of blogging, I have entered the digital world by writing blogs focused on doctrinal issues, theological issues, societal issues, political issues, and others. This is an avenue that is wide open for anyone who will take advantage of it.

Some have the ability to teach the Bible in classroom settings. If you are one of them then please consider using that God-given ability in a discipleship class, or a small group you invite into your home for the purpose of studying the Scriptures together.

And still others enjoy mentoring in small groups or even one-on-one. This is such a vital need in the church today. Discipleship has suffered tremendously in the recent past. I have served as pastor of churches in the past in which I was told plainly that they were not interested in attending a discipleship class if they were going to be required to complete daily assignments of prayer, Bible study, and journaling. If our Christianity is not worth enough to us to invest a small amount of time and energy in striving to grow in our walk with the Lord, then it is of extremely little value to us.

These are just a few suggestions for us to consider as we think about how we can become more involved in being better stewards of the mysteries of God. The protection, the profession and the propagation of the mysteries of God are all our responsibilities. We need to prayerfully seek God's guidance in determining ways we can personally be involved. And we need to remember: Paul says that it is required of a steward to be found faithful.

In addition to what Paul has taught us about being good stewards of the mysteries of God, Peter adds that we should be good stewards of the manifold grace of God.

> As each one has received a gift, minister it to one another, as good stewards of the manifold grace of God.
>
> (1 Peter 4:10)

As has been stated throughout this book, it is by grace that we are enabled to serve our Lord. Each chapter has dealt with a different manifestation of His grace. Every aspect of the believer's life, from the very moment of salvation, until the moment of physical death, we are empowered, enabled, gifted, and grown by grace.

It is my prayer that those who read the pages of this book will be encouraged and strengthened in their life of faith; that they will be compelled and motivated to deepen their faith walk; and they will be convicted and challenged to go farther in their faith walk than ever before.

POINTS TO PONDER

1. In you own words, define stewardship.
2. What is the difference between a natural talent and a spiritual gift?
3. Paul encourages us to be good stewards of the mysteries of God. How would you describe these "mysteries"?
4. The author suggests three ways we can be involved in being good stewards of the mysteries of God. Explain in your own words how you, personally, can be involved in:
    a. Protecting the mysteries.
    b. Professing the mysteries.
    c. Propagating the mysteries.

It's All About Grace

This book has been all about grace. But that makes perfectly good sense, especially in the life of a believer in Jesus Christ. Why? Because our lives are, indeed, all about God's grace. We live by His grace. We have health by His grace. When our health wanes, we maintain a life of commitment to Him, by His grace. We learn to enjoy the bounties of life by His grace, and we learn to handle times of need by His grace. We make it through the valley of the shadow of death when a loved one passes away, by His grace. We sit by the bedside of a loved one whose mind is slowly deteriorating by the ravages of Alzheimer's or dementia, by His grace. We experience the prosperity of riches by His grace, and we endure the poverty of loss by that same grace.

It is all about grace.

This book has reminded us, in a very limited way, about some of the different aspects of grace that are clearly evident in the pages of Scripture. Perhaps you found a reflection of yourself as you read through the pages of a particular chapter. Maybe you have recently experienced a loss in your life, and you were reminded of God's sustaining grace. Or perhaps you have gone through a grueling experience that caused an undue amount of stress, and even found yourself in a time of distress. It was during that time that you found God's strengthening grace to be more than sufficient to get you through.

It is all about grace.

God's grace is in plentiful supply. It has been for the duration of the human race up to this point and will continue to be so until the Lord returns for His bride, the church. And even beyond that coming event, we will still dwell in the presence of God by the grace of God.

It is all about grace.

I have read hundreds of books in my lifetime. One of my regrets is that I did not try to really commit to memory some of the extremely important things I learned. Oh, yes, I have learned so much by reading the writings of others, and I am so thankful for their influence in my life. Yet, there is so much more I could have, and should have, learned. So, now that you are reading these last pages, I would like to make a couple of suggestions for your consideration.

First, perhaps it would be a wise investment of time to go back to the end of each chapter and review the author's "Points to Ponder." If you jotted down any thoughts as you considered the questions, review those, maybe adding more to them so as to give more clarity to your understanding.

If, by chance, you did not make any notes, then perhaps now that you have finished reading the book in its entirety you could go back to those questions and work through them one by one. To do so would be a great aid to help remember things that you learned as you read.

Second, perhaps you have learned some things about grace that you did not know before, or that you became a little more knowledgeable of. If so, then share those new tidbits of knowledge with others. If you know of someone who might need some encouragement in one of the areas discussed in the book, share with them some words of comfort and compassion, and then pray that God would use that knowledge to motivate them to dive more deeply into the pages of the Bible for themselves.

Third, maybe you would like to begin a discussion group with a few of your friends, family members, or fellow employees. Share with one another insights gleaned from the book, utilizing the "Points to Ponder" as discussion starters. Then, allow time for each individual in the group to share their own insights gleaned from the book, or directly from the pages of Scripture. Some may even have insights that they have learned through the classroom called life.

Fourth, and finally, consider giving the book away. Once you have read it and made your own personal notes to refer back to when needed, allow someone else to read. This could be a valuable tool that can be easily passed around to friends and family.

I would like to personally thank you for taking time to read my thoughts. Some of them were probably a bit wandering – preachers have the tendency to do that on occasion! But my prayer is that you were encouraged, strengthened, and helped as you read these pages.

I would love to hear from you. Your thoughts would be an invaluable asset to me as I prayerfully consider writing on more biblical topics that I pray would encourage us along this pilgrimage of life. You can email me at stevestewart532@gmail.com, or through my website, steve-stewart.org.

And once again remember:

It is all about grace!

Printed in the United States
by Baker & Taylor Publisher Services